Gems No. 6
South Asians and the dowry problem

Edited by Werner Menski

with a Preface by Himendra Thakur

G E M S
★★★

Trentham Books and School of Oriental & African Studies

First published in 1998 by Trentham Books Limited
Trentham Books Limited
Westview House
734 London Road
Oakhill
Stoke on Trent
Staffordshire
England ST4 5NP

British Cataloguing in Publication Data
A catalogue record for this book is available from the British Library
ISBN 1 85856 141 8 (hb 1 85856 139 6)

Designed and typeset by Trentham Print Design Ltd., Chester and printed in
Great Britain by Professional Books Supplies Ltd, Oxford.

Ethnic Minority Studies at SOAS

is a series of monographs and collected papers that focus on current issues in the study of ethnic minorities in Britain and elsewhere in the world.

The series is edited by Dr. Werner F. Menski, Senior Lecturer in South Asian Laws at the School of Oriental and African Studies and the Chairman of GEMS, the Group for Ethnic Minority Studies at the School.

No. 1 Sanjiv Sachdeva
The primary purpose rule in British immigration law

No. 2 Werner Menski (ed.)
Coping with 1997: The reaction of the Hong Kong people to the transfer of power

No. 3 Claudia Mortimore
Immigration and adoption

No. 4 António Cruz
Shifting responsibility: Carriers' liability in the Member States of the European Union and North America

No. 5 Richard Jones and Gnanapala Welhengama
Ethnic minorities in English law

No. 6 Werner Menski (ed.)
South Asians and the dowry problem

Acknowledgements

Many people have contributed to the production of this book and a few words of thanks and recognition would seem to be the least one can do to acknowledge that this book was truly a team effort, dedicated to the major, longer-term objective of trying to save young South Asian women, anywhere in the world, from a cruel, premature death.

First of all, without the pioneering spirit and energetic encouragement of Mr. Himendra Thakur, the series of International Dowry Conferences would never have started, nor would this book exist. My colleague Dr. Julia Leslie, who herself played no small part in all those Conferences, has duly acknowledged Thakurji's key role in chapter 2 of this book. At Harvard, Professor Michael Witzel and his team ensured that the first two International Conferences went smoothly and provided a congenial atmosphere for the lively and – given the nature of the subject – often quite stressful discussions.

The Third International Conference on Dowry and Bride-Burning was held in London on 14th and 15th November 1997. It was made possible through financial support from the Dharma and Gender Working Group of the DHIIR in Cambridge, which is gratefully acknowledged here. Key members of that group, in particular Dr. Julius Lipner (Cambridge) and Dr. Kim Knott (Leeds), took an active role in ensuring that the Conference took place. During the London Conference, too, personal testimonies of several dowry victims were given. These were not recorded and do not appear in published form. The courageous, unnamed women who spoke during that deeply disturbing and draining afternoon session deserve much appreciation for sharing some of their most personal insights and experiences with those of us who, as academics, researchers and students, have been trying to understand how it is possible that some people appear to take pleasure in inflicting mindless violence on women who are manifestly in need of support and care, rather than further hurt.

The enthusiastic assistance of leading lights in our Students Against Dowry group at SOAS, especially Lara Mustafa and Dr. Urmila Goel, helped to shape the organisational framework, thereby setting a model for future groups of students to follow. Largely in the background but quietly effective, Agnelo Barreto, Preston Andrew and Rajesh Bhavsar contributed to the organisation of the conference on behalf of GEMS and helped to produce the manuscript for publication.

Last, but not least, it has again been a joy to work with Dr. Gillian Klein, who is one of the most efficient, and yet patient, publishers and editors one might ever wish for. The team at Trentham Print Design, as is customary by now, have been absolutely wonderful, and have also been responsible for the speedy appearance of this book.

The Authors

Dr. Rohit Barot is Senior Lecturer at the Department of Sociology at Bristol University. He was one of the founders of the Centre for the Study of Minorities and Social Change at Bristol University. He has written extensively on Hindus in Britain, mainly the Swaminarayan Movement and on questions of social change. His work on dowry among Gujaratis in Britain will hopefully be continued in the near future.

Ms. Manjaree Chowdhary, from Chandigarh in India, was a lecturer before she became a postgraduate law student at SOAS, where she obtained a distinction in the LLM in autumn 1996. She has since been practising as a lawyer in New Delhi, specialising in legal issues concerning women's rights and family law. She plans to be actively involved in future Dowry Conferences.

Ms. Jagbir Jhutti is currently completing a DPhil in Social Anthropology at Wolfson College, University of Oxford, on the subject of changes in marriage practices among British Sikhs. Her contribution arises from fieldwork connected to this intensive long-term study, which she hopes to continue after her doctorate.

Dr. Julia Leslie studied Sanskrit and Indology. She is a well-known and prolific author of books and articles particularly on the position of women in Hindu culture and is now Senior Lecturer in Hindu Studies at SOAS. Her study of *The perfect wife* (1989) and subsequent work on the status of Hindu women provided an important foundation for research on the position of South Asian women.

Dr. Werner Menski studied Indology and modern South Asian Studies in Germany and is Senior Lecturer in South Asian Laws at SOAS, University of London. He has taught and researched the subject of dowry in South Asian laws for the past fifteen years and has supervised dissertations and theses on the topic. He is author of a large number of papers on South Asian laws, including the dowry problem.

Dr. Bisraam Rambilass is a descendant of indentured labourers who migrated to South Africa in 1860. He is actively involved in both government and non-government structures that promote Indian studies in the Republic of South Africa. He is a Senior Lecturer in Sanskrit at the Department of Indian Languages, University of Durban Westville, South Africa and author of several books.

Dr. Bisakha (Pia) Sen completed her undergraduate studies at Presidency College, Calcutta and obtained a PhD in Economics in the Department of Economics, Ohio State University, Columbus, Ohio. She is Assistant Professor in Economics at the University of Central Florida in Orlando. An active member of the International Association for Feminist Economists, she has conducted research on many socio-economic issues affecting women's lives, both in India and in the USA.

Mrs. Usha Sood has been a practising barrister in Britain and a law lecturer at Nottingham Trent University for many years and has recently been instrumental in bringing dowry-related litigation before English courts. She is a member of EMAC, the Ethnic Minorities Advisory Committee of the Judicial Studies Board in London.

Mr. Himendra Thakur has worked for many years as a senior Civil Engineer in the USA. He is Chair of the Board of Directors of the International Society Against Dowry and Bride-Burning in India, based in Boston, MA. As author of *Don't burn my mother* (1991), he is well-known as an international activist, whose main aim is to highlight the continuing problem of dowry-related murders.

Contents

Preface

Himendra Thakur

Each year, in India and in South Asian communities almost anywhere in the world, thousands of innocent brides are burnt, killed or maimed in the prime of their lives, by husbands and in-laws. The most likely cause is that the father of the bride has been unable to meet demands of dowry (defined as demands from the husband's family as a consideration of marriage) which kept on increasing after the wedding. The tragedy of dowry-related violence and bride-burning (the term includes all kinds of atrocities that lead to the murder or suicide of the bride) is one of the most brutal scourges of humankind today. It is a baffling paradox that it occurs in one of the oldest civilisations, one which claims to honour and respect women.

Dowry murders are different from 'domestic violence', most of which stems from fits of rage between husband and wife. Bride-burning is usually perpetrated by the mother-in-law, sister-in-law, husband, father-in-law or other relatives in the marital home of the victim. It is calculated, cold-blooded murder. In World War II, in Nazi death camps and in Japan's chemical warfare laboratories, where prisoners were used as guinea pigs, at least the perpetrators of the atrocities could be identified as uniformed military personnel, trained to kill. In today's South Asian communities, those who burn brides or drive them to suicide wear no uniforms; they cannot be distinguished from other members of the community. After killing, they continue their normal lives, attending religious festivals, gatherings or temple services, or social events like a birthday party or even another wedding, as though nothing had happened. Their jobs or businesses do not normally suffer, nor does the community ostracise them. On the contrary, if the father of the victim raises his voice, he may be treated as a troublemaker.

Notwithstanding the clear messages of India's *Dowry Prohibition Act*, enacted in 1961, an undercurrent of tacit social approval of dowry violence and bride-burning continues in the dowry-infested areas of India, and the perpetrators seem to feel no guilt when they burn a bride. The enormity of this crime may be better understood if we compare it to the toll taken by land-mines which has evoked world-wide understanding recently. As statistics produced by the UN and various important concerned international organisations (e.g. Human Rights Watch and Associated Press) have confirmed, land-mine accidents kill or maim about 26,000 people annually throughout the world. About 80% of these victims (roughly 21,000) are civilians. Dowry and bride-burning kill or maim at least 25,000 innocent brides every year in India alone. Moreover, land-mine accidents are not treated as culpable homicide. Bride-burning is clearly culpable homicide, cold-blooded murder, perpetrated by identifiable criminals, members of the victim's marital family.

In terms of geographical distribution, it is interesting to note that dowry and bride-burning are not practised uniformly all over India. The geographical distribution of dowry death figures from India is given in Table 1 below, which we printed for the first time in the Souvenir Volume of the 1995 Harvard Conference. In addition, Table 2 below gives an idea of the intensity of dowry deaths per million Hindu population in different parts of India. The figures are drawn from statistics published by the National Crime Bureau of the Government of India, which reports about 6,000 dowry deaths from many parts of India every year. This is due to gross under-reporting; the reality is much worse.

From these two Tables, it can be seen that there are no reported dowry deaths in Arunachal Pradesh, Meghalaya, Manipur and other Eastern states of India. There is no dowry murder or bride-burning in the Assamese or Nepalese communities. The highest intensity of dowry deaths is found in Delhi, closely followed by Panjab, Haryana, Uttar Pradesh, and other North Indian states. Maharashtra and Assam claim that the reported number of dowry deaths in their states is inflated by settlers from other parts of North India. These data need to be investigated and researched further to understand why dowry and bride-burning became more prevalent in the Northern states of India.

A matter of growing concern is that people of mainly North Indian origin have now carried the practice of dowry to their new homes in the UK and North America. While dowry problems are also rampant in Mauritius (as reported by Bunwaree-Phukan, 1995), a notable exception seems to be found in South African Indian communities (see chapter 4 in this book). Another exception is India's Assamese community, which still carries the burden of male supremacy and adherence to traditional principles,yet has no dowry and no bride-burning, disproving the claim of many activists that these are brought about by male supremacy and Hindu scriptures. Such evidence needs to be further researched, since the solutions to the problem of dowry murders may be hidden behind such exceptions.

The burning of a bride often takes place in the secrecy of her kitchen. No one knows when or where it will happen, or to whom. By the time others learn of the event, the victim is already a charred body. There may be little evidence; there are often no witnesses other than the perpetrators. Prevention is almost impossible and in a court of law it often remains difficult to obtain a conviction because of lack of evidence.

There are evident links between such dowry and the historical practice of female infanticide in some parts of North India, which is now replaced with foeticide – selective abortion following modern ultrasound tests. It is no coincidence that there are far fewer women than men in the dowry-infested areas of India, compared to the Eastern states of India and Kerala, where women outnumber men.

The notion that education will eradicate dowry and bride-burning is powerfully disproved by the fact that people with lesser education, like tribal communities in various parts of India, do not indulge in such evil practices. Dowry problems are rampant among what one would call educated families, often highly educated, who should know better.

Efforts to combat dowry by making women economically valuable have not succeeded so far. A significant example is the death of Sangeeta Goel, who had a PhD in solid state physics and was employed as a highly paid scientist, who should have been very valuable to her husband economically. Her father failed to meet the dowry demands, and Sangeeta was found dead in her marital home in April 1994, barely five months after her marriage.

From the available evidence, many people conclude that dowry murder is a middle class crime. However, we have received reports of dowry-related atrocities also from the rich upper class. We must face the truth, therefore, that dowry and bride burning is a very complicated problem sprouting from unidentified seeds in history, mixed with old practices of caste, joint family tradition, male supremacy and misunderstood values like saving the family honour and, increasingly it seems, a desire to impress others through conspicuous consumption. The victimising of women in this context is a serious cultural abnormality which needs to be further researched and tackled. No other cultural tradition in the world inflicts this kind of violence on women and indulges in such gruesome destruction of precious young lives.

It is not possible to explain in a few words how dowry problems 'happen'. In a social context of arranging marriages, at all levels of society, mate selection involves considerations of caste ranking, education, financial status and personal character. The complex mechanisms of bride-giving and wife-taking in South Asia's mainly patriarchal cultures are premised on concepts of male supremacy, so that the girl's father is automatically treated as inferior to the boy's father and the wife-givers have to 'serve', as it were, the wife-takers. The wife-takers are thus tempted to exploit their stronger position and may go to the lengths of making demands, explicit or unspoken, that certain goods or property be given to them. Social conventions indicate, therefore, that the girl's family is mainly responsible for the 'giving away' of the daughter and has to bear the bulk of the marriage expenses. After the wedding, a bride normally goes to live in her husband's joint family and, in the extreme, becomes a member of that family, with more or less complete severance of her ties to her natal family.

Dowry problems are not an inevitable element of all South Asian marriages. But if dowry demands remain unfulfilled, an innocent young bride may become totally vulnerable and insecure in her husband's family. Should her birth family fail to produce the expected goods, she is likely to become the object of taunts and torture in her new home. She walks a perilous terrain, similar to a minefield, with no certainty about when and where death might strike. She knows that her life is in danger, but she has no means to protect herself against the impending disaster, nor has she anywhere to go.

A bride's parents are equally torn between giving in to dowry demands and resisting them, knowing that their daughter may be at risk if any wrong steps are taken. But what is right or wrong? Social norms seem to dictate that it is not acceptable to encourage a newly married daughter, who will feel insecure and vulnerable in many ways, to return to her natal home. The husband's family would most probably view this as interference and resent it. In a social environment where 'family honour' and the desire to save marriages at all costs are paramount, even women who have already been subjected to dowry-related violence would not easily contemplate leaving their tormentors. Moreover, a bride is at the pro-creative stage of her life, full of hope, faith and love. Together with her husband, she hopes to build a family. She has a strong belief that she will be able to win everyone with her love and does not want to give up that faith. Even when she knows that her life is in danger, she may hope that everything will turn out right one day and she feels that she cannot just move away.

It is well-known that brides in this difficult situation are normally told by their natal family to 'stick it out'. Even officials in shelter homes and police stations encourage them to return to the perpetrators of violence. Given the potential victim's desperation, everyone simply hopes for the best but actually waits for disaster to strike, suddenly, like a land-mine. Many brides are killed soon after they return to the husband's family.

Given the urgency of the problem, we invited scholars to scrutinise the problems of dowry murders in a series of International Conferences on Dowry and Bride-Burning in India. I must express my gratitude to several persons who encouraged me to continue the struggle. I cannot forget the late Sarah Rosenbloom, who passed away at the age of 90. Apart from the contributors to this book, I am also grateful to Mrs. Naomi Rosenberg of West Palm Beach in Florida, Mr. Inder Kapur of Hawaii, Dr. Renuka Sharma of Melbourne, Australia, Professor Michael Witzel of Harvard University, my wife Jyoti, and many others whom I cannot mention here for lack of space. Without their support it would have been difficult for me to continue.

Two conferences were held at Harvard University in 1995 and 1996 and a third at London University in 1997. The fourth conference will again be held at Harvard in November 1998 and further activities are planned, since the magnitude of the dowry problems we uncovered, and the considerable public interest in this matter, demand further detailed study. The present book is a beginning, pulling together the most relevant papers from the conferences held so far. I am grateful to all the contributors for their efforts in trying to save the lives of young Indian brides all over the world.

TABLE 1: Geographical distribution of dowry-deaths in India
Source: National Crimes Bureau, Home Ministry, Government of India

	Name of States or Union Territories	1987	1988	1989	1990	1991	1992	1993	1994
1.	Andhra Pradesh	98	113	216	248	411	424	575	396
2.	Arunachal Pradesh	0	0	0	0	0	1	0	0
3.	Assam	3	3	7	8	14	1	19	13
4.	Bihar	120	139	265	303	263	170	338	298
5.	Goa	0	0	0	0	0	1	2	0
6.	Gujarat	23	27	51	58	103	123	114	105
7.	Haryana	133	154	293	336	144	209	166	191
8.	Himachal Pradesh	4	5	9	10	30	18	18	4
9.	Jammu and Kashmir	10	12	22	25	9	30	20	1
10.	Karnataka	83	96	183	210	227	209	266	170
11.	Kerala	2	2	4	5	13	18	10	9
12.	Madhya Pradesh	220	254	485	556	423	350	370	354
13.	Maharashtra	250	289	551	632	828	727	746	519
14.	Manipur	0	0	0	0	0	0	0	0
15.	Meghalaya	0	0	0	0	0	2	0	0
16.	Mizoram	0	0	0	0	0	0	0	0
17.	Nagaland	0	2	4	0	0	0	0	2
18.	Orissa	2	2	4	5	63	152	254	169
19.	Punjab	70	81	154	177	99	101	147	117
20.	Rajasthan	113	131	249	286	152	250	369	298
21.	Sikkim	0	0	0	0	0	0	0	0

TABLE 1: Geographical distribution of dowry-deaths in India (continued)
Source: National Crimes Bureau, Home Ministry, Government of India

	Name of States or Union Territories	1987	1988	1989	1990	1991	1992	1993	1994
22.	Tamil Nadu	49	57	108	124	97	75	79	83
23.	Tripura	3	3	7	8	7	3	5	6
24.	Uttar Pradesh	553	639	1,219	1,398	1,597	1,783	1,952	1,977
25.	West Bengal	97	112	214	245	538	179	256	349
26.	Andaman& Nicobar Islands	0	0	0	0	0	0	0	1
27.	Chandigarh	0	0	0	0	2	1	3	3
28.	Dadra and Nagar Haveli	0	0	0	0	0	0	1	0
29.	Daman and Diu	0	0	0	0	0	0	1	0
30.	Delhi	79	91	174	200	133	121	107	132
31.	Lakshadweep	0	0	0	0	0	0	0	0
32.	Pondicherry	0	0	0	0	4	6	0	4
33.	TOTAL FOR INDIA	1,912	2,209	4,215	4,835	5,157	4,954	5,817	5,199

TABLE 2: Geographical distribution of concentration of dowry-deaths per million Hindu population
Source: National Crimes Bureau, Home Ministry, Government of India

	Name of States or Union Territories	1987	1988	1989	1990	1991	1992	1993	1994	6 year average
1.	Andhra Pradesh	2	2	4	4	7	7	9	6	6.17
2.	Arunachal Pradesh	0	0	0	0	0	0	0	0	0.00
3.	Assam	0	0	1	1	1	0	2	1	1.00
4.	Bihar	2	2	4	4	4	2	5	4	3.83
5.	Goa	0	0	0	0	0	0	0	0	0.00
6.	Gujarat	1	1	1	2	3	3	3	3	2.50
7.	Haryana	10	11	21	23	10	14	11	12	15.17
8.	Himachal Pradesh	1	1	2	2	6	4	4	1	3.17
9.	Jammu and Kashmir	4	5	9	10	3	11	7	0	6.67
10.	Karnataka	2	3	5	6	6	5	7	4	5.50
11.	Kerala	0	0	0	0	1	1	1	1	0.67
12.	Madhya Pradesh	4	4	8	9	9	6	6	5	7.17
13.	Maharashtra	4	5	9	10	13	11	11	8	10.33
14.	Manipur	0	0	0	0	0	0	0	0	0.00
15.	Meghalaya	0	0	0	0	0	0	0	0	0.00
16.	Mizoram	0	0	0	0	0	0	0	0	0.00
17.	Nagaland	0	0	0	0	0	0	0	0	0.00
18.	Orissa	0	0	0	0	2	5	8	5	3.33
19.	Punjab	10	12	22	24	13	14	19	15	17.83
20.	Rajasthan	3	4	7	8	4	6	9	7	6.83
21.	Sikkim	0	0	0	0	0	0	0	0	0.00

TABLE 2: Geographical distribution of concentration of dowry-deaths per million Hindu population (continued)

Source: National Crimes Bureau, Home Ministry, Government of India

	Name of States or Union Territories	1987	1988	1989	1990	1991	1992	1993	1994	6 year average
22.	Tamil Nadu	1	1	2	3	2	2	2	2	2.17
23.	Tripura	1	1	3	3	3	1	2	2	2.33
24.	Uttar Pradesh	5	6	11	12	14	15	16	16	4.00
25.	West Bengal	2	2	4	5	10	3	5	6	5.50
26.	Andaman & Nicobar Islands	0	0	0	0	0	0	0	0	0.00
27.	Chandigarh	0	0	0	0	4	2	6	5	2.83
28.	Dadra and Nagar Haveli	0	0	0	0	0	0	0	0	0.00
29.	Daman and Diu	0	0	0	0	0	0	0	0	0.00
30.	Delhi	12	13	24	26	17	15	13	15	18.33
31.	Lakshadweep	0	0	0	0	0	0	0	0	0.00
32.	Pondicherry	0	0	0	0	6	8	0	5	3.17
33.	TOTAL FOR INDIA	3	3	6	7	8	7	8	7	7.17

Chapter 1

Introduction: New concerns about abuses of the South Asian dowry system

Werner Menski

1.1 The need for action

The background to this book and its topic requires some explanation, which will also help readers to place the growing concern about dowry-related violence among South Asians into a wider context. This GEMS study is a pioneering effort which will probably be followed soon by other studies on the dowry problem among South Asians, in India and overseas. In this book, which is more than just a collection of the main papers from three international conferences on the subject so far, we have pursued a variety of aims. The main motivation was clearly a desire to try and help save lives, the lives of South Asian women who are burnt, otherwise killed, maimed or disfigured, every day of the year, because somehow their closest relatives through marriage are not satisfied with them or with what they brought with them into the marriage. One of the most worrying aspects of this problem has been that such murders and other dowry-related violence have been on the increase and now occur no longer only in Delhi or somewhere far away in South Asia, but also in London, other British cities, and in the urban centres of North America.

Many efforts have been made to deny this fact, to discredit our research and to silence us. All three International Conferences on Dowry and Bride-Burning generated fierce debates about different approaches to the dowry problem itself. Because of the constantly growing strength of our evidence, the inevitable result of our efforts has been a collection of articles which may be seen to cast South Asian people in a bad light. Many of us have been troubled by this, since we want to help solve a grave socio-legal issue specific to South Asians, a problem which is literally burning. There is no hidden agenda of destroying goodwill and, in the context of modern transnational South Asian studies, to undermine intercultural harmony and communication. Still, if we want to protect South Asian women from dowry deaths, it is not enough to engage merely in polite talk or detached academic discourse. Gruesome death figures with upward tendencies constantly reminded us that we have a grave problem before us and that no easy solution seems to be available.

Media attention for the conferences which led to this book has been remarkably intense, but not always for the right reasons. While we have tried to avoid being misused for essentially racist purposes, we have still been accused, in various ways, of throwing mud at the very people whom we say we want to help. Indeed, many Asians in Britain and North America are not keen to talk about the problems surrounding dowry transactions. Their defensive reactions confirm that the dowry problem constitutes a huge social problem in the communities themselves. While we may respect the right of individuals not to talk about such problems, we cannot simply condone the fact that a growing number of South Asian women has been falling victim to dowry-related violence. As Julia Leslie reiterates in chapter 2 below, there was a strong feeling that we needed to act, and act now.

We learnt, through the conferences and in our own research, if we did not know it before, that the dowry problem is an immensely complex and complicated phenomenon in South Asian societies and that no quick-fix solutions can be offered. We are painfully aware that South Asian women will continue to burn, every day, while this book is being read. I am afraid we even have indications that some of the people who discussed the problems of dowry with us then went away and exploited the system even more skilfully than before. Knowledge, as always, can be put to a variety of uses.

Nevertheless, instead of defining the problems away and closing our eyes to such disturbing aspects of current daily reality as the systematic murder of South Asian women, we have pursued the path of trying to understand how dowry-related violence is brought about and how such violence might be restricted. Speaking for a moment as someone with a specific interest in legal aspects of this problem, I want to highlight the fact that the various legal protection mechanisms developed by South Asian legal systems, in particular, have led to some prosecutions of murderers, but overall they have not been sufficiently effective to control, let alone stop, dowry murders. In contrast, North American legal systems and English law have only just begun to take notice of legal problems relating to dowry among South Asians in England, the USA and Canada. In those countries, as we found, the absence of culture-specific knowledge about dowry problems among South Asians adds to the dangers for South Asian women in diaspora, increasing their isolation and helplessness in situations of crisis.

Dowry-related violence is clearly not just a matter of criminal law or property law. It has complex economic and social dimensions which need to be unravelled, and which any remedial strategy must not overlook. Significantly, it became impossible for participants in the three Anti-Dowry Conferences so far to stick to tempting slogans like 'Dowry is bad! Abolish dowry!'. As we heard again and again, the truth of the matter is that many South Asian women actually expect, want and more or less demand dowries or their equivalents. While many contributors to the discussion argued that women should have no need to rely on dowries (see Julia Leslie in chapter 2 below), researchers like Bisakha Sen (chapter 5 below) argue that there are even hard economic reasons why women, and their natal families, count on the use of dowries as part of overall economic family strategies.

In the process of researching the subject, we found that the basic definitions of 'dowry' have remained unclear. There are definitely several concepts of dowry which interlink with each other and the picture is complicated, as this book reveals. Definitions apart, strong evidence to the effect that bringing a dowry helps and supports South Asian women in various ways means that it cannot be claimed that the dowry system is altogether negative for women. In other words, simple feminist, women-centred arguments have proved to be self-contradictory and have offered no useful analysis for how to tackle dowry-related violence. At the same time, there is no doubt that the customs of dowry exchanges can lead to dowry-related violence, which often kills women, on a growing scale and increasingly world-wide. Dowsing the flames of dowry seems, therefore, an important task, but the conferences made it very clear that outright abolition of 'the dowry problem' is just not an option. Many of us reluctantly approached an uncomfortable basic starting point for further discussions therefore, to the effect that South Asians anywhere in the world would have to learn to live with dowry arrangements without killing women in the process. But quite what is 'the dowry problem'? At first sight, it looks like an element of South Asian traditions which is anti-women, typically patriarchal, and therefore inappropriate for today's world.

1.2 Blaming tradition

It appears to have become increasingly tempting for modern researchers to portray dowry problems among South Asians as evidence of a barbaric traditional system which does not know how to treat its women as human beings and therefore violates with impunity the human rights of women. Indeed, in modernist discourses, dowry-related violence often serves as an illustration of systematic human rights violations perpetrated against South Asian women in the name of tradition and culture. But is this really so simple? Can one just blame tradition for the current violence against South Asian women? While it would be foolish to deny that there may be elements of tradition which feed the roots of the dowry problems which South Asians face today, dowry as a phenomenon is too complex to yield to any one-dimensional explanation of its origin and development into a custom of questionable pedigree. Given the internal diversity and long history of Hindu traditions specifically, and South Asian traditions more generally, one could 'prove' almost anything by reference to 'tradition'.

As Professor Michael Witzel showed during the First Conference on Dowry and Bride-Burning in India at Harvard (Witzel, 1995), the ancient Sanskrit texts mention a number of relevant aspects and subjects which relate to the dowry problem. Witzel noted in particular the fact that brotherless daughters could inherit property and could also become an 'appointed' daughter, which meant that such a daughter's son would then be acknowledged as continuing his grandfather's patriliny and would inherit the maternal grandfather's property. This was obviously a clever device, a legal fiction, as it were, to ensure the continuity of a bloodline which was in danger of being discontinued. As a general statement on whether daughters can inherit property, it rather shows the opposite of what modernists would like to see: normally, a man's sons would inherit the family property, while the daughters, in classic patrilineal and patri-local fashion, would move away to follow the husband. In normal circumstances, daughters did not inherit immovable property but took only movables with them into marriage.

What the old classic fiction about the daughter's son also tells us, however, is that ancient Indian tradition was flexible enough to take account of emergencies and of difficult situations. Old Hindu law is not a rigid rule system which cannot cater for change or is oblivious to pressures for finding a proper balance between patrilineal and matrilineal ideologies. Therefore, it would be wrong to claim in principle that a Hindu daughter could never inherit the family's property. What, for example, of the institution of the *gharjamai,* the son-in-law who agrees to move to the wife's home and who then takes on the business of looking after the family's economic affairs? There are many variations within South Asian traditions, Hindu, Muslim and others, so that no one regime of property relations was absolutely dominant.

With regard to marriage and dowry, the old sources appear to be familiar with the concept of dowry in the sense that a bride would bring possessions with her to the new home. These possessions, crystallised in the rather wider term *vahatum,* signifying all the things that are brought with the bridal procession, may be exclusively the woman's property, or they may not be – we simply do not know about this topic directly from the texts themselves. However, we should be aware that, in common with many other non-Western legal traditions, Hindu law views any form of property, in philosophical terms, as a matter of trust. Thus, whatever an individual owns is perceived to be only held in trust so long as that person lives – on death, property has to pass on to others, who in turn are just trustees. In that sense, no property right in Hindu law is absolute, since everything 'belongs', if that is the right term, to a higher entity. All humans, during their lifetime, therefore enjoy the right to own, but only in the sense of a usufruct rather than an absolute claim. It is apparent that Western legal concepts of individual ownership have later dominated legal rules as well as thought patterns.

While we do not know with certainty what ancient Hindu society thought of the property rights of women, there is evidence of 'dowry in a mild form' (Witzel, 1995: 7). As Witzel has shown too, the position of women themselves is ambivalent. To the extent that they may be seen as property of the husband, or of the family, anything they own will be owned by the family rather than the individual. But it would be misleading to assume that Hindu traditions spoke on this important issue with one voice. There never was *one* Hindu tradition to which everybody was supposed to adhere. Far from being owned by others as chattels, Hindu women were also perceived as individuals in their own right. After all, they constituted the most precious element of human creation, since it was all too evident that women alone could give birth and thus ensure the continuity of humanity. There seems to be much unspoken agreement in the specialist literature that the birth monopoly protected ancient South Asian women against annihilation. It had the effect that killing a woman, and certainly killing a bride at the point of entry to that phase of life in which she was supposed to be most productive, would become viewed as the most heinous of violations of the eternal Order (*rita*) that the Hindu worldview revolves around (see Miller, 1985). In view of this conceptual context, Witzel (1995: 9) argued that, within such traditional frameworks of reference, 'bride burning or dowry deaths, of course, do not occur at all. Such behavior goes against the Shruti rule not to kill any woman – a fact that has to be stressed today'.

It is evident from the literature that later conceptualisations of this superhuman Order do not stress the key role of women to the same extent. In a sense, the refusal of modern women to accept a predestined role as 'birth machines' is matched by the relative de-recognition of the female birth monopoly.

We know quite a bit about ancient Indian society and its development, but it is apparent that new research is required to answer new questions that now arise about the relevance of traditions. Asking why South Asian women today are subjected to killings of the type we have seen, and being given explanatory models which contain references to the insufficiency of dowry, we need to know more about what 'dowry' actually is and why it is considered so essential for the success of a marital relationship.

Another contributor to the First Dowry Conference at Harvard, R. N. Tripathi (1995), referred to the so-called eight forms of marriage among Hindus as a potential source of further information about the value attached to dowry transactions. In this context it is highly significant that the best form of marriage, the *brahma* form, is the one in which the bride herself is the sole consideration (see in detail H. Chatterjee, 1974: 369-

417). In other words, the solemn transfer of the bride to her new home is undertaken not for any financial gain but for the sake of continuity of mankind, signified in the sacramental tie between a specific husband and wife.

Notably, the less prestigious forms of marriage, albeit still good ones, are those in which either the wife's procreative potential or the goods that she brings with her form part of the contractual relationship that is being established (H. Chatterjee, 1974: 418ff.). Contrasting with that we find another form of Hindu marriage in which the husband (or his family, of course) have made a payment to acquire the bride, in other words, a form of bride-price. The dominant ideal model within Hindu tradition is therefore, it seems, the transfer of a virgin bride to the husband's family for no consideration at all. If we look at this contract in its social context, the absence of any direct consideration may well be a sign that the wife-giving family would, in turn, be entitled to expect that it was given wives from the other side.

At this stage of our research on 'the dowry problem' among South Asians today, far too little is known about why and to what extent brides were given something in marriage which we would call 'dowry'. Already the ancient material makes it clear, however, that there are various aspects of dowry transactions which can be distinguished. The treasure chest of the old *vahatum* probably contains many different things. The idealised – and idealising – old texts appear to suggest that these were willingly given. But it is equally clear that women were not killed and maimed because the dowry they brought with them was insufficient.

Thus, tradition involves South Asian women in some form of dowry transaction, but before one condemns this outright, one ought to reflect whether what we now refer to as 'dowry problem' might not be a more recent phenomenon. At the same time, giving presents to a daughter on her wedding looks also like some kind of ancient, universal phenomenon. In other words, what is 'Hindu' about giving one's daughter something on her way to the new home? Would it not be a rather bad reflection on a society of any kind if it allowed daughters to be sent away to a new home with empty hands? Such questions highlight the potential for conflict between arguments that dowry protects and assists women, and that it exploits and commodifies them.

Assuming that firm conclusions on the role of tradition in this context may ultimately be possible, we will not get any clearer answers unless a good deal of specific research is conducted on such questions. The resources for this, in the form of texts and material, are available in suffocating magnitude. What we need is researchers who can undertake this kind of painstaking work, and who are not merely excellent linguists but are mindful also of the social contexts within which the textual statements need to be interpreted. This remains a task for indological research which has been severely neglected, probably to the detriment of the discipline as a whole. The existing papers on this issue so far merely scratch the surface and Professor Witzel (1995) has convincingly highlighted the need for further detailed research.

Other work which we also did not include in the present volume of essays reflects the frustrations of concerned South Asians who, when faced with evidence of such barbaric customs as dowry murder, seek for explanations and find at once that their own tradition is blamed for this. The paper by R. N. Tripathi (1995) sought to identify certain scriptural elements which oppose the idea that dowry should be given. However, lack of focus on the dowry issue and constant interference by the train of thought that later historical events, as it were, impeded the development of Hindu cultural traditions, create an impression that, somehow, the current excesses of dowry-related violence are blamed on non-Hindu influences. It is manifestly too simple to blame Muslim influences in South Asia, in particular, for the current dowry problems. Such hidden agendas do not appear productive for comprehensive research on the South Asian dowry dilemma, although it is helpful to remind us that 'tradition' did not stop thousands of years ago.

1.3 The International Conferences on Dowry and Bride-Burning

So far, three International Conferences on Dowry and Bride-Burning have been held, two at Harvard (30th September to 2nd October 1995 and 22nd to 24th November 1996) and one at the School of Oriental and African Studies, London University on 14th/15th November 1997. At least three more such Conferences are currently being planned, another one in Harvard, one in India in 1999 and a further conference in London.

The first two conferences were organised jointly by the International Society Against Dowry and Bride-Burning in India (ISADABB) in Boston, Massachusetts and by the Committee on South Asian Studies at Harvard University. Both conferences took place at Harvard and the first one, in particular, attracted much attention among North American South Asians as well as international participants. In the first conference, eighteen papers were presented and lively discussions continued throughout the three days of the event. A Souvenir Volume collecting the papers from the first conference was issued, but its circulation has been limited (Witzel and Thakur, 1995). Some of the papers, together with other work, have been published in the electronic *Journal of South Asia Women Studies 1995-97* (see Garzilli, 1996), but that journal does not focus particularly on the dowry problem and looks at South Asian women's studies more generally.

Julia Leslie introduced the discussions at Harvard with a keynote paper, a revised version of which appears here as chapter 2. Recounting her own journey of discovery about the extent of the dowry problem in India today, she, too, argues for serious thinking about the links between past and present and calls for more attention to be given to the connections between dowry and female property rights generally. Another keynote paper from the first conference (see chapter 3) seeks to provide an overview of the issues surrounding dowry-related violence and also offers a preliminary literature review. It is argued that, at the end of the day, dowry-related violence represents a breakdown of civilised behaviour, akin to a serious form of bullying. In other words, this becomes a form of domestic violence, ultimately denying the newly married woman even the right to live. In this paper, too, the need for investigating the links between past and present is emphasised and the discussion highlights the need for greater reliance on traditional norms of internal self-control, rather than external pressures by agents such as the modern state law, which have proved to be inefficient in protecting endangered women's lives.

The issues covered in the first conference ranged from a discussion about the absence of dowry and *sati* problems in Vedic literature by one of the leading classical indologists in the world today (Witzel, 1995), to the most recent evidence of dowry murders. Professor Witzel showed clearly that ancient Hindu law did not underwrite dowry extortion, but that dowry in the sense of presents made to the bride by her parents and natal family, was known. As discussed above, in the ideal order of things, the bride herself was the main consideration and the most precious asset, on which all ritual and social attention was focused. What a contrast between this idealised depiction of tradition and a detailed presentation given during the same conference about an actual case of dowry murder affecting a South Asian family in the USA! Even today, the unresolved dowry murder case of Sangeeta Goel continues to be stark proof of the ineffectiveness of legal protection mechanisms for South Asian women.

At Harvard, several papers focused on domestic violence generally and the marginalised position of women, arranged marriages and their consequences, as well as various marriage practices linked to dowry and gift-giving (Witzel and Thakur, 1995). Some of these papers could not be included in our present collection. Ms. Bandita Phukan emphasised in a brief paper that sons are not essential for the execution of Hindu rites and that daughters can act in their place, thus seeking to oppose the gender-based ideology according to which daughters are only burdens and no asset to a Hindu family (Phukan, 1995). Uma Narayan (1995; see also Narayan, 1993) examined the effects of modernisation on patterns of marriage arrangements in India and concluded that the process of modernisation, by itself, has not benefited women, that it has in fact made marriage arrangements more prone to hazards which could negatively rebound on women, making them more vulnerable to violence.

A fieldwork-based study by Vijayendra Rao, which we could unfortunately not include, confirms that dowry-related violence has been on the rise in the subcontinent, even among villagers in South India (see Rao, 1995). On the other hand, Leslie's evidence to the effect that many so-called 'dowry problems' are not in fact directly related to dowry also appears in this context. Rao's research establishes direct correlations between perceived or actual dowry shortfalls and the extent of dowry-related violence, showing that this has negative consequences not only for women subjected to such violence, but often for their children, too.

Bisraam Rambilass presents the interesting argument that South African Indians did not and do not indulge in the demanding of dowry and claims that such practices are largely absent in his country (see chapter 4 below). At the same time, he provides evidence of the inflation of expenses surrounding marriage, a theme which several other contributors have also picked up as an indicator of spiralling anxieties in relation to dowry problems (see chapters 8 and 9 on Asians in Britain). While it therefore seems correct to argue, as Rambilass does, that for various historical reasons Indian South Africans do not experience dowry-related violence, there is no guarantee that in the future such inflation may not engender new forms of abuse.

During the sometimes heated discussions, the first Harvard Conference gradually shifted away from the classic approach of simply blaming the male side, or the husband's family, and began to look more closely at the roles played by the wife's family. It was found that the simple binary opposition of male-female does not make sense in this discussion, since in most cases the wife-givers of today would be the wife-takers of tomorrow. Several contributors showed clearly that the dowry problem was integrated with many other socio-psychological issues and that an exclusive focus on 'dowry' could not explain why South Asian women suffer dowry-related violence and continue to die. As a result of that first conference, it was even more obvious that further research was needed to explain and elucidate certain specific points.

The second Harvard Dowry Conference was much smaller than the first and gave space, as planned, to a more specific analysis of the economic and legal aspects surrounding dowry problems. Specialist papers had been produced for this conference and were discussed in detail. Our discussions focused in particular on the economic aspects surrounding dowry and the effectiveness of legal control mechanisms. Bisakha Sen's paper (chapter 5 below) explained why dowry still persists in India, using economic models which show convincingly that the wife's family actually benefits – or thinks it benefits – from offering and giving dowry. This challenging paper, which we have included although it is primarily addressed to a more specialist readership of economists (who have had their own discussions about dowry problems) confirmed the earlier preliminary view that one-sided blaming of male extortion might not be sufficient to explain why dowry problems have continued with such vigour among South Asians. Finding that the socio-economic conditions in South Asia so strongly operate in favour of continuing the transfer of resources to the bride and the groom's family on the occasion of marriage, Bisakha Sen began to explore the next logical step, asking how it can be made more certain that any resources transferred in this way would actually benefit the woman. The suggestion that this is a 'law-job', as it were, may be correct, but surely this is a matter not only for the law, but in the first instance for members of society? It will surely be useful to explore the economic rationales of Bisakha Sen's paper further and to contrast scenarios in which women do benefit economically from the dowry given to them on marriage with situations where such assets or their use are withheld from the woman because the husband or members of his family appropriated them as soon as they could. This kind of research would link well with further work on the property rights of South Asian women generally.

On the legal front, the law paper which I presented at the second Dowry Conference (see chapter 6) assessed and analysed in some detail how modern Indian law has sought to control the dowry problem. It was found that the almost universal perception that the Indian anti-dowry law has been a complete failure was correct until recently. However, beginning in the mid-1980s, the legal control and retribution mechanisms for dowry murder in Indian law have been strengthened by a number of new enactments which have gradually led to more strictly enforced judicial supervision. Still, despite growing evidence of convictions for dowry murders, it was found that those strict legal deterrents remained largely ineffective because only very few prosecutions for dowry murder or dowry-related violence were ever brought to the courts. It transpired that there are continuing problems of implementation of the anti-dowry laws at ground level, and it became evident that further research would be needed on this aspect of the legal control mechanisms.

More practical questions about the prevention of dowry tragedies were explored by Himendra Thakur, who outlined in some detail his plans for the establishment of shelters for dowry victims in India. This continues to be an important matter of abiding concern and we have included here a modified version of this contribution as chapter 11.

The London Dowry Conference on 14th/15th November 1997 was sponsored by the Dharma and Gender Working Group of the Dharam Hinduja Institute of Indic Research (DHIIR) and was jointly organised by the Group for Ethnic Minority Studies at SOAS, the SOAS group of Students Against Dowry (SAD), the Centre for South Asian Studies at SOAS and the International Society Against Dowry and Bride-Burning in India, based in Boston, MA. This conference had two major aims. It wanted to bring together our current knowledge about dowry-related violence among South Asians and to apply this to case studies reflecting specifically on the British Asian experience.

The morning session was devoted to a round-up on existing research on the dowry problem, provided by Julia Leslie, Kim Knott and myself. Following detailed discussion, the economic and legal aspects of the dowry problem were addressed through Bisakha Sen's paper on the economic dimensions of dowry (see chapter 5), presented in this Conference by Dr. Urmila Goel (SOAS) after extended transatlantic e-mail discussions. On the legal front, the detailed analysis of Indian case law on dowry was used as a basis for further discussion on legal strategies to combat dowry-related violence (see chapter 6). It was confirmed that it is no longer correct to assert categorically that Indian courts currently do not convict dowry murderers. A more updated analysis of the Indian *Dowry Prohibition Act*, 1961 shows, however, that despite many amendments to the anti-dowry law in India, women continue to be killed. Is appears that the legal deterrents by themselves do not lead to a decline in dowry-related violence. Earlier, we saw that the law has many loopholes, only some of which were plugged during the 1980s. While the legal definition of dowry has now been tightened, the giving as well as the taking of dowry are still crimes, and many participants in the discussion felt that this remains a major drawback. Further research on this issue remains to be done.

In view of the disturbing fact that most cases of dowry murder in South Asia never even go to court, specially commissioned research by Manjaree Chowdhary from India (see chapter 7) threw some light on the reasons for such legal inefficiency and anti-women collusion. The evident non-implementation of the anti-dowry law in India, presented as a powerful first-hand account, starkly illustrated why dowry crimes are still not pursued with the required vigour by Indian enforcement agencies.

The special focus of the London Conference on dowry problems among Asians in Britain today led, as expected, to animated debates following two papers based on fieldwork, presented by Rohit Barot (Bristol) on dowry among British Gujaratis (see chapter 8) and Jagbir Jhutti (Oxford) on dowry among Sikhs in Britain (see chapter 9). Jhutti's paper is part of a larger pioneering ethnographic study related to marriage arrangements of British Sikhs and contains powerful evidence of the deep-rooted complexity of dowry transactions among British Asians. Following several moving accounts of the dowry problem from various victim perspectives, a further paper by Usha Sood (Nottingham), an Asian woman barrister who has worked hard to bring such dowry cases before British courts, focused on the dowry problem in its legal context in Britain (see chapter 10). This contribution to the ongoing discussion showed that, in British legal practice, South Asian dowry problems have begun to achieve a higher profile, as a growing number of Asian women in the UK are currently fighting for their rights through the courts in Britain. However, the English legal profession as a whole is not sufficiently educated about South Asian family laws and the specialist issue of dowry-related violence to be able to make decisions which would help to curb the growing problems for South Asian women. In its own way, therefore, the Third Conference, too, has confirmed the awful truth of the continuing escalation of dowry-related social and legal problems among South Asians all over the world.

The three Dowry Conferences held so far have each identified a set of focal points of concern and established an agenda for further research (see chapter 12), which will be pursued in a series of further conferences. We have begun to link dowry-related violence with studies on domestic violence generally, and the need for more fieldwork-related explorations of the subject has become very evident indeed. With particular reference to Asians in Britain, we need to explore further to what extent specific research on dowry-related violence could assist law enforcers in the UK, as well as the countries of North America, to gain better knowledge and awareness about the dowry problems among South Asians.

The ultimate aim, as passionately put by Himendra Thakur, is to save thousands of young women from a gruesome death (see chapter 11). For the moment, though, our efforts seem to be frustratingly ineffective in the short run. Writing a book on dowry does not dowse the flames that kill. Dowry-related violence and the associated problems have continued to escalate, irrespective of various legal measures in the countries of the subcontinent, and despite much social censure against dowry-related violence in the overseas Asian communities of Britain and North America. As a group of socially-conscious academics and activists who seek to save lives, we have been painfully aware of such limitations. During all three conferences, there were moments of sheer despair, frustration, and outright horror at the scale and extent of dowry-related violence. All three heard personal testimonies from victims of the dowry problem, from relatives who had lost a family member or women who had been fortunate enough to escape from probable death or destruction of their personality.

While the ultimate aim is to save women's lives, we have an enormously long way to go. Writing a book on the subject clearly has no direct spin-off – it does not in itself prevent dowry-related violence. But not writing a book would be worse! Many of us felt strongly that a start must be made to break the vicious circle of dowry-related violence. Mr. Thakur himself, and the various organisations which have now developed as a result of his pioneering efforts, need and deserve the fullest possible support.

1.4 The conundrum of dowry

As the conferences confirmed, and our readers will soon discover for themselves, even the basic definitions surrounding the dowry problem remain somewhat unclear and some of the contributions in this book tackle only specific aspects of dowry-related problems. That, of course, has been part of the first big problem in understanding the difficult and extremely complex subject of dowry-related violence. Trying to establish a common language and terminology around the problems we decided to debate has not been easy. And I would argue in favour of maintaining a variety of perspectives and approaches, given that the dowry problem is such an immensely complicated conundrum and that no one explanatory model on its own seems to give us satisfactory answers. We have seen that simple sloganeering about the desirability of abolishing dowry altogether misses important points. Similarly, any laws which envisage a total ban on dowry or its outright prohibition are not going to be effective in social reality.

If a total ban on dowry is not a realistic option, because the people with whom – and about whom – we are concerned want to have some form of exchange, gift-giving and transfer of property, what other avenues of curbing dowry-related violence can we think of? For many conference participants, there was a need to think – with however great reluctance – about acceptable forms of exchange that fall under our definitions of dowry. But how can one ensure that, in the process, women do not get killed? In many ways, it seems that our discussions about dowry so far have replicated Madhu Kishwar's personal process of coming to terms with the pervasive existence of dowry. As a leading Indian social activist with a focus on women's rights, Kishwar initially tried to use techniques of public protest and boycott to highlight abuses of the dowry system and to call for the total abolition of dowry transactions. She was then told by women who had benefited from dowry transfers that, in essence, she had no business to tell other women to renounce their dowry claims. This story of an activist's self-discovery is recounted in detail by Kishwar herself (see Kishwar *et al.*, 1980; Kishwar, 1986 and 1988).

It appears that the dowry conferences held so far have taught us similar lessons. When it comes to dowry, we cannot throw the baby out with the bathwater; we have to co-exist with the fact that various dowry systems are operated by people in their respective social circles. Rather than condemning South Asians as stupid or misguided, we ought to apply ourselves to how to curtail and avoid any abuse of dowry transactions, in particular when it results in violence against brides and recently married women. To me, there is no doubt that this is a law-job, but that is by no means all that needs to be done.

Without wishing to be prescriptive, we hope it will be useful for readers who are unfamiliar with the subject if we indicate briefly that there appear to be at least three aspects of the dowry problem and what they are. They are closely interrelated but must be distinguished.

1. The term 'dowry' is generally used for what a woman brings or takes with her into the new home. These forms of property may be given by her parents and/or family, though she may have earned it herself. This form of dowry may cause its own problems because of inflation, and inflated expectations, but this is property that, in normal circumstances, belongs to the woman, should be owned by her absolutely, and should help her to build up her status as a married woman in the new home.

2. Also included in the wider definition of dowry, and at any rate closely linked with its social problems, is what a woman's natal family spends on the marriage celebrations, the feasting and the gift-giving that goes on around it. Much of this expense is non-recoverable, for example the food consumed, the costs for the venue, entertainment and other items of expenditure. In addition, presents to the

husband's family made as part of the wedding ceremonies and gift exchanges on that occasion, once given, would appear to belong to the recipients. Similarly, gifts received by the bride's family would become the recipients' property. There are many complex customs and conventions relating to economic transactions on the occasion of family celebrations, such as weddings, often subsumed under terms like giving-and-taking (*len-den*) and other forms of exchange systems. Here again, inflation and inflated expectations might cause problems, but the social customs as such are, at least in their origin, positive elements of social exchange and of bonding between the two families. In this context, it is very difficult to determine what precisely is 'dowry' and what is not.

3. The real crux of the dowry problem appears to lie with what the leading Indian sociologist M. N. Srinivas has called the 'new dowry': property or cash demanded or in various forms expected by the groom's family. This often turns out to be a grave burden on those families who have agreed to be trapped into unequal exchanges along hypergamous lines. It may still be that once such demands and expectations have been fulfilled, whether fully or partially, everybody is happy and the new couple (and at any rate the husband's family) is a little (or maybe considerably) richer than they might otherwise be. However, if it turns out that the husband's side claims to be dissatisfied with what was ultimately given – and that often includes the woman herself – or continues to make further demands after the marriage, we find what appears to be the real dowry problem, culminating in a scenario with burning bodies.

If we are concerned here to understand what 'dowry' means and involves, and aim towards the elimination of violence arising from dowry transactions, we must recognise that not all dowry transactions result in violence. Many South Asians marry with immense splendour and spend a great deal on the wedding as well as on dowry items, but nobody ends up getting killed. It may therefore still be argued that there is nothing wrong with those kinds of dowry transactions. However, the matter becomes quite different as soon as there is evidence of dowry-related violence against the newly married woman.

Our research so far has confirmed that dowry-related violence is not an inevitable consequence of dowry transactions. It only arises in particular situations, which can be referred to in terms of a breakdown of the customary concepts and contracts of exchange on the occasion of marriage. Problems appear to arise mainly in three types of scenario:

- If the wife's family promises too much dowry, perhaps as a kind of 'sweetener' for the groom, and afterwards cannot deliver what was agreed to be given. To take a British Asian example, the bride's father may have offered (for reasons good or bad) to buy the bridegroom a BMW as part of the marriage transactions, but he ultimately produces a Ford instead. We need to research in more detail, of course, why such offers are made in the first place. Or are they, as Jagbir Jhutti's work seems to suggest, not real offers but promises made under the duress of extortionate expectations? So much is certain: disputes get even more complicated if so many gold sets of jewellery or sets of clothes were agreed to be given and the other side then claims that these were not of high enough quality. Madhu Kishwar, among others, has made it clear that by criticising the dowry in such a way, the husband's side was indirectly criticising the woman, or rather, the 'package deal that she represents' (Kishwar, 1988: 12). There may be ritual elements of 'putting the other side down' involved in such disputes, but if the repercussions of such strategic bargaining turn into violence against the woman, something has gone seriously wrong.

- A variation of this theme is found when the girl's family did not actually offer to provide all kinds of dowry items but there exists an unspoken, silent expectation that certain gifts will be made as part of the dowry. Thus, as indicated, the young man or his family in the example above may simply have expected to receive a BMW (for whatever reason) and if that expectation is frustrated, then the young bride may be made to suffer. The same goes, more so in practice, for the quantity and quality of jewellery and clothes that are commonly exchanged in South Asian marriages.

- Dowry problems also arise when the groom's side, after an agreement about exchanges has been reached, actually violates that contract once the girl is married, or even during the marriage ceremonies themselves, by continuing to demand more and more. It appears that once a bride's family has agreed to be trapped in this way, there may be no end to dowry demands. The safest exit from such a breach of contract is clearly to terminate the marriage negotiations, if that is still possible. If this scenario arises only after the marriage, the predicament for the young bride can be extremely dangerous.

In this book, we progress in our analysis of dowry and dowry-related violence among South Asians from a journey of discovery, recollected by Julia Leslie, and an overview of the issues, provided by myself, to several attempts at legal, historical, cultural, economic and social analysis of the dowry problem. Dowry is clearly a complex interdisciplinary problem, and this is reflected in the research conducted on the subject. None of our contributors has been able to stick to one particular discipline or perspective and we have not even begun to include the important work which has been conducted by researchers in medical-related subjects.

It seems impossible, at this stage, to pronounce on definite conclusions about how to get round dowry problems, in particular how to abate dowry-related violence. The discussions and analyses we present here highlight that one of the key problems in the dowry debates continues to be that South Asian women themselves are in certain circumstances perceived as property that is passed on and exchanged between families. It is too simple to say that this mind-set occurs in all patriarchal contexts, for this is manifestly not true in social reality, where only certain families stoop so low as to kill a new bride or daughter-in-law.

Our research so far seems to suggest that once a woman is perceived merely as property, or the bearer of property, any individual woman's rights to property given by her parents on the occasion of marriage (or indeed brought by the woman herself in her own right) is, in a sense, assumed to be transferred to the ownership of the new family. When a mother-in-law virtually confiscates a new bride's possessions and gives them to her own daughters or to someone else, we find clear evidence of abuses of the dowry system which can have disastrous consequences. Again, it would be too simplistic to blame traditions like the joint family system, for such abuses do not occur in all joint families. Dowry-related violence is decidedly not an integral part of marriage arrangements among South Asians anywhere in the world; it is evidence of a grave social illness that has infected some people belonging to those social groups, not everyone. So there is no need for South Asians to be so defensive about the topic of dowry, for we are not saying that dowry is bad *per se*, while we do say, clearly and loudly, that torturing or killing women in the name of dowry is inexorably a despicable crime. If, as the evidence suggests, this crime is on the increase among South Asians, then there is a strong need to do something about it. Hence, to return to our starting point, there was an urgent need to compile this book and to propel some very necessary discussions which will keep us busy into the next millennium.

Chapter 2

Dowry, 'dowry deaths' and violence against women: A journey of discovery

Julia Leslie

I first met Himendra Thakur, Chair of the Board of Directors of the International Society Against Dowry and Bride-Burning in India, at the Ninth World Sanskrit Conference in Melbourne in January 1994. Prior to our meeting, he had sent me a copy of a book he had written, a fictionalised account of a dowry death in India (Thakur, 1991). His intention in writing that book was to provoke an emotional response to an emotive topic, and it worked. Having read the book, and being already sympathetic to its message, I was not surprised by Mr. Thakur's impassioned presentation in Melbourne. He outlined what he saw to be the current situation in India regarding dowry deaths: that the custom of demanding dowry is spreading throughout India, and that the number of dowry-related deaths is on the increase. He explained that he had been trying to do something about this within India for over a decade but without any real effect. Finally, he begged the conference participants most earnestly to do everything in their power to bring international public opinion to bear on the matter.

The response from the floor, from mainly Indian delegates, was uninspiring but understandable. One speaker suggested that this was an inappropriate topic for a Sanskrit conference. Another implied that Mr. Thakur was doing India a disservice by 'washing her dirty linen' in public.

When I stood up to support Mr. Thakur's call, it was an instinctive response. I had done no research on the topic myself. My own work (see bibliography) had been on gender ideology in classical Hinduism with a particular bias towards teasing out the implications for women. In this context, dowry deaths seemed an especially worrying modern variant of the general oppression of women, and one that I ought to know more about. I should like to thank Mr. Thakur formally for making me shift my focus for a while from the ideals of the classical past to the uncomfortable realities for South Asian women today.

2.1 'Dowry deaths' in the news

The following summer, I went to Bangalore to spend the better part of my sabbatical year. Alerted by Mr. Thakur's appeal, I kept an eye open for reports of dowry deaths. For this purpose, I ordered several papers on a daily basis and soon built up an unsystematic selection of cuttings which strike to the heart. The headlines say it all: 'Housewife ends life following dowry harassment' (*The Deccan Herald*, 20 November 1994); 'Woman commits 'suicide'' (*The Hindu*, 25 November 1994); 'Woman alleges dowry harassment' (*The Deccan Herald*, 13 February 1995); 'Girl dies of burns' (*The Hindu*, 16 February 1995); 'Dowry death: Husband held' (*The Deccan Herald*, 17 February 1995); 'Dowry harassment case: Bangalore doctor absconding' (*The Indian Express*, 20 February 1995); 'Dowry death: Life term for 5' (*The Indian Express*, 27 February 1995); 'Young woman set on fire' (*The Hindu*, 10 March 1995); 'Suspected dowry death reported' (*The Deccan Herald*, 13 March 1995). An article by Frederick Noronha in *The Deccan Herald*, 20 March 1995, entitled 'Goa: Alarm over women burning to death' begins:

> Women in Goa are burning to their death, and nobody seems to know why... Shockingly, some 109 predominantly young women died of their burn injuries in a 20-month period, and women activists suspect that many of these cases are linked to dowry-demands and post-marriage harassment.

There was also a disturbing report by Charu Lata Joshi in *India Today* (15 October 1994, pp. 122-129), entitled 'Civil Services: Give dowry, will marry', which detailed the astronomical amounts openly demanded by grooms in the Civil Services in today's marriage market. Such reports led me to wonder how long 'dowry deaths' had been receiving such attention.

A recent book on the role of the media in projecting gender issues (Joseph and Sharma, 1994) provided some answers. Media attention was drawn to dowry-related deaths in 1978-79. Following Tarvinder Kaur's death, a campaign against dowry was launched in Delhi (see R. Kumar, 1993a). This, in turn, drew attention to what became known as 'bride-burning'. Media coverage during this period reflected the general assumption that the problem was restricted to Northern India. By 1983-84, however, it was beginning to be recognised that the problem afflicted many parts of the country. 'Bride-burning' became front-page news, and the subject of editorials and in-depth comment. However, as Joseph and Sharma (1994: 42) quietly note, only the 'alternative media' went further, to 'highlight structures which perpetuate patriarchy and oppression'.

At this point, my own appreciation of the issues underlying dowry deaths was simplistic. Parents are unhappy when a girl child is born because the widespread assumption is that they will need to pay a dowry when she marries. If they are lucky enough to have a son as well, they will see his marriage as an opportunity to bring in the money for the dowry of their daughter. Inevitably, for some grooms' families, marriage becomes a way to make money. Greed for more leads to the harassment of brides.

Kishwar (1986: 2-4) had tackled such popular belief from several angles. First, the notion of 'greed' is usually linked with the influence of Western consumerist culture. However, greed in Western cultures has not led to dowry demands and to the burning of women, which is a peculiarly South Asian response. A second, related idea is that dowry becomes 'evil' only when the groom's family is unnaturally greedy, the implication being that 'voluntary giving' on the part of the girl's family is acceptable. Kishwar (1993: 14-16) also discussed in what sense such giving can be termed 'voluntary' in the context of current social expectations.

In extreme cases, so much I learnt quickly, murder or suicide is the direct result of dowry-related harassment. If a bride dies, her husband can marry again for a second dowry, often without apparent difficulty. The giving of dowry in the first place is traditionally justified in terms of giving the daughter her 'inheritance' at the time of marriage (see e.g. Teja, 1993: 94-96). As Madhu Kishwar (1994a: 10) found when the Manushi-led boycott of dowry-marriages failed, this is the argument most often used by women themselves to justify their own dowries:

Why should they be forced to give up a dowry, they argued, when they knew their parents would not give them a share in the family estate? If I did not have a means of ensuring that daughters got their due share in parental property, what business did I have to prevent them from getting dowries? In their view, it would only serve their brothers' interests, as they would get an even larger share of the inheritance.

However, only a small proportion of that dowry may be intended for a woman's own use. Even more disturbing is the balance of power implied by dowry: both families seem to agree that it is necessary to pay the groom's family to take on the burden of a bride.

My own experience showed that the fears of the parents of daughters were real. When I left Bangalore, my once-weekly cook was desperately trying to raise Rs. 75,000/- for the dowry of the eldest of her three daughters before the young woman turned twenty; for then, she assured me, the groom would raise his price. She had tried to find a young man who would take her daughter without a dowry, but in vain. Now she had no more illusions: The full amount (more, if possible) had to be found, or her daughter might be in danger. Another example was provided by a middle-class friend. To protect his daughter's life, he cancelled her supposedly dowry-free wedding when he received a demand for cash and gifts just days before the ceremony.

At this point in my journey of discovery, after reading whatever I could lay my hands on and talking to whoever would listen, I drew three seemingly obvious conclusions. The *problem* was the harassment of wives; 'dowry deaths' and 'bride-burning' were real. The cause was dowry. The *solution* was the eradication of the dowry system. But how was this to be achieved? As we have seen, anti-dowry campaigns seem to make no difference. In this context, it made sense to me that the debate on dowry should concentrate on legal issues: defining dowry, prescribing penalties, ensuring the enforcement of the anti-dowry law. If existing or amended laws could only be enforced, if dowry-giving could be eradicated, then surely 'dowry deaths' and 'bride-burning' would belong to the past. This is also the usual stance of the media (Joseph and Sharma, 1994: 42). A leader article in *The Deccan Herald* (10 March 1995, p. 8) entitled 'Fair deal to fair sex' argued:

...if the concept of fair deal to women in all walks of life were to mean something more than a utopian ideal, there is an urgent need for taking other effective measures to enforce the co-parcenary rights of women as regards property and also the laws against payment of dowry to men at the time of marriage and harassment of women who fail to fetch dowry.

However, I am not a lawyer, and so the matter was left there, at least for the moment.

2.2 Dowry as a middle-class phenomenon

My next question focused on the scale of the problem. How prevalent is the custom of demanding and giving dowry? Are 'dowry deaths' and the system of dowry generally on the increase? How big is this problem?

I spoke to several activist groups in Bangalore. Were they tackling dowry? Was the question of 'dowry deaths' on their agenda? Again and again, I was informed that, in the context of women's issues generally, this was a minority topic. Dowry deaths are numerically and statistically few, I was told, and the dowry problem is still largely restricted to the wealthier urban middle classes, especially in the North of India. This was an argument I had heard and read many times before. As far back as 1928, for example, M. K. Gandhi had written in *Young India* (21 June 1928), quoted in Gandhi (1947: 58):

> A correspondent sends me a newspaper cutting showing that recently in Hyderabad, Sindh, the demand for bridegrooms has been increasing at an alarming rate, an employee of the Imperial Telegraph Engineering Service having exacted Rs. 20,000 as cash dowry during betrothal, and promises of heavy payments on the wedding day and on special occasions thereafter. Any young man who makes dowry a condition of marriage discredits his education and his country and dishonours womankind.

Apart from the actual figures of the cash transaction, Gandhi could have been describing an agreement made today. The dowry system, termed 'marriage by purchase' by Gandhi, was considered heartless and he argued that it should be abolished:

> There is no doubt that the custom is heartless. But so far as I am aware, it does not touch the millions. The custom is confined to the

middle class who are but a drop in the ocean of Indian humanity... This, however, does not mean that one may ignore the dowry evil because it is confined to a comparatively small number of the people of this country. The system has to go. (Gandhi, 1947: 59)

For Gandhi, however, dowry abolition was never a major target for reform. It remained a minority issue confined to the upper levels of society, and so not a serious menace to Indian culture as a whole. In fact, Gandhi was much more concerned with the abolition of child marriages and the offensive idea of old men buying child brides according to the custom of brideprice (see Gandhi, 1947: 55-58). This view has persisted despite statements to the contrary by several eminent researchers.

The earliest detailed Indian study on the dowry problem found, as part of a survey of attitudes towards dowry among Scheduled Castes and Backward Classes in some areas of Delhi, that the main concern was not to escape dowry demands but to persuade the Government to raise their incomes, so that they could spend and give even more than they did (Hooja, 1969: 87). In 1976, M. N. Srinivas publicly highlighted the fact that dowry was no longer confined to the upper levels of society but 'has now spread even to so lowly a group as sweepers in Calcutta' (Srinivas, 1978: 26).

Recent studies make it plain that the custom of giving and taking dowry has expanded and that it is spreading further fast. While studies of rural women are still in their infancy, the trend is clear. It must suffice here to note only one example from Southern India, an empirical study of rural women in the Bangalore District of Karnataka in 1979-80 (Khan and Ayesha, 1982). Of the 390 women covered in the survey, 86% were Hindus, 12% were Muslims, and 2% Christians, thus establishing a fairly representative sample. In the context of dowry, the researchers commented, at pp. 172-174:

One of the salient features of modern marriage customs is the emergence of the dowry system. This unethical system has grown so strong and spread so wide that it is said to have been accepted and practised by all the religious groups and caste groups...

...Though it was admitted by all the religious groups that payment or demand of dowry had no sanction in the concerned religion, dowry system prevails among all the groups. However, among the Hindus, the incidence is extensive and penetrative though 76 per cent are against this...

...the amount paid by the Brahmins was generally the highest among the Hindus. Lingayats are also very much concerned with this system. Exceptions are rare. The dowry system has entered the lower castes also. But the rigidity is not as much as found among the Brahmins and Lingayats.

For a long time the Scheduled Castes remained outside the clutches of the dowry system. But according to the Scheduled Caste women respondents, during the last two decades, even these people have begun to adopt this custom. However, this is generally confined to the rich and the educated among them. But the poor people are not totally free in general.

Muslims...pay both dower and dowry, the former from the boy's side and the latter from the girl's side and further the former is generally a deferred amount, whereas the latter is [an] immediate one.

If this pattern is found elsewhere, as seems to be the case, (especially if I look back to my collection of press cuttings and Noronha's article on Goa, referred to above), then the spread of dowry appears to be in all directions: from urban to rural communities, from higher to lower levels of society, from Hindus to non-Hindus.

2.3 Who is to blame?

Interestingly, 83% of the women respondents in the study by Khan and Ayesha spoke against the system of dowry. However, when group discussions were held separately with the men and women of the community regarding who was thought to be responsible for the perpetuation of the system, the sexes disagreed:

The consensus among the men is that their women are responsible for this. Left to themselves, they are prepared to give up the practice. On the other hand, women feel that they have little say in decision making and therefore, men alone are responsible. (Khan and Ayesha, 1982: 172-173)

Blaming women is a common tactic in this context. In particular, mothers-in-law are blamed for being behind the constant demands and the brides themselves are described as taking pride in the lavish dowries they bring. At an early stage of her own personal journey of discovery, Kishwar (1986: 10-11) was forthright in her rebuttal of this point of view, saying that 'blaming the women as the major perpetuators of dowry is like blaming the soldiers on the battlefield for fighting... Dowry, as practised in India, is a war declared by men against women, using women as pawns'.

The findings by Khan and Ayesha corroborated my own observations: everyone is against dowry on principle, and yet everyone feels compelled to take part, the men by the women, and the women by the men. Both dowry-givers and dowry-takers term the custom iniquitous, then acquiesce. This has led to the notion that anyone can be victimised by the dowry system, even men.

2.4 Can men be the victims of dowry?

When I first came across this idea, I thought it extraordinary. In Bangalore, two letters to the *Deccan Herald* caught my eye, both written by men. On 6 January 1995, Ravi Mario wrote about 'Harassment of husbands', speaking of the victimisation of innocent men by scheming wives who accuse them falsely of dowry-related harassment. The second letter, by Mani Parameswaran, was entitled 'Unfair Dowry Act' (*Deccan Herald*, 13 March, 1995) and complained bitterly that 'many men are suffering at the hands of their wives', adding that such men 'are afraid of the Dowry Act under which the already suffering husband has to undergo further suffering'. I found that such warnings had earlier been voiced by Ram Ahuja (1987: 120), who wrote that 'stringent pro-bride laws will become tools in the hands of unscrupulous people to exploit innocent husbands and in-laws'.

On investigation, such claims are not as ludicrous as they may seem. Indeed, Madhu Kishwar told me not long ago that she was giving legal aid to a family who had been taken to court by just such a daughter-in-law. One may also be struck by the parallel with cases of rape and sexual harassment in the West, where men's fears of being falsely accused are well-documented; Michael Crichton's best-seller *Disclosure* (London: Century, 1994) derives its unusual tension and unsettling popularity from just such a scenario.

Another uncomfortable example is provided by Elisabeth Bumiller's study of Indian women. Bumiller (1990: 48) begins on apparently firm ground, with official statistics:

In 1987, the government released figures in Parliament that showed that the cases of registered dowry deaths nationwide numbered 999 in 1985, 1,319 in 1986 and 1,786 in 1987. These figures almost certainly do not reflect the actual number of dowry deaths in a country where most people do not report domestic violence. In India, violent deaths are common, but the dowry deaths are especially startling.

But when Bumiller seeks out a severely burnt survivor of such violence, nothing seems straightforward. After several visits to the young woman in question, after listening to both sides of the story, after speaking to both families and both sets of lawyers, Bumiller does not know what to believe and writes, at p. 61:

To this day I still wonder what happened and I suppose that I always will. If I were forced to decide, I would have to agree with the defense lawyer, as odious as that is to me, and say that her burns were self-inflicted in an attempt to frame her husband and sister-in-law. But my judgment is based on instinct, not evidence.

In the context of her evident sympathies for Indian women, this is a courageous conclusion. It is difficult to admit uncertainty, even more difficult to allow for the opposite conclusion to that which one has set out to find.

Bumiller's analysis of female infanticide in Tamilnadu provides a similarly discomforting conflict of loyalties. Her informants place the blame squarely on the custom of dowry, never on the parents or grandparents who carry out the killings. Bumiller (1990: 102) writes:

No one knew for certain... how prevalent female infanticide really was... But the phenomenon was sufficiently widespread so that the government-employed midwives who lived in the area told me they feared for a newborn's life if it was so unfortunate as to be the third or fourth girl born into a poor family of farm laborers. Such a family could not possibly afford the price of another girl's dowry, a custom which in Belukkurichi had spread to lower castes that had not observed it even a decade before... To some villagers of the valley around Belukkurichi, 'putting a child to sleep', as they called it, seemed their only choice.

The reader's shock is not easily digested, embracing as it does the murder of a baby, the dreadful choice faced by parents, and the even more dreadful rationalisation of their decision.

But we must be careful here. Our sympathies for the parents of the murdered baby girls in Tamilnadu should not blind us to the fact that it is the girls who die. Similarly, our sympathies for a husband possibly framed by a temporarily unhinged wife should not make us forget that it is the women who burn. Whatever the justifications, whatever the rationalisations, the violence is inevitably experienced by the female: in the womb, at birth, at marriage. While men may perceive themselves to be 'victimised' in a particular case (having to poison their own baby, having to find the money for a sister's dowry, having to pay more and more to keep a daughter safe), this is not to be compared with the death of women or with the torture of constant harassment. Violence against women is the norm (see Verghese, 1980; Ghosh, 1989; Omvedt, 1990; Sood, 1990; Mitter, 1991; Kapur, 1993; Jung, 1994).

At this point in my investigation, the scenario still seemed fairly clear. Despite the protestations of both men and women against the dowry system, few are able to resist the demands. The self-respect of the groom's family depends on attracting as large a dowry as possible. This factor cannot be dismissed lightly. A small dowry may be seen as an insult to both families. A groom 'without a price tag' is often assumed to have something wrong with him; whether or not this is the case, he and his family are liable to be treated badly (see Khan and Ayesha, 1982: 173; Kishwar, 1993: 14). The bride who brings a handsome dowry earns respect in her new home. On the other hand, as the Karnataka study (Khan and Ayesha, 1982: 173) demonstrates:

...if the amount is low or secured after a lot of bargaining, the girl is not safe in the hands of the in-laws. She is harassed, insulted, humiliated not only by her in-laws but also occasionally by her husband, according to respondents.

Again, the conclusion seemed obvious: dowry is the root of the problem, the eradication of dowry the answer. But I still had some doubts.

2.5 Is dowry really the problem?

I had read various estimates of the numbers of women whose deaths were termed 'dowry deaths' and the figures were always shockingly high. For example, in 1994 in Uttar Pradesh, a total of 1,852 dowry deaths were registered, as against 1,606 in 1993 and 1,444 in 1992 ('Crime against women increases in U.P.', *The Hindu*, 10 March 1995, p. 9). We already saw above that Bumiller (1990: 48) cited official nationwide figures for 1987.

But I had also heard it said that most of these deaths were unrelated to dowry. For example, a Delhi Police Commissioner in charge of an anti-dowry cell in Delhi is quoted as saying that 90% of the so-called 'dowry deaths' are in fact suicides or murders due to what she chillingly terms the bride's 'inability to adjust to marriage'. In each case, she is quoted as saying that the issue was made out to be one of dowry in order to take advantage of the 'prevailing pro-bride wave' (see details in Ahuja, 1987: 115).

It is important to be clear here. There is no disputing that women and girls are dying. Furthermore, as I hope to have shown, most media reports and investigative studies take dowry to be the primary problem. If this assumption is correct – and again, this we must find out – then our urgent task must be to dismantle the dowry system. But if there is a flaw in our argument, then anti-dowry campaigns – ours included – may be missing the point. This was my area of discomfort. Is dowry really the problem?

Clearly, I needed more facts. I shall cite one example here. From 1979 to 1989, a total of 147 cases of marital violence were reported in *Manushi* (Nos. 1-50). In 79 of these cases, the woman died. The other 68 cases involved beatings, torture and attempted murder. In the lethal group, dowry was cited as the primary cause of violence in 36 cases; dowry was mentioned but other causes cited as primary, in eight cases; and dowry was not mentioned at all in 35 cases. In the non-lethal group, dowry was cited as the primary cause in 10 cases; dowry was mentioned, but not as the primary cause, in nine cases; and in 49 out of 68 cases dowry was not mentioned at all. Out of the total of 147 cases, therefore, only 46 cited dowry as the primary cause. Kishwar (1989a: 5) summarises these preliminary findings:

A pattern we noticed in the reporting was that when the woman spoke or wrote about the violence she suffered, dowry was almost never

31

mentioned as the sole cause and, further, that most of the reasons were merely pretexts, the violence being actually irrational and causeless, merely an expression of power. When a third person who was not a continuous witness to the violence such as the woman's parent, sibling, other relative, or an activist, reported the case, the description tended to be briefer and more unidimensional, and more frequently focused on dowry as the only or primary cause of violence.

This pattern is evident from the fact that in cases where the woman had died, and had left no account of her suffering, about half the cases (reported by others) were ascribed simply to dowry (36 out of 79). But in cases of torture or attempted murder where the woman either reported herself or would have spoken to the person reporting, only 14.7 percent cases cited dowry as the sole cause, 13.2 percent cited other causes as primary while mentioning dowry, and 72 percent cited other causes, or none, not even mentioning dowry. It is noteworthy that the violence in these cases was not of a negligible kind, ranging from attack with an axe to chopping of nose to repeated rape by father-in-law to severe battering and sadistic torture.

It is clear from reading these and other cases, and from the Deputy Police Commissioner's comments quoted earlier, that 'dowry deaths' are not always what they seem. The media, the police, the social worker or activist, even the woman's own family, all have internalised the urgency of the label. Harassment of women not so labelled, even extreme forms of violence, are more likely to be dismissed as a domestic matter. We are left with the day-to-day brutality of violence against women. Sometimes dowry is the pretext used by the perpetrators, sometimes it is a convenient label for those who wish to press charges. Clearly, we need to know more precisely what is going on. To my mind, however, it is the violence that matters, and the vulnerability of women in South Asian societies – indeed, the institutionalisation of that vulnerability – that allows it to happen. The real problem, as I see it, then, is the perceived internalised and socially reinforced ideology of the inferiority of women. In this respect, the Legal Aid Handbook of the Lawyers' Collective in Delhi suggests:

Wife-beating knows no class, race or religious distinctions. Woman battering is not just an aberration in the behaviour of a number of disturbed men; it is a violent manifestation of male domination over women and the patriarchal attitude that sees women, especially wives, as the property of men. (Lawyers' Collective, 1992: 5; on theories of female subordination see generally Bhasin, 1993).

2.6 What should we campaign for?

The aims of the International Society Against Dowry and Bride-Burning in India fall into four important categories:

- **Support for the victims of violence.** This should cover both practical help, such as medical and legal assistance or work training, and psychological and social support in the form of women's shelters, or counselling.

In this context, Kishwar (1994b: 16) warns against naive assumptions regarding the oppressed. As she points out, the poor and vulnerable are no more virtuous than the powerful and wealthy: 'A woman who seeks aid because she is suffering marital abuse may be abusive to others herself, or there may be mitigating factors for the husband's violence'.

- **Education and awareness.** This ranges from the education of children – boys and girls – to a major national and international campaign to galvanise public opinion in India and abroad against the varieties of violence against women, including those perpetrated in the name of dowry.

This is not a new agenda item, of course. In 1928, Gandhi (1947: 28) wrote that change could only be brought about by the educated youth: 'A strong public opinion should be created in condemnation of the degrading practice of dowry, and young men who soil their fingers with such ill-gotten gold should be excommunicated from society'. In 1976, M. N. Srinivas pointed out that the passing of the *Dowry Prohibition Act*, 1961 had had no real effect and concluded that only a powerful social movement among educated youth could have any impact on this great evil (Srinivas, 1978: 26). The significance of this conclusion is undermined, however, by Srinivas' insistence on two dubious benefits of dowry: first, that the custom has helped to raise the age of marriage of girls, because it takes so long for their parents to raise the necessary cash; second, that this in turn has helped to spread female education.

It should be pointed out that education for girls is a complex pheno-menon with serious consequences. For example, it is the norm for a bride to be married to a man with more education than herself. But a more educated groom expects or requires a larger dowry. Highly educated girls, therefore, need a massive dowry to catch a suitable husband. As dowry demands increase, young women become yet more vulnerable to their in-laws (see Jeffery and Jeffery, 1994: 148-157). Again, we need to know more about the issues involved in female education in the different regions of India and at the different levels of society. Two major actions are needed:

- **Fact-finding and research**. This should include in-depth studies of incidents recorded as 'dowry deaths' and 'bride burnings' to ascertain the facts of the situation, research into the theory and practice of the dowry system in different parts of India, and broader theoretical analyses of how dowry fits into the wider pattern of misogyny and violence against South Asian women.

- **Law enforcement**. This seems more problematic in view of a percep-tion of widespread lawlessness in India today. It is evident that legal attempts to enforce the anti-dowry laws have failed abysmally. Baxi (1986: 62) has claimed that people in India do not even know that dowry is prohibited by the law. I follow Madhu Kishwar's lead in strongly arguing that we focus on the laws relating to inheritance rights for women instead of looking narrowly at the dowry problem.

2.7 Inheritance rights for women

As we have seen, a daughter clings to her dowry because that is all she is likely to see of her parental inheritance. Men (fathers, brothers, male rela-tives) resent having to find large sums of cash and movable items as dowry, but they would far rather pay dowry than give a daughter or a sister equal inheritance rights. As Madhu Kishwar (1989a: 4) wrote:

It is significant that historically, any attempt to ensure women's inheritance rights has been violently opposed by women's fathers and brothers (the supposed victims of the dowry system). For instance, a perusal of the parliamentary debates in the years preceding the passing of the Hindu Succession Act, 1956, is very instructive in this regard. Men were united across party lines in opposing equal inheritance rights for women on the ground that it would create discord between brothers and sisters. In other words, they virtually admitted that a key element in the asserted harmony between brothers and sisters is the disinheritance of the women. While some brothers accept their obligation to give dowry, few are willing to concede inheritance rights to women.

But this dowry is no real inheritance. However large a sum it may be, it is always pitifully small when compared to the brother's share. Furthermore, most of it may go not to the bride but to the groom's family. Thus it may never provide for a woman's future security in the way that her brother's share, large or small, can. By associating the daughter's 'inheritance' with marriage and by handing most of it to her husband's family, Indian society treats her as a perpetual minor, deprived of what little she is given. In contrast, her brother will receive his inheritance as an adult and will, by and large, control what he gains.

But let us imagine a different scenario. Girls and boys have the same opportunities for education and work training. They are brought up, both at home and at school, to treat each other as human beings. They are treated equally in their natal home. When they marry, they marry as adults (physically, socially and psychologically), whether they live with her family or his, or on their own. Wife and husband treat each other as equals with equal rights to decision-making. The wife loses none of her inheritance rights. She receives her full share of parental property at the same time as her brother receives his, and therefore not at her marriage. When she marries, she loses none of her rights to her natal family. She can visit her parents or even live nearby; she and her brother are equally responsible for their ageing parents.

Imagine if this were the case. A bride would then no longer hanker after dowry for her own protection, and her male relatives would no longer have the incentive to pay her off. The question of dowry would fall away of itself. I therefore urge that we focus the legal aspects of our campaign on demanding inheritance rights for women. We need to separate property rights from marriage, both in our minds and in reality. This will cut at the deepest root of the pernicious dowry system. Once that root is cut, the dowry tree itself will wither away.

Chapter 3

Dowry: A survey of the issues and the literature

Werner Menski

3.1 The problem and the potential for solutions

There is now a fair amount of writing on the dowry problem and my students always find this one of the most difficult and challenging topics in modern South Asian laws to understand, research and write about. Significantly, most writers in this field are women, reflecting particular concern among female scholars and activists about dowry-related issues although, to be fair, in family law generally there are significantly more women writers than men. Still, the dowry problem is clearly an illness of society as a whole, not specifically a women's issue, even though women are so obviously the main victims.

To construct a literature survey, one could follow the literature in chronological order. However, that seems hardly a suitable strategy because it would probably just reproduce the various confusions around the dowry problem in a rather messy order. For it is a sad fact that writers have just gone round in circles during the past few decades, while the dowry problem has become worse and worse. A look at a major old study on the position of women in India shows this at once. Altekar (1978: 71-72) wrote:

> In ordinary families, however, the amount of dowry was a nominal one. It was a voluntary gift of pure affection and presented no impe-diment in the settlement of the daughter's marriage till the middle of

the 19th century. It is only during the last 50 or 60 years that the amount of the dowry has begun to assume scandalous proportions...

It is now high time for Hindu society to put an end to this evil custom, which has driven many an innocent maiden to commit suicide. There are signs to show that this custom is becoming unpopular and odious, but public opinion must assert itself more emphatically. The youth must rise in rebellion against it.

This text, originally written in 1938, shows us (I have left out several related portions) that the problem we discuss here in the late 1990s had already excited public opinion decades ago and that the definition of dowry itself has not been quite clear. Is it, as Altekar seems to suggest, the case that the voluntary gifts of affection are causing the dowry problem? What precisely is the key issue here?

This chapter attempts to clarify what the dowry problem actually is and to isolate its various aspects and sub-questions which have arisen over time. I therefore focus first on definitions and various aspects of the problem before addressing the question of how to curb the manifest evil. My reading of the literature suggests that neither legal reform nor social action movements by themselves can achieve significant improvement unless they take into account the crucial role of individual self-restraint.

Where does this leave us when thinking about the eradication of dowry and bride-burning? Indeed, we need to discuss human psychology and morality rather than law and social policy issues. Dowry violence is not something that can be abolished by law, or administered away; it is evidence of a growing human deficiency in self-control. We will need to discuss this in more detail.

Surveying the literature, one finds that most writers about dowry pursue their own larger or specific agenda at the same time and thus actually devote less attention to remedies for dowry violence than one would hope. It seems we all do that. So let me pursue my own agenda as a human being thinking about the dowry problem, not as a male or a scholar of Hindu law. Since what I say here could immediately be misunderstood as some form of attempt to raise Hindutva consciousness, I must ask for patience.

Having read everything about dowry that I can lay my hands on, it seems to me that the key to improvements of the situation seems to lie not in arguing in a broad sweep for gender equality or more specifically for increased property rights for women. These are no doubt important legal agendas. Still they are illusions because human life always turns any equalising formal provisions into diffuse unequal realities. Significantly, the very first Indian study on the dowry problem (Hooja, 1969: 222) immediately argued that if inheritance rights for daughters would be introduced, men would simply marry girls with the most property rather than the highest dowry! Rather, the key to effective solutions lies in a basic moral message, which any human society may find difficult to implement because it depends on individual self-restraint when it comes to exploiting dowry as a tangible financial benefit. Yet, while greed is undoubtedly a core issue, it does not by itself explain why South Asian women are dying as a result of so-called dowry disputes.

A careful reading of the literature shows that we should learn to see dowry murders as the negative outcome of a conflict resolution strategy in which one side sits in judgement over the other and faces few restraints on its bargaining power. It needs to be questioned whether this is fair and humane, and we must therefore tackle the individual human tendency to exploit the other's weaknesses regardless of the consequences. This is a much more complex issue than the imbalance of gender relations, although the dowry complex is manifestly part of the bipolar gender struggle that many writers depict.

Verghese (1980: 185) portrays an image of anti-dowry campaigners as a group of mice nibbling away at the huge net that ensnares the ferocious lion of dowry. We have certainly had fascinating discussions in the Anti-Dowry Conferences so far, but there has been the constant danger that too many different agendas compete and clash, making us forget that the main task was to nibble away at the ensnaring net. This net is, in a wider sense, the ubiquitous human quality of unbridled egoism. Unless we ourselves overcome this, we will not even be able to have a meaningful discussion of possible solutions to the dowry problem. This remains a danger for future Conferences also, which some people might be tempted to use as fora for their own publicity, riding the bandwagon of dowry debates.

Reading the literature confirmed my latent cynicism about the force of self-control, which is also reflected in ancient arguments in Hindu philosophy to the effect that selfishness and greed are ubiquitous forces in the world and that self-controlled order is not something that can be expected simply to happen by itself. Hindu philosophy and Hindu law show that *dharma* – doing the right thing at the right time – needs to be promoted, by the state, by moral education, by the good example of individuals (in Hindu legal terminology *sadacara*), the behaviour of model figures in society, who need not be elderly men who claim to know some sacred sources. This model behaviour does not have to be seen in terms of *dharma* (or, for that matter, *shariat*, its Muslim equivalent); it could be perceived in terms of human rights, but the message ought to be meaningful to the addressees in a particular socio-cultural environment. For ultimately individuals are the agents of self-control and self-restraint. Let us just note that this element of reflection on one's human duty, a form of conscious abstinence from bullying, seems to be lacking in the perpetrators of dowry violence.

How does one instil self-restraint in greedy or abusive individuals? So far, the arguments we can read in the literature all relate to and focus on external force: blacken the face of dowry tormentors, boycott dowry weddings, ostracise those who beat women for cash, fridges and scooters, demonstrate against dowry murderers, drag them to court, even hang them in public! None of these deterrent strategies seem to work fully. While all of them nibble away at the ensnaring net in some form, thousands of women continue to get killed every year. We should consider, therefore, whether perhaps the crucial locus of control of the dowry problem lies not in the street or the courtroom, nor within the binary opposition of men and women, but within the individual mind. Saying this is not calling for a return to Hindu values because there is nothing inherently 'Hindu' about self-control, but I do think that a South Asian public, to whom any reform messages would need to be addressed, would benefit from reminders about the basic human value of self-restraint, in cultural terms that make sense to the people concerned. Thus, while we may also blame westernisation and modernisation for the ills of the dowry problem, it would appear that its roots go deeper and are local, too. Otherwise, how would we explain that evidence of dowry murders is found mainly among South Asians, in fact concentrated among certain kinds of South Asians, not spread throughout the social field? While it could be argued that greed is found in any human society, this argument does not explain the manifestly uneven distribution of dowry deaths.

Tackling the dowry murder problem in this way seems to end up as an argument for moral education, which again is no guarantor for instant success in combating the dowry problem, but would be an important element of a comprehensive strategy. For self-control under threat of sanction will evaporate as soon as the threat seems less powerful. If we do not want a police state, we need a society composed of individuals who are able and willing to exercise self-control. But how does one achieve self-control in relation to the dowry debates?

3.2 Literature on dowry: History and definition

Complex psychological issues aside, even the definition of dowry remains a somewhat thorny issue, as we saw in chapter 1. While it could be argued that the dowry syndrome is an ancient element of South Asian societies, the problem of dowry violence is clearly a thoroughly modern phenomenon. Thus, there is no need to rewrite Hindu scriptures – a ridiculous suggestion anyway, because one cannot undo the past. The Hindu cultural texts, arguing from within the *dharma* complex, do not, as we have seen, underwrite cruelty to women for the sake of material possessions (*artha*). At the same time, there is much scope for re-interpreting traditional sources in the light of today's new concerns about dowry-related violence.

In essence, most writing uses 'dowry' in at least three senses. The first is presents, jewellery, household goods and other property taken by the bride to her new home or given to her during the marriage rituals. These are items to be used by her, or by the couple, as a sort of foundation for the new nuclear household unit or sub-unit being established, either on its own or within the context of a larger, joint family unit. It is often seen as a form of pre-mortem inheritance for the daughter, which has given rise to a long, complicated debate about female property rights (see below). Another, closely related issue is the nature and extent of the bride's individual property rights over these items. In families where the new bride herself is perceived as property, there are bound to be disagreements over the ownership of this form of dowry, which should be the absolute property of the bride, but may not be treated in this way.

I have already shown that a second form of dowry may be constituted by what families, particularly the bride's family, conspicuously consume on the occasion of the marriage celebrations. In this respect Srinivas

41

(1984: 27) stated unequivocally that 'Indian weddings are occasions for conspicuous spending and this is related to the maintenance of what is believed to be the status of the family'. Such expenditure on the marriage only benefits the couple indirectly, probably in status terms rather than directly in a financial sense. Otherwise, the exorbitant costs of celebrating weddings these days ultimately provide benefits to skilful service providers, many of whom have grown fat on such inflationary trends in what is undoubtedly a growth industry. Several contributors to this book appear to focus on the costs of weddings as an element of the dowry problem (see especially chapters 8 and 9 with fieldwork from Britain). I would argue that this is a different kind of dowry problem, related because of the cost and status elements, but it does not quite hit the key area of concern. We can hardly imagine that South Asians would stop celebrating marriages in style, although the *Marriages (Prohibition of Wasteful Expenses) Act*, 1997 in Pakistan became instantly quite popular and has brought about important changes, which need to be further researched. On the other hand, these kinds of expenses, often exorbitant, add to the tensions around marriage arrangements and therefore contribute to the dangerous climate in which newly married brides may get killed.

The third type of dowry, the really problematic aspect of the phenomenon, is dowry as property expected or even demanded by the husband, more often by his family, either as a condition for the marriage itself, or at a later stage. This is the 'consideration' for the marriage that the legal textbooks, and Indian anti-dowry law itself, talk about.

There is much scope for these three forms of dowry to become intertwined and mixed up, in the minds of writers as well as in social reality. Many writers remain unclear about basic issues of terminology and thus fail to identify precisely what the dowry problem is. The main reason for such confusions appears to be that dowry has been attacked and viewed simply as a form of suppression of women, a manifestation of the inferior status of women, who are at best given presents, but have no full rights over them. This then gives rise to typical ideologically motivated sweeping statements which fail to pay attention to detail and therefore miss important points. A recent example of such ideological round sweeps is found in Kumari (1994: 104):

The problems of violence against women in the form of rape and dowry are to be looked [at] from a wide perspective of unequal status of women in the Indian society. The solution also will have to be worked out accordingly. Isolated efforts to meet the challenge of dowry or rape as separate problems are, therefore, insufficient.

This clearly puts the dowry problem in the wider context of gender inequality. I do not disagree with portraying the dowry problem this way, but authors who pursue this line of argument inevitably end up suggesting that only legal equality can provide a solution and therefore fail to address the essence of the dowry scenario. In my view, such generalised, utopian arguments have been unproductive for the dowry debates, and also for other questions relating to South Asian women's rights. Even the most advanced legal systems in the world have not achieved gender equality, and may never do so (see Monsoor, 1994 and 1998). Thus, it seems a long way off to recommend this arduous route of legal change to Asian and African people just because the West fools itself into thinking that it has invented legal equality. Such hypocracies can be traced back to Christian doctrine (see Kelly, 1992: 105), with remarkable parallels among Muslims whose retort to accusations of gender suppression is that everyone in Islam is equal. This means, however, as in Christian doctrine, equality only before God, not in real life! It may be necessary for a full analysis of the dowry problem to take explicitly into account that in South Asian societies women are definitely not perceived as equal to men. Arguing for gender equality as a remedy for dowry-related violence closes one's eyes to the immediate, burning issue of daily dowry murders and postpones solutions to an unbearably distant future. This is not good enough in view of the gruesome facts.

What then, more specifically, are the central elements of the dowry problem? Is it merely a continuation of the old *kanyadan* syndrome, the giving away of the daughter as the key ritual of marriage, or in fact a new economic trick of the unscrupulous, even a 'money-earning racket' (Awasthi and Lal, 1986: 1)? It has been easy to blame Hindu tradition, but the overwhelming evidence (see already Altekar above) is clearly that the real dowry problem has little to do with religion and is an economic issue, in other words, more of a secular, modern phenomenon. Still, Indian legal textbook writers in particular, who seem to ignore recent sociological writing when they produce their introductions and turn to old textbooks on Hindu law instead, insist that various forms of dowry appear to have existed in ancient India (Awasthi and Lal, 1986: 1). This then leads to conclusions that 'dowry is of an ancient origin which assumed abnormal proportion in later times' (Awasthi and Lal, 1986: 2). Without any further reflection, this simply blames tradition for feeding the deepest roots of the problem. The result is that this approach excuses, at least to some extent, modern unacceptable behaviour. I find such explanatory models deeply unsatisfactory and patently dishonest.

An important early study on dowry is the much-cited book by Hooja (1969), whose foreword clearly indicates that the problem of dowry may have its origin in affection but has, in course of time, grown into a commercial practice causing untold misery (Hooja, 1969: xi). The author herself immediately emphasises the 'element of competition, carrying a 'demonstration tendency" (Hooja, 1969: 1). However, Hooja fails to draws a clear enough distinction between the traditional form of dowry as property that a girl brings with her on marriage and the modern forms of extortion that cause so much trouble. She recognises the link with absence of inheritance rights (Hooja, 1969: 17) but then seems to assume, in essence, that the old custom of the *kanyadan* type has simply taken an acute form in the present century (Hooja, 1969: 18). It is evident that we need to know more about that crucial link, if indeed this is a key element.

However, to others it may seem that dowry is not so much some religious obligation run amok, through which the past asserts its hold over women, but rather a modern, consumer society phenomenon. Towards the end of her study, Hooja (1969: 212) indeed refers to dowry as 'unspiritual in nature', with 'no ethical value'.

Verghese (1980: viii), in an informative early study, also imagines a process of deterioration 'from being gifts of affection to becoming a means of extortion and exploitation' and thus clearly links the two forms of dowry together. Several other authors do the same but seem unaware of the consequences of doing so.

Notwithstanding the considerable tradition of dowry extortion, so-called dowry murders are in my view a different aspect of the problem; they are also a still more recent occurrence, much more dangerous than the dreaded widow-burning (*sati*), precisely because *any* South Asian woman, of whatever religion, could fall victim to it at any time. As we noted, so-called 'dowry-murders' also occur in Pakistan, especially in Lahore. *Sati* differs in that respect, too.

It is important to isolate such distinctions from the start. Fuming about the *sati* syndrome, feminist arguments which a *priori* challenge the fact that Hindu women are attached to men and are given away in marriage miss several important points. Notwithstanding local customs, especially the patriarchal patterns of Northern India, young Hindu women are first of all precious commodities, not in a commercial sense but because women alone can bear children. Older women, and of course men, have always resented this, but this is never verbalised. Modern writers overlook such basic cultural factors and therefore draw fundamentally false conclusions. Thus Kumari (1994: 116) is wrong to assert that 'Kanya is no different from any other thing worth giving away'. Saying so strongly that a girl is just a commodity ignores precisely – purposely, one must conclude – what modern feminists know to be the most precious element of womanhood for society, the capacity to bear children. It is therefore too simple to see the continuing frequency of dowry deaths merely as evidence of the powerless position of women in Indian society (see Parashar, 1992: 25, 26).

Every society needs a next generation. The gift of a daughter, thus, manifests primarily not her subjugation in a patriarchal society, but the honouring of a family's duty to society, having reared a girl child who will be of value to another family rather than her natal clan. If this kind of thinking is repulsive to modern feminists, so be it, but in a discussion on dowry-related violence we cannot shut out such traditional thinking as though it did not exist and is irrelevant. This societal burden-sharing is still expressed in various forms of bride-price, but that is not the issue here. The critical point is that such burden-sharing is reciprocal and roughly equitable: much of the writing seems to forget that the wife-givers of today will be the receivers of wives tomorrow. Much so-called activist scholarship seems to have overlooked this, simply falling into the trap of binary opposition, whereas life is so much more complex.

Challenging this complex exchange mechanism as evidence of Hindu chauvinism, religious suppression of women and a manifestation of continued female subordination through marriage, reflects so-called modern thinking which places individual egoism before duties to society. Regrettably, such analyses by themselves offer no productive routes for understanding how South Asian societies work and why some South Asian women suffer. They simply dismiss everything South Asian, 'religious' and 'indigenous' as inferior and bad. Such deficient approaches offer scant scope for understanding, let alone resolving, the serious social and legal problems surrounding dowry.

I therefore find that an important research job has remained neglected so far. Traditional indological scholarship and modern sociological research need to get together to identify in more detail how transactions which could fall under 'dowry' were viewed and developed in earlier times and how people themselves view the links between the two kinds of dowry today.

3.3 Dowry as part of complex marriage transactions

Dowry transactions are clearly part of something much more complex, namely the intricate marriage arrangements among South Asians. Subject to many local variations, these are immensely diverse. Having identified the transfer of the woman herself as not necessarily central to the dowry problem, we need to look at the financial or material transactions. I do not agree with Julia Leslie's position that these can be separated from marriage transactions; it is so manifest that South Asians themselves treat them as important elements of such arrangements.

It is well-known that such transactions are reciprocal but often show a marked imbalance between the wife-giving and the wife-receiving group. This imbalance, again, should not be read simply as evidence and confirmation of female subordination. Only some dowry transactions lead to violent deaths. In situations where everyone agrees about these loaded reciprocal transactions, and they are even carried out in public (mainly because that is part of the status game being played), there is no dowry problem, even though millions of rupees or takas, or thousands of pounds or dollars may have changed hands. The 'dowry problem' is therefore not measurable in financial terms, because it can arise among millionaires as well as lower class families who barely have the resources for a 'decent' marriage. Marriage exchanges, as everybody knows, are public affirmations of status and are used to acquire status (see Srinivas, 1984: 27, cited above). Thus, spending on marriages, and not just in India or among South Asians, has become a fashion (which we may deplore) but this does not help us to uncover the dowry problem itself. If South Asians regularly go crazy about spending vast sums on the *tamasha* of *shadi*, the spectacle of a splendid wedding, as new fieldwork in Britain clearly confirms (see chapters 8 and 9) that is still not, perhaps, a core issue of the dowry problem.

Many different agendas have thus been mixed into the dowry discussions and one needs to separate them out to grasp the core of the issue. As discussed already, it evades the problem to insist that the core of dowry-related violence is female subordination. Let us be very clear: dowry problems occur as part of relationships between males and females, but they occur only when there is a breakdown of the reciprocal arrangements around such a relationship, whether at the point of a marriage or afterwards. Problems only occur when there is a violation of the customary arrangements and expectations concerning a particular marriage. We only come to know of dowry problems when one side refuses to honour its part in the arrangements or when the other side exploits its assumed position of strength and superiority by demanding more and more.

However, this is only one explanatory model, which we need to pursue further. Two further models are likely to yield relevant results. The first relates to dowry violence against a woman as an individual who is found wanting in some respect. Often, criticism of this individual is phrased as a dowry dispute, although the real issue is not the dowry. As Julia Leslie also found (see chapter 2), Madhu Kishwar (1988: 12) expressed this issue well when she argued that 'criticising the dowry, like criticising her family, is a way of criticising her, and the package deal that she represents'.

I do not yet see another explanatory model adequately reflected in the literature. This relates to so-called 'dowry deaths' as a result of marital breakdown. To put it more sharply, dowry murder has evidently also become an alternative divorce strategy – a dead woman cannot demand maintenance payments and other ancillary benefits. Thus, it has become cheaper and quicker to get rid of an unwanted wife through 'dowry-murder' than to negotiate her exit from an unsatisfactory marriage. This is cruel reality, especially in the Pakistani part of Panjab, where some fieldwork has been conducted, which needs to be further pursued, showing that dowry is not a Hindu problem but an illness in South Asian societies of any description.

To clarify the complexity of marriage transactions, a small list of the various exchanges may help to locate dowry problems:

[Key: G = girl; B = boy; GP = girl's parents; BP = boy's parents;
}}} = transfer; {{{ = reciprocity]

0. Non-negotiable in principle:

GP　}}} BP　the girl herself = she becomes part of BP

　　{{{　　wife-giving rules between communities/families

　　　　BP community may give Gs to GP community

　{{{　　(sometimes: bride price)

1. Negotiable between GP and BP:

a) GP　}}} G　ornaments, clothes, household goods = **dowry?**

　　　　= women's property (*stridhanam*) ?

　{{{　　nothing, but touching their feet = respect

b) GP　}}} BP　cost of the wedding arrangements and reception

　　{{{ BP　may contribute, or hold their own reception

c) GP　}}} BP　clothes and ornaments, other presents

　　{{{　　some reciprocity, but often a clear imbalance

　　　　we can locate the **real dowry problem** here

2. Negotiable:

GP　}}} B　gifts, ornaments, clothes, cash　= B's property?

　　{{{　　nothing, but touching feet = respect

　　　　potential for **dowry problems** here, too

3. Negotiable:

BP　}}} G　ornaments, wedding dresses, clothes = G's property or BP's?

　　{{{　　nothing, but touching feet = respect

4. Depends on family arrangements:

BP　}}} B　gifts (esp. when B and B=G do not stay in the family and move out)

　　{{{　　nothing, but touching feet = respect

5. Negotiable, but really part of 1 above:

B　}}} G　ring or some other sign of marital link

　　{{{　　something similar or equivalent

6. After the marriage: further scope for **dowry problems**

GP　}}} BP

GP　}}} G

GP　}}} B　These depend on custom and family arrangement.

Dowry in the traditional non-hazardous sense is thus found in 1a), but the dangerous dowry problem is located in various rubrics of the list above and, notably, also in the time after the marriage solemnisation is long over. This confirms the finding that there are indeed important links in people's minds between the two main concepts of dowry. If dowry-grabbing in-laws have taken not only to expecting but to actually demanding that the bride should arrive in her new home with specified amounts of goods, not only is the bride herself devalued, but the old form of dowry has been intermingled with, and virtually incorporated into, the new dominant form of the demanded assets that are to come with the bride, just as the early study by Hooja (1969) suggested. This is a further reflection of the fact that some women, apart from the goods they bring, are seen as property of the family. As several researchers have begun to indicate, this is a dangerous constellation and one of the potential scenarios for dowry-related violence, for it is easy to claim that the newly arrived chattels, including the human addition to the family, are not of adequate quality.

However, it would be too simple to blame the strength of traditional South Asian family concepts for the dowry woes of individual women. It remains a fact that there will be no dowry problem in one household and family, while in the next there will be a murder. South Asian joint family ideology does not by itself underwrite the murder of women and does not explain why we find selective violence – there are complex other factors at work which need to be explored. But what are they? One important nexus, highlighted by many researchers and campaigners, has been the nature of the links between female property rights and dowry-related violence.

3.4 Dowry and inheritance

For a number of reasons, giving increased inheritance rights to women has become a prominent new topic in relation to the dowry debate. There is considerable legal action on this front, too. I have already argued, with reference to Hooja (1969), that giving inheritance rights to women will not by itself alleviate dowry-related violence. Most writers seem to agree, but the agenda for female inheritance rights are of course much wider than the dowry issue.

The early literature on dowry in the context of marriage arrangements is of a more sociological than legal nature, since the anthropological interest in marriage arrangements and exchanges pre-dates legal concern about dowry abuses. I do not propose to go into that literature, which rehearses the well-known patterns of exchanges and subordination in South Asian marriages in the context of kinship studies.

Among the writers on dowry, already Hooja (1969: 32 and 41) found that well over 90% of her Scheduled Caste respondents were unwilling to advocate the abolition of dowry. This kind of evidence could easily be dismissed as a sign of undeveloped consciousness or of backwardness. Hooja (1969: 197) clearly saw it as evidence of greater honesty: Since dowry benefits daughters, and to go empty-handed to a new home does not make sense nor create a good impression, women have an interest in securing dowry from their parents.

On the other hand, among Hooja's interviewees from the three upper castes, less than 10% favoured the retention of the dowry system (see in detail Hooja, 1969: 90-193). In social reality, however, it was found that all castes adhered to the practice of dowry (Hooja, 1969: 197), so that there was divergence between theory and practice for the upper castes and greater honesty among the lower caste group.

On the traditional realm of dowry, I found Derrett (1984) and Sharma (1984) most useful. Both concentrate on the property aspects of the dowry problem. Derrett (1984: 185) emphasises, like Hooja (1969: 15), that there is in fact no Sanskrit word for 'dowry' in its modern sense, that dowry is part of a complex pattern of exchange (Derrett, 1984: 188) and that its main function is to secure and enhance the bride's status (Derrett, 1984: 192). Therefore, a bride with inadequate dowry, i.e. a woman who comes to her new home with little to show, is seriously penalised in status terms (Derrett, 1984: 183). This confirms again that the two main forms of dowry have become linked together in people's minds, even though they are different. Derrett, arguing for further legal reforms, also concluded that if one really wanted to help the wife as an individual, one would have to secure her absolute property rights.

In an excellent article, Ursula Sharma (1984: 66) has reiterated that within the *kanyadan* complex, bringing a dowry gives women status. However, she also shows that this dowry property is not in fact individual property (Sharma, 1984: 64-66) and that dowry is therefore wealth that goes (or comes) with women rather than being owned by them absolutely. Sharma (1984: 70) writes:

> Contrary to the dominant ideology and the terminology of traditional Hindu law, dowry property is not women's wealth, but wealth that goes *with* women. Women are the vehicles by which it is transmitted rather than its owners.

As a result, Sharma (1984: 71) argues, the dowry transaction has become more important than the girl herself, a significant and, to that extent, correct observation. I have already said that nobody speaks in sufficient detail about the procreative power of the young woman, but surely this also remains a key element, unspoken because it is so obvious to the insider.

Thus, if so-called modern wife-takers today claim that they want 'only the girl', they might be saying that they are not really interested in what the young woman might bring with her, because they want, first of all, a future mother of their children. On the other hand, the very same statement might also mean that the wife-takers want nothing much to do, in terms of future social relations, with the wife-givers. In this case, too, they are saying that they want only the girl, precisely because her main value is her procreative potential. The resulting difficulties for a new bride in this outrightly patrifocal context, where the wife-takers do not even wish to keep family relations with her natal family, can turn into nasty scenarios that may not be called a dowry problem, but are relevant here in the context of dowry-related violence. For what happens to a girl who was given on the understanding that she is not to contact her parents any more, but who quite naturally wishes to do so? The flashpoint here may not be the insufficiency of dowry, but this dangerous scenario is only a tiny step away from a situation where anyone in the family can express criticism of the tormented bride in terms of her insufficient dowry. After all, this young woman was given away on the understanding that only she was to be given! We see here a further reason why inheritance rights for daughters would be considered problematic: they would necessitate some kind of continuing link between the bride and her natal family. This, at least in North Indian patrilineal ideology, is certainly not wanted, thus contributing to the difficult isolation of the newly married woman who has to bear the burden of adjusting to a new position in life.

Sharma (1984: 71) also comments on the fact that the law has not been effective in controlling dowry problems and then turns to the feminist agenda of opposition to dowry. Here she notes two major issues. First, dowry offerings, within a hypergamous pattern of marriage arrangements, now enable lower-caste women to 'marry up' through financial incentives to the man's family. This facilitates more inter-caste marriages and thus increases competition in the marriage market (Sharma, 1984: 72). Secondly, as her article argues throughout, women remain divided over dowry because they are at the same time beneficiaries and victims of it. Her overall assessment is clearly negative, in the sense that 'dowry has during the present century come to be regarded as a social evil by Hindus themselves, but somehow as an evil which no-one knows how to stop' (Sharma, 1984: 71).

Feminist writing on this topic can be traced back to the earliest issues of the magazine *Manushi*. Already in its first issue, Sadagopan and Kumar (1979) highlighted the dowry problem and documented cases, including letters written by women who were contemplating suicide. Such writing has been important to inform and rally supporters but does not extend to critical analysis. However, there is a serious and sustained attempt to come to grips with the dowry problem, reflected in a fascinating series of articles by Madhu Kishwar and published in *Manushi*. By 1980, she had focused attention on an anti-dowry campaign which concentrated on boycotting dowry marriages (see Kishwar *et al.*, 1980). However, some years later she candidly discussed the futility of that strategy and emphasised the importance of dowry for women:

> While in many cases, the woman is not allowed to enjoy her dowry, in many other cases, she does have some enjoyment, partial or total, of it. To go dowryless is to be deprived even of this chance. Hence, women's common sense desire [is] for a dowry...

> In many cases, therefore, dowry is a woman's lifeline. To ask her to do without it is like asking workers to protest against wage slavery by working for free and abstaining from taking their wages (Kishwar, 1988: 10).

This is evidently recognition of the fact that dowry itself is an asset to women, an often very valuable security, and of potentially enormous benefit to them all their life. To demand that right-minded women should renounce dowry, Kishwar's argument goes, may be ideologically correct but does not offer a solution to the problem in practice.

I should add here my own recent observations about the marriage practices of poor Hindus in Kerala, South India. In such cases, the whole debate about inheritance rights for women seems pretty irrelevant, since there is no property for daughters to inherit, and all they can hope for is to have a 'decent' wedding paid for by their parents and relatives (Menski, 1993b). The daughter from a very poor family is still going to have her marriage arrangements, however simple they may be, financed by her family. She will come to her new home with some minimal equipment and whatever possessions they can afford to give her. Tough luck for the brother of several sisters in those circumstances! He may have to wait until all his sisters are married off, by which time he is probably in his thirties, still very poor, and none the wiser as far as dowry is concerned, because he now hopes that his wife (if he can find one) will bring at least some clothes and utensils with her. No question of big extortionist demands, because he is not a high-class, high-status groom in whom Bisakha Sen's calculating parents of a marriageable girl would 'invest' a large dowry (see chapter 5). Significantly, Kerala is one of the Indian states with a low rate of dowry-related murders. While dowry murders linked to extortionate demands or unrealistic, oppressive expectations appear to be more of a middle class phenomenon appearing in Northern India, there seem to be other triggers for dowry-related violence in Southern India (see Rao, 1995; 1997; 1998).

Returning to Madhu Kishwar's arguments, we find her engaged in her own rethinking, soon starting to argue for more emphasis on female inheritance rights:

> Today, I find it irrelevant to talk of abolishing dowry. Instead, we should singlemindedly work to ensure effective inheritance rights for women – not on paper alone (Kishwar, 1988: 13).

Lamenting in the following year that this limb of her argument had not been taken as seriously as she had hoped, Kishwar (1989a: 6) reiterated her conviction that dowry serves the interests of men:

> Unless we are clear about whose interests dowry serves, we cannot know whom we should primarily address to eradicate it. Dowry is not a natural phenomenon like a disease which affects the whole popula-

tion, and in whose eradication everyone has an equal interest. It is a societal phenomenon from which one set of people – men – gain overall, while another set – women – lose overall, despite exceptions and apparent contradictions. But the anti-dowry campaign has not made this distinction clear. Its call to eradicate dowry as a 'social evil' has been vaguely addressed to everybody, as if the whole population would immediately and equally benefit from the eradication.

It appears that this perception then gives rise to the argument that only female property rights can strengthen the position of women in this context. This line of argument has been more recently pursued, in particular by Bina Agarwal (1994) and was also taken up in further research (Desai, 1996), which found that simply giving better property rights to women was not going to be the key element that turned the tide of dowry murders – the key still lay in societal assumptions about women in relation to marriage and patrifocal concerns.

As we saw, the argument that giving women better property rights would alleviate the dowry problem was already questioned by one of the earliest writers (Hooja, 1969: 222). Kishwar's approach to the need for property rights has recently been critiqued by Kumari (1994: 123-125) as an unrealistic strategy. In principle, I find myself in agreement with this critique. This does not mean that I am opposed to inheritance rights for women, merely that I cannot see this, by itself, making any significant change to the problems of dowry violence. We can also refer back to Hooja (1969: 222), to the effect that if we replace dowry by property rights, men will still seek to marry the woman with the largest property.

In my view, therefore, the feminist inheritance or property agenda for getting round the dowry problem downplay the fact that dowry violence is not primarily a binary male-female problem, although it seems based on that polarity. In fact, more dangerously, focusing on the property dimension avoids or sidesteps the issue of domestic violence in relation to dowry. In this respect, the uncomfortable truth is that women themselves are among the worst perpetrators of dowry-related violence. Anyone doubting this should read chapter 1 in Verghese (1980: 1-20), a fine and perceptive account of a dowry suicide, which is neither unrealistic nor unrepresentative.

If the dowry problem, in the sense of dowry-related violence, has to do less with property rights and more with violence, we enter the realm of criminology and psychology. How and why is it that certain families kill for dowry, while others do not? What, other than allegedly insufficient dowries, triggers off the killing of young women in their thousands?

3.5 Dowry and self-restraint

Such questions raise a different issue in the dowry debate altogether, namely the question why violence is perpetrated in the name of dowry. I suggest that one should see and treat dowry-related violence as a form of bullying, exploiting a strategic advantage over others to an ultimately unbearable extent. In fact, many writers, as I show below, have alluded to this mental and moral sphere of the dowry problem rather than dwelling on the financial aspects alone. The credit for pointing out most clearly that dowry is not simply a matter of male-female power relations and of money and property, but a deeper issue of morality and decency, would appear to be due to Madhu Kishwar. Typically, her valid and valuable arguments are buried in a round sweep of feminist rhetoric. In a later article (Kishwar, 1989a: 7-8), she proceeded to detail a whole catalogue of desirable changes to the norms for marriage in India, in essence seeking to implement equality for women in all aspects of life. Again, this goes well beyond the dowry issue and embraces such wide agenda that the particular concerns around dowry violence have been overshadowed.

However, a careful perusal of Kishwar's arguments brings to light a number of relevant points which appear to have been overlooked and underplayed in the heated debates on women's rights. They need to be brought out for our present discussions of how to control the dowry problem, which clearly is more than just an issue of gender relations or of property. Research published in *Manushi* (see also Kishwar, 1989a: 5) shows very clearly that dowry is not the real killer of Indian women.

What, then, is the key problem, and how do we tackle it? Kishwar (1988: 12) recounts her own experience of listening to dowry victims and comes up with significant comments which show us that criticism of the dowry is in fact veiled criticism of the woman herself, often taunting for the sake of troubling the newcomer and allocating her an inferior place. I would suggest that this often takes ritualised forms, which individuals simply act out, without meaning to challenge the individual on a personal level. While the literature clearly shows that married women, over time, gain status and power, to be ultimately themselves found in the dread figure of the mother-in-law, recently married women are the most vulnerable victims of such ritualised role playing, which can easily deteriortate into bullying. Kishwar (1988: 12) is brutally realistic:

There is almost no attribute – negative or positive – which a woman may possess, which cannot be used against her if her husband and in-laws wish so to use it. Clearly what requires rectification is not her attributes or possessions but her position of dependence and helplessness which forces her to put up with harassment and violence.

The analysis is helpful, yet the conclusion drawn here, somewhat typical for a Delhi-based feminist activist, is in my view an ideological sop, especially if we see the above comments in the context of Kishwar's wider argument about increased property rights for women. Giving women property rights will obviously not save them from malicious taunts. So the only way to avoid such trouble is not to get married!

The alleged inevitability of distress and looming trouble for the newly married South Asian woman throws us back to the issue of morality. Indeed, if we read carefully, we find many allusions to precisely this element in the writing on dowry. Madhu Kishwar herself has much to say on this issue. Discussing the predicaments of a newly-wed woman, Kishwar (1988: 13) writes:

The wellbeing of such a girl is at the mercy of chance – whether husband and in-laws are good enough to refrain from exercising the arbitrary power they have over her life. If they decide to do so, she will be well treated, dowry or no dowry. *If they decide to be nasty, no amount of dowry or lack of it can help her*. Most women realise this. That is why they are not convinced by the argument that to refuse dowry would be to ensure their own welfare. They are aware that as their lives are structured today, the chance of getting a kindly disposed husband will play a more important role in their welfare than anything they can do. (italics supplied)

Thus, the key issue is self-restraint on the part of those persons who have power over a newcomer in the family, refraining from using a power that one has. This applies at two levels: not using bullying tactics to trouble the woman, and not using the same or similar tactics to demand more dowry. There are undoubtedly shades of differentiation here, but ultimately the former would seem to be more dangerous, because it might not stop short of physical violence and could lead to the woman's death, whether by murder or suicide.

As we saw, Kishwar (1989a: 7-9) produced a sustained attempt to rephrase the marital expectations of Indian couples along gender equity lines. Again, the domination of the feminist agenda disguises the essentially humanistic message and obfuscates the analysis with reference to dowry violence. Other writers have, albeit in an unsystematic and almost hidden fashion, made reference to the same syndrome of unbridled violence against the less powerful, confirming what I have emphasised earlier about the pernicious role of women in this context. Thus, Hooja (1969: 207) wrote, all those years ago:

> Among the in-laws, a very great role in solving the dowry problem falls on the shoulders of the girl's mother-in-law. Her attitude towards the dowry of the daughter-in-law is usually aggressive and critical. This creates unpleasant feelings in the family...

I have already referred to the dramatic case study in Verghese (1980). This author also emphasises the need to see brides as human beings (Verghese, 1980: vii), while Kanta Grover (1990:1), noting that there is no progress and that today's youngsters want all sorts of things at once (Grover, 1990: 3), asks for a code of ethics to improve the situation. This ends up as a sweeping generalised call for social improvement and becomes almost poetic (Grover, 1990: 9-10):

> There should be a code of ethics for the young men, to be responsible and make good husbands, fathers, brothers and members of society. The monumental uphill task is to improve the thinking of the older generation. The parents of the boys, by and large, start the rows. The irritating grains of sand in the eye spread fast, and soon the young couple finds itself in the cyclone of unhappiness.

Significantly, what Madhu Kishwar and others write and advise in this respect refers us back to very basic issues of human morality and, as one needs to point out, the old Hindu *dharmic* concept of self-controlled order with its core elements of individual conscience (*atmanastusti*) and 'model behaviour' (*sadacara*). Appeals to social ostracism of dowry marriages and of murderers for dowry all address the sphere of *sadacara*. Such advice was, during the 1980s, influenced by widespread disillusion with the modern legal machinery and its protective mechanisms for women in the context of dowry. The exasperation among activists of such more or less public campaigns (see in some detail Verghese, 1980: 183-184) was widespread. Loss of faith in legal protection is strongly reflected in Kishwar's argument that neighbourhood control and surveillance remain a most promising strategy (Kishwar, 1990; 1994a). Indeed, unpublished research on the so-called 'stove-blast' dowry murders in Lahore has found that the daily case-load of burnt wives comes only from certain localities, precisely those in which there is no effective neighbourhood control.

Ultimately, then, refraining from dowry violence in its various forms is a matter of individual conscience, for men and women alike. Significantly, the existing literature has not put this in terms of traditional Hindu law, presumably because that would be too 'traditional' and therefore politically incorrect and against the secular spirit of Indian discourses about reform. Writing from the distance of London, and wilfully disregarding such pressures, I would argue that it is a fruitful line of pursuit to bring in reflections about the need to improve individual moral considerations. Kishwar is by no means alone in advocating this kind of strategy, although she does so in secular, feminist terms. Kumari (1994: 120-122) argues rightly for increased *locus standi* for women activists who would otherwise appear to 'interfere' in issues of family life. I suggest that under India's recreated public interest consciousness, dowry-related violence can and should also be covered (see Menski, 1996). At the end of the day, though, individual men and women have to stand up, in their own home environment and without the involvement of any law or social activist group, against the temptation to use dowry issues as an excuse for mental and physical torture. How easy is it to say that one must resist such temptations, and how much more difficult to actually do it!

There is another aspect of this problem which has not even begun to be examined by academics. Recent reports from India focus on increasing evidence of breakdown of marriages, often at a very early stage, pinpointing as a major reason that many young women today are not willing to tolerate any form of criticism. It is evident that traditional assumptions of gender roles (which may include ritualised disparagement of the newcomer) and modern expectations about married life clash in many ways. As we saw, dowry provides a convenient flashpoint of arguments, but is often not the actual reason for the dispute.

The present survey is clearly too short to do justice to all writing on the subject. However, it is no exaggeration if I reiterate that many writers have continued to go round in circles. The reason is not so much the inadequacy of scholarship but the nature of the problem and the continuing distractions presented by a variety of wider feminist agendas. Julia Leslie's observation to the effect that women's groups in Bangalore did not put dowry high up on their agenda confirms the point that activist theory delays any action on dowry problems *ad infinitem* by placing wider agenda above the narrower issues.

At source, the problem of dowry-related violence appears to concern human morality, particularly the question of checks and balances on taking advantage of the other's weaknesses. Marriage presents a structural point of institutionalised weakness for women. As we saw, no amount of property given can protect newly-married women against the abuse of greedy or merely mischievous individuals who enjoy bullying others and use dowry-related arguments for that purpose. Nothing can protect a newly married woman from the sadistic desire to torment an insecure new member of the family. To this extent, the dowry problem is an inseparable aspect of human predicaments. Arranging marriages may well secure the future of the next generation, but in the process everyone concerned may create new troubles for themselves and each other.

Some of the recent writing on dowry has sought to analyse the impact of anti-dowry legislation, found in the *Dowry Prohibition Act* of 1961 and its various amendments during the 1980s in India. Hooja (1969: 214ff.) already proposed a diagnosis to the effect that the anti-dowry legislation was not effective. Indeed, it would be difficult to argue that the law alone has brought significant improvements. Dowry, more than any other legal topic, illustrates the limited role of legal intervention in people's lives and the tangential legal impact on individual morality. The progression of amendments to the original anti-dowry legislation during the 1980s may be a model lesson in criminal law strategies and their lack of real impact in society. The existing writing reflects such inherent contradictions but is also full of confusions about what the law actually is. Even recent authors seem unable to put together a clear brief summary of the law (see e.g. Kumari, 1994: 117).

No matter how carefully the law and its amendments have tried to check the social evil, dowry-related violence continues to exist and appears to have become worse. Despite being a law-focused researcher, I find myself fortified in the view that the dowry problem is a matter of individual conscience, and therefore a social rather than a legal issue. It seems clear that we need to debate and analyse how to put a stop to individual greed and the exploitation of bullying tactics, rather than trying to tackle the huge agenda of gender equality and women's rights. Dowry violence is certainly not just a 'men on women' issue; it goes much beyond the gender division, and our debates must address that fact, however uncomfortable it may be to the researchers.

Chapter 4

Why dowry does not exist among Indian South Africans

Bisraam Rambilass

Preliminary investigations in the form of interviews with elders in the Indian community affirmed my view that dowry was a non-issue in South Africa. As an insider I argue in this chapter that dowry is not practised, and often not even heard of, among the present generation of Indian South Africans.

4.1 The custom of dowry

The term 'dowry' is used in relation to current practice as a perceived social evil in India. During the 1930s, Altekar (1978: 71) summed up his findings about the dowry problem as follows:

> The extraordinary pride which the Rajputs took in their ancestry, was mainly responsible for this development. A Rajput youth of the bluest blood would be desired as a son-in-law by a large number of people, and so his price in the marriage market would soar [sic] high. The dowry system had become a positive evil of great magnitude in Rajputana from about the 13th or 14th century A.D.

> In ordinary families, however, the amount of the dowry was a nominal one. It was a voluntary gift of pure affection and presented no impediment in the settlement of the daughter's marriage till the middle of the 19th century. It is only during the last 50 or 60 years that the amount of the dowry has begun to assume scandalous proportions.

The improvement in education, lucrative appointments and learned professions placed the prospective groom high on the social and economic ladder and made him a valuable commodity as a prized son-in-law who could fetch a high price in the marriage market. The addition of articles to the dowry list which were difficult to produce in a restricted consumer market, such as HMT watches, scooters and motor cycles, or refrigerators, added to the woes of the bride's family. Altekar (1978: 71-72) offered an appropriate solution:

It is now high time for Hindu society to put an end to this evil custom, which has driven many an innocent maiden to commit suicide. There are signs to show that this custom is becoming unpopular and odious, but public opinion must assert itself more emphatically. The youth must rise in rebellion against it. The custom is really as heinous as the counter custom of bride-price, which has been so vehemently condemned by our culture. Proper female education, marriage at an advanced age, mainly settled by the parties themselves, and the awakening of the public conscience seem to be the only remedies that will eventually stamp out the custom.

Altekar's reference to bride-price, also termed bride-wealth, is relevant because this system prevailed among the African people as part of the indigenous wedding ceremony. Called *labolo*, it is as complex a problem for the African people as dowry is for the Indians. Depending on the status of the bride, according to Dolphyne (1991: 7):

...a man may give anything between twenty and sixty cows for a wife. In some of these societies, such as among the Swazi, where the man cannot provide the total herd of cattle required as bride-wealth at the time of marriage, an arrangement can be made for him to provide them in instalments. If he is unable to provide all of it before his death, his son will have to do that for him; otherwise it will be a source of disgrace for both the man and the woman.

The intricacies of the practice of an indigenous tradition in a community greatly influenced by urbanisation has had devastating effects on African society. Inability to afford bride-price is a major cause of the widespread illegitimate relationships in African communities, resulting in abortions, unwanted pregnancies and babies, infidelity, abuse and the disempowerment of women. Be it bride-price or dowry, the unfortunate victim seems always to be the woman. Africans who contract marriages by common law can and often do conclude *labolo* agreements in respect of such marriages.

In India, according to Ghadially and Kumar (1988: 167), it is customary for the bride's parents to give gifts in the form of dowry to their daughter, the groom and his family. These authors do not define what 'dowry' means but cite Srinivas (1984), Sambrani and Sambrani (1983), Rajaraman (1983) and Nair (1978) who have amply documented the nature and origin of this custom and the general economics involved in its practice. Ghadially and Kumar (1988: 167) state that:

> In contemporary times, however, dowry is no longer a gift but rather a demand for cash and/or goods made by the groom and his family on the bride's parents. Increasingly, it has became difficult to meet these demands and many a young woman has died for not fulfilling the expectations of the groom's family.

Such comments suggest that dowry, once a harmless custom of giving gifts to the bride and the groom's family, has become in India a social evil of monstrous proportions, as the following statistics cited by Antony (1995: 1) indicate:

> According to the National Crime Records Bureau of the Ministry of Home Affairs, the number of crimes against women reported was 53,860 in 1987. It rose to 74,903 in 1991. For the same years, the number of dowry death cases were 1,912 and 5,157 respectively. In the category of 'cruelty by husband and his relatives' the rise was from 11,603 to 15,949.

This chapter seeks to demonstrate that dowry, in the form that it has assumed in present-day India, is relatively unheard of among South Africans of Indian origin. An empirical study was needed to ascertain what forms, if any, the practice of dowry has taken on in South Africa.

4.2 Semblance of dowry among Indian South Africans

A pilot study in the form of interviews with five members from each of the four main language groups, viz. Hindi, Tamil, Telugu and Gujarati was initially conducted. The youth, and even young married couples, were relatively ignorant about the practice of dowry in India or South Africa. They were also unaware of aspects of the religious ceremony of marriage and evidenced a startling lack of basic appreciation of the significance of the Hindu wedding, the taking of vows and other important components of the ceremony. The purchase of clothes and jewellery was seen merely as a traditional exchange of gifts – practices that did not warrant any detailed discussion. For these respondents, dowry was a non-issue and did not merit serious research. A second survey was then undertaken among married respondents aged fifty and over and who had some knowledge of the economic transactions linked to the occasion of marriages. Such selective sampling was essential for the researcher to ascertain whether the dowry system was practised locally and to what extent the giving of gifts was a vestige of it.

The responses in all four language groups clearly indicated that exchange of gifts was common and that it was an important aspect of the wedding ceremony. The interviewees could not tell, however, whether it constituted a marriage ritual or was just a traditional practice. The following epitomises the drift of responses: 'When I was married, my parents bought these items and my in-laws gave such and such gifts'. Generally, this was done as a matter of course, with great delight, bustle and excitement. It also gave women their due importance by making them key players in the ceremony.

The gifts exchanged did not vary significantly in the four groups. The groom's parents usually bought a set of jewellery and clothes for the bride. The bridal *sari* and the complete outfit that the bride wore for the ceremony, was purchased by the groom's family. The bride's parents gave the groom a set of clothes which the groom would perhaps wear for the wedding. The parents of the bride also buy jewellery for the bride.

There were many cases where these clothes were exchanged in the initial stages of the wedding. The bride would change into the bridal outfit and then the rest of the nuptials would follow. Many also exchange these gifts at a function on the day before the wedding so the bride could come fully attired and go through the nuptials without having to change her clothes at the wedding hall. In many cases the bridal *sari* given as a gift just before the ceremony proper was merely a token and the bride did not change her attire.

All the respondents discounted the association of gifts given to brides with inheritance of any sort. The inclusion of the question of inheritance into the questionnaire was prompted by an article by Veena Das (1976:

142) declaring that it is the Hindu position that 'property can be inherited only in the male line, though women are entitled to gifts from their natural families... The property gifted to women is seen [as] individual property, and its social value is less than the social value of corporate property'. Nanda (1976: xiv) endorsed the view expressed by Das:

In patrilineal societies there is no recognition of a continuous descent through women, and property over which women have rights becomes alienated from the property of the group. Hence among Hindus, daughters are usually given marriage gifts, but no share in land and other immovable property. Islamic law sanctions share in property to daughters, but in practice, this share is either not given, or is sought to be retained within the family by the custom of arranging marriages between children of two brothers.

According to the general opinion of the respondents, Indian South Africans, through exposure to Western influences, have inevitably become affected by modernisation and inheritance and are not governed by rigid orthodox Hindu laws. There are many instances where daughters inherit as much as sons do. Daughters have occasionally been sole beneficiaries in the father's estate. Such situations arise when parents, cared for in their old age by their daughters, become disillusioned with the son who, under his wife's influence, cares more for her own parents than his. The question of inheritance is therefore relatively fluid and is determined by the circumstances of a case rather than by any general norm. The practice of sons being the natural inheritors of property and the scions of a patriarchal lineage has not been totally abandoned, however. Instances abound which amply attest an innate desire to cling to Hindu tradition and to perpetuate a patriarchal society.

Among the Hindi and Gujarati speaking communities, the bride's party is the host and will pay for the catering, hall hire, and the priest, whereas in the Tamil and Telugu communities, it is the groom's responsibility. Interestingly, one of the respondents stated that it is not unusual to find in the Tamil community an amicable arrangement whereby both parties share the costs. This happens when both are well-disposed to the match but one party is less well off financially. Where the groom's party meets the expenses, the practice does not qualify as 'bride-price' because there are no stipulated amounts of cash or prescribed gifts given to the bride's parents.

As part of the pre-wedding nuptials, among the Hindi and Gujarati speaking communities, the maternal uncle of the bride (the *mama*) is expected to buy a set of clothes for his sister, the bride's mother. Among the Gujaratis, it is the *mama* who gives away the bride. While in India this may be viewed as a veiled form of dowry in that the bride's mother and family can be put to enormous expense, in South Africa the practice is a harmless one and performed with much pride by the uncle.

The Gujarati community still persists in some of the orthodox practices. To some extent, this is simply a result of their affluence. They are the descendants of a trader class of passenger Indians. They remain very caste-conscious, because as passenger Indians they were not subject to the problems of the indentured labourer (Chattopadhyaya, 1970: 85). Dowry is not practised as in India, but the giving of gifts can assume extravagant proportions.

Professor Anshu Padayachee, who heads the Advice Desk for Abused Women at the University of Durban Westville, feels strongly that when emotional abuse of a wife takes place, the inferior status and financial standing of the wife's family surfaces and during domestic quarrels the wife would have to tolerate such taunts. When respondents, both male and female, were asked about this type of abuse, they were guarded about reading insinuations of dowry into instances and preferred to dismiss them as excuses for the abuse of women.

4.3 The wedding ceremony and the giving of gifts

Dowry – the bride's parents giving gifts to the groom – can be traced to the Hindu wedding ceremony itself. From the interviews it can safely be concluded that of the four language groups that make up the Indian Hindu community, the Hindi, Gujarati and Telugu follow, with negligible differences, the same ritual procedure for the *godana* ceremony, which in Sankrit means literally 'cow-gift'.

As a pre-nuptial practice, the bride's father receives the groom and his party. The wedding ceremony proper begins with the receiving of the groom by the bride. This is done by a series of rituals that mark the deferential and gracious welcoming of the guest with due decorum. The bride (or her parents) offers the groom a seat (*vistara*). Then there is the offering of water (*argha*), which the groom sprinkles on his face, hands and feet, a symbolic gesture of auspicious oblations marking the commencement of a religious act. Thereafter there is the purificatory ritual where water, offered to the groom by the bride, is sipped thrice from the palm of the hand as a symbolic act of purifying one's inner being. The next step is the taking of curd and honey (*madhuparka*) offered to the groom by the bride, an act signifying sustenance of life through proper and healthy nourishment. The different sense organs and limbs are also anointed with drops of water (*angasparsa*) while the accompanying ritual verses ask for purity, good health and longevity.

This is followed by the actual *godana* ritual in which a mantra is chanted: '*om gaurgaurgauh pratigrhyatam*' ('May this cow be accepted'). The groom accepts this gift, pronouncing the mantra: '*om pratigrhnami*' ('I accept'). Repeating the word 'gauh' thrice does not imply that three cows have to be given. The ritually significant words during the marriage ritual, such as 'seat' (*vistarah*), 'feet' (*padyam*) or 'mixture of curd and honey' (*madhuparka*) are also chanted thrice, in keeping with the symbolic value which three enjoys as a Vedic numeral.

The bride then makes the symbolic gift to the groom. The ritual of *godana* is performed by pressing a coin into a ball of dough which is probably meant to be a figurine or symbol of the cow. Thereafter other gifts will also be given to the groom. Among those that subscribe to the Arya Samaj, a Hindu reformist sect which is opposed to excessive ritualisation, the ritual of the dough is normally dispensed with. The priest usually explains the practical value of the cow in Hindu society and therefore the giving of the cow to the bridal couple to start them off in life. Since this is not practical in the situation that obtains not only in South Africa but also in India, the gift of a cow is replaced by a gift that would befit both the occasion and the means of the bride's parents. This gift has become fixed as a traditional practice and normally comprises a shirt and tie, a suit, some sweetmeats and cash ranging from fifty to a hundred Rand currently less than £10 or $16. We found no evidence of inflation of the gift-giving in connection with these rituals.

This is followed by the ritual of 'the holding of the girl' (*kanyagrahanam*), popularly known in Hindi and Sanskrit as the *kanyadan* ritual, the giving away of the bride. The South African variant seems to emphasise the acceptance of the bride by the groom, so has a contractual element. The ritual requires the placing of the bride's right palm in that of the groom while the acceptance *mantra* is recited. Then the groom gives the bride a set of clothes which she might wear to perform the main wedding rites. The traditional bridal *sari* and the rest of the suit may be quite lavish and an average family will spend about three to four thousand Rand on it. There are no rigid distinctions between the exchange of gifts and that of the sets of clothes (*vastradana*). Often both are dispensed with as part of the *godana* ritual. In some weddings the bride will come attired in the bridal *sari* and will wear it throughout the ceremonies.

Paupuja, literally meaning 'worshipping the feet', was originally a ceremonious washing of the feet of the groom by the bride's parents and was part of the welcoming rituals. This practice seems to have its sources not in the Vedic Kalpasutras, the earliest extant texts on the procedure for nuptials, but more probably in the *Ramayana* (see Gopal, 1983: 229ff.). In South Africa today, women, sometimes thirty or more, will each give the groom a daintily wrapped tray of sweets and fruit. Originally a brass plate (*thali*), or a goblet (*lota*), the main traditional Indian utensils, were given (Singh, 1989). In describing marriages among the early indentured labourers, Chattopadhyaya (1970: 87) observed:

A salient feature of the marriage-celebration in South Africa's Indian society is the provision for marriage gifts. The practice with the Tamil and Tel[u]gu immigrants is that gifts are to be given by the bride-groom's parents to the bride, whereas among the Hindi-speaking immigrants the practice followed is just the reverse. The gifts usually include the traditional brass trays and vessels, clothing, coconuts and cash money. Cash money as a part of dowry is required by the parents to meet the wedding expenses and is called 'credit without interest'.

Hilda Kuper (1960: 162 ff.) provided a detailed account of wedding ceremonies as performed by each of the Indian language groups in South Africa. She tabled various rituals that comprise the wedding ceremony to enable a comparison between the orthodox and reform practices in the Hindi/Gujarati and Tamil groups. Here again there is no reference to dowry, and the fact that it is not mentioned can be taken to confirm that it did not exist as either a practice or a concept.

4.4 Probable reasons why dowry does not exist

The history of the arrival of Indians as indentured labourers in South Africa and the circumstances under which they came are important to the present study, for they reveal some of the reasons for the non-existence of dowry.

Several factors led to the migration of Indians as labourers to the British colonies. After the abolition of slavery in the middle of the 19th century, the British desperately sought for a legitimate system to replace the slave labour they had used in their colonies (Kuper, 1960: 1). South Africa, Mauritius, Trinidad, British Guyana and Fiji, all British colonies, had proved ideal for farming sugar-cane. The Indians, who were largely agrarian, were known for their skills in farming, particularly of sugar-cane. Because of abject poverty in India, particularly in Eastern Uttar Pradesh, Bihar, Bengal and Tamilnadu, the Indians there were easily lured as labourers to the sugar plantations in British colonies. India, as a British colony, could easily be exploited as a source of ready labour.

Bhana (1990: 61ff.) examines how the socio-economic developments in India during the 19th century affected the caste and class composition of the migrant labourers. British policy undoubtedly influenced the very fabric of Indian life. The introduction of British goods on the Indian market threatened a thriving indigenous cotton handicraft industry. The impact was felt unevenly but many parts of India suffered crippling effects. As these industries slowly collapsed, thousands of jobless weavers and tanners were forced to join an already overcrowded farming work-force. Greedy feudal landlords (*zamindars*) and money-lenders (*baniyas*) created massive problems of exploitation, land alienation, famine and attendant problems. It is not surprising, then, that those who migrated to the province of Natal were mostly agricultural workers, uprooted peasant farmers and artisans.

Could dowry have been practised to any significant extent in the Indian communities that were plagued by such poverty? It is difficult to imagine that they brought along with them a tradition of dowry practice, given the poverty in the areas from which they emigrated. Even today in India, the problem of dowry is more a middle-class malaise.

The early plight of indentured labourers has been researched in some detail. In 1860, the first batch of Indian migrant labourers arrived on the ship 'Truro' at Durban, then called Port Natal. The historic landing of 'coolies' in batches from 1860 to 1924 has been well-documented. From these records it is evident that indentured labourers lived under trying circumstances. Bhana noted that the transition from life in India, which was caste-based and governed in every detail by the village *panchayat*, to a new setting without village elders or communal family life and with people of different castes, created serious disorientation. Bhana (1990: 115) notes:

Leadership emerged; attitudes changed; and old habits gave way to new ones. The feeling of togetherness generated bhaiyacharya (brotherhood); caste consciousness weakened because the village structures were not there to reinforce it.

This statement may offer some explanation for the changes that occurred to the customs that had prevailed in India. The changed social order, customs and traditions were tailored to the new environment in which the immigrants found themselves. Their caste was in reality the one uniting caste of poverty, and this probably forced them to abandon the practice of dowry if it had indeed been practised back home.

One major reason why dowry does not prevail among South African Indians was the gender distribution among indentured labourers. Bhana (1990: 19) gives detailed graphs and tables indicating the gender distribution among the two main groups, the Madras and Calcutta batches. From 1860 to 1866, of the total of 6.446 arrivals, 4,552 were male, 1,846 were female and 48 unknown. For the period 1860-1902, of the total of 95,382 newcomers, 61,473 were male, 26,804 female and 7,105 unknown (Bhana, 1990: 22 ff.). Although Bhana mentions that the indentured Indians experienced a shortage of women throughout the period, he does not discuss its implications. With a ratio of seven men to three women, there could be little scope for the practice of dowry, since it was not the bridegrooms who were in demand.

Beall (1990) describes the plight of immigrant women and the humiliation, abuse and servitude they suffered as a result of their disproportionately small numbers (see also Bhana, 1990: 89 ff.). Bhana and Bhana (1990) analysed the primary reasons for suicide among indentured Indians for the period 1875-1911. Marriage or dowry-related deaths do not feature anywhere, while 'personal problems', which account for 23.7% of such deaths, are described as 'love problems' or 'domestic disputes'. Padayachee and Singh (1995) also speak of the ratio of men to women and the abuse of women precipitated by the imbalance, but there is no mention of dowry as a cause of such abuse.

Henning (1993: 121) observes that 'one of the most demoralising aspects of indenture remained the shortage of women, who were forced into either insecure marriages, concubinage or polyandry which in turn gave rise to endless disputes between the men and even led to suicide'. Again, nowhere does he mention dowry. His book, however, contains an interesting document (Appendix 27: Law 12 of 1906 – Indian Marriages), a Bill 'To make certain provisions relative to marriages of Indian Immigrants' (Henning, 1993: 239), which later became *Natal Act* No. 2 of 1907. Two sections of this Bill are relevant here:

3. If the parents of an Indian girl or either of them shall hold out to any Indian man the promise of giving such girl in lawful marriage to him, and shall receive from him any presents, money, or goods in expectation of such marriage, and shall thereafter refuse consent to such marriage, or shall give the girl in marriage to some other person, or shall otherwise directly or indirectly break such promise, they, or the one of them shall be liable upon conviction before a Magistrate to the same punishments as are hereinbefore mentioned, unless it shall be shown to the satisfaction of the Court that they so acted for good and sufficient reason unconnected with any fraud, deception, or bad faith.

4. The person by whom such presents, money or goods have been given or paid, shall in the circumstances mentioned in the foregoing section, and subject to the same exception as is therein mentioned, have the right to sue for and recover, all such presents, money, goods or their value.

Nothing in this or the previous section shall be deemed to apply when to the knowledge of the intending husband, the marriage was to have taken place before the girl was of a legal age to be married, or the marriage would otherwise be illegal.

The Bill actually speaks of cash payment for girls who could be procured in marriage and details the laws that would apply to such arrangements (Henning, 1993: 239). The author himself stated in an interview that this Bill was, in all probability, a result of a court case where a man had purchased a bride for a hundred pounds and then the father had sold off the girl to another suitor for a higher price.

All the books and articles on indentured labourers in Natal speak of the three pound poll tax and annual one pound tax payable by women, which helped to regulate their numbers and also gravely undermined their position, but none of these speak of any links to the practice of dowry.

A different perspective arises in the context of social reform debates. Naidoo (1992: 169) asserts that the Arya Samaj, in its programme of reforms aimed at improving the status of women, also fought against the dowry system:

> The dowry system which was also introduced in South Africa was totally banned by the Arya Samaj. The system had obtained in India for centuries bringing untold hardships to many families. The system which required the bride's parents to place large sums of money, jewellery and other possessions in the care of the groom before a marriage could be solemnised, left many families in deep debt for many years after the marriage, thus making them virtual slaves to a system they neither loved nor supported but followed only to satisfy the whims of a customary practice that had no logical explanation.

Naidoo's statement that the dowry system was introduced in South Africa is not attested, however. There is no doubt that the Arya Samaj played a tremendous role in the liberation of women in South Africa (Vedalankar and Somera, 1975) but in the absence of precise details regarding the actual steps taken against the practice of dowry, if it did exist, it is very difficult to determine the exact role played by the Arya Samaj in the elimination of dowry. It seems more probable that the socio-economic factors were largely responsible for the spontaneous demise of any customs that could be treated as relating to dowry.

The most arduous task in hand has been the tracing of evidence for a malpractice that most probably never existed among South Africans of Indian origins. While poverty, ratio of men to women, literacy, westernisation, religious reform, caste mobility and other factors have been offered as likely reasons for the demise of dowry in South Africa, these reasons have been advanced for the elimination of a problem that, in all probability, did not exist in the first place. All respondents and informants in this empirical study seemed to find difficulty in recalling the practice of dowry as a social evil at any time in the history of the indentured labourer. Another compelling consideration is the definition of dowry, always being qualified as initially a harmless and even laudable practice of giving or exchanging gifts. This contrasts starkly with the transformation of dowry from giving by the bride's parents to demanding by the bridegroom's family. The most satisfying answer seems to lie in dowry becoming a bane in India only in more recent times, well after the indentured labourers were long settled in their homes abroad and their descendants remain untainted by the decadence of dowry into a system that has racked a society at its very roots.

Chapter 5

Why does dowry still persist in India? An economic analysis using human capital

Bisakha Sen

5.1 The task in hand

Dreze and Sen (1995: 177-178) have argued that 'the persistence of extraordinarily high levels of gender inequality and female deprivation are among India's most serious social failures. Few other regions in the world have achieved so little in promoting gender justice'. Of the many obstacles that confront India on her road to economic and social justice for all, one of the largest continues to be the custom of 'dowry'. The custom is responsible for a plethora of ills perpetrated against India's women, the most serious being the problems of abuse of wives and bride-murder. There has long been a consensus amongst India's intelligentsia and legislators that it should be abolished.

Unfortunately, the *Dowry Prohibition Act* of 1961 has been spectacular in its failure to eliminate the custom, or even to check its spread beyond the upper echelons of the Hindu society where it originated. There is even evidence that dowry is becoming increasingly popular among tribal groups, as well as among Muslims and Christians in India. Some fault undoubtedly lies in the provisions of the Act itself. Most notably, by holding both the givers and takers of dowry guilty of the offence, it provides an effective disincentive for the bride's family to report dowry cases. *Ex post*, it is virtually impossible for a third party to distinguish between dowry and voluntary gifts. It also imposes serious psychological costs on the bride if any women's group chooses to investigate the matter, for she realises that if the fact of dowry comes to light, her parents may be legally liable. Thus, the victim, too, becomes an accomplice in the conspiracy of silence.

In a wider perspective, the root of the problem lies in the treatment of dowry as an autonomous phenomenon rather than as one outcome of a patrilineal society. Attempting to eliminate the custom exogenously rather than investigating and removing its root causes is a classic case of treating the symptoms rather than the disease.

While the effects of dowry have been extensively analysed in socio-logical and economic literature, there is a relative paucity of formal studies exploring the causes of dowry. Not all Indian brides are married with dowry, nor are dowry givers a purely random sample of the Indian population. To eliminate the custom effectively, it is necessary to assess the characteristics of those who abide by it, and those who take advantage of it, so that policies may be formulated to target these specific groups. This chapter makes a beginning in that direction by systematically analysing the causes of dowry within the framework of economic thought. Dowry is explained as a result of inter-sex differentials in the accumulation of human capital. The analysis at least partly explains the phenomena of abuse and dowry murders, and allows us to advocate certain short-term measures to alleviate the custom's evils. I hope that it will be the basis for further empirical research on dowry and its abolition.

5.2 Dowry definitions

Traditionally, dowry has been broadly defined to include the totality of assets transferred from the bride's family to the groom's at the time of marriage. It has played two roles, that of a vehicle for property transfer to the woman, and that of a 'marriage payment' (Basu, 1996). Authors such as Sambrani and Sambrani (1983), Narayan (1993) and Oldenberg (1993) have argued that in a patrilineal society, with women prohibited from directly inheriting parental property, the primary role of dowry was to provide a vehicle whereby part of a woman's parental property could be transferred to her affinal home, thereby increasing her own standard of living. Therefore, they claim, dowry was in essence given voluntarily by the woman's parents. Nonetheless, there must have been considerable scope for extortion, where a groom's family could appropriate a more than fair, or voluntarily given, share of wealth from the bride's family as part of the marriage payment. This scope was provided by the strong societal and religious dictates that demanded a girl's marriage to a man of appropriate caste and class before she attained puberty. Failing this, her family would be subjected to the gravest censure and disgrace. In the tight-knit, semi-autonomous village economies of India, societal condemnation carried with it the weight of economic penalisation, for the errant family would find itself losing employees, customers and goodwill in the market. This of course created sufficient imbalance of bargaining power in the marriage market, and dowry essentially became the maximum price a family was willing to pay in order to safeguard both social standing and economic livelihood by procuring suitable husbands for their daughters. Among many others, Rabindranath Tagore commented on this. My translation of the following passage is from 'Lok sahitya' (in Bengali), published in Vol. 13 [1961] of *Rabindra Rachanavali*:

> We are compelled by society's dictates to marry off our daughters by a given age, and within a limited circle. Such an exaggerated compulsion by itself artificially hikes up the value of a groom; his virtues, attributes or economic prowess become of little consequence.

The *Hindu Succession Act* of 1956 grants all offspring equal inheritance rights and should have made redundant the need for any means of indirect inheritance for women. There has been a general trend towards liberalisation of social attitudes regarding the imperative of marriage, and Indian law has set minimum ages of marriage well beyond puberty. The legal minimum age of marriage for women in India is now 18 years (21 years for men), which is higher than in most Western countries.

All this reduces the potential for coercive power that grooms can wield in the marriage market. True, the laws and attitudinal changes have not reached many parts of rural India which remain steeped in orthodox tradition, and there dowry continues for the reasons just outlined. But the main concern of this chapter is to explore why dowry prevails even among the economically advanced, seemingly modernised urban communities.

There is no denying that in spite of much modernisation, there still exist large differences in power and status between the genders in India. But in the rationale of Robert Pollack (1985), to attribute the phenomenon of dowry in its present form to vague 'power differences' merely emphasises that the custom actually has no legitimate reason for existing. It neither serves to explain why the custom does exist, nor does it offer any concrete guidelines to combat it. To do that, we must identify the precise areas where relevant power differences come into play and pinpoint the routes by which they nurture the custom.

For the purpose of policy formulation, the definition of 'dowry' needs to be revised, for in modern times the totality of assets which are transferred with the bride may be divided into three parts. First, the property transfer to the bride, which is part of her inheritance and should be legally under her control. Second, gifts which are part of a ceremonial exchange symbolising the union between the families, and are matched by reciprocal gifts of equivalent value from the groom's family, as in the customs of *namashkari* in Bengal. Third, dowry constitutes assets given as 'marriage payments' with the explicit understanding that without them the marriage contract will be voided. I would argue that only the last item can truly be categorised as 'dowry'. This redefinition is in keeping with the legal terminology, as found in section 2 of the amended *Dowry Prohibition Act* of 1961, to the effect that dowry is the transfer of assets from the bride or her kin to the groom or his kin 'in connection with the marriage'. The redefinition also underlines the fact that there is no rationale for controlling or limiting any gifts which parents choose to give to their daughters.

5.3 Dowry and 'gains from marriage'

The identifying characteristic of this dowry definition is that, by itself, dowry yields no utility, i.e. well-being, to the giver. It is prompted neither by the bequest motive, as are voluntary gifts to a daughter, nor by a desire for conspicuous consumption, as may be the case for the ostentatious wedding ceremonies calculated to impress the community. Yet, in the absence of legal or socio-religious compulsions, marrying a daughter off at the cost of a dowry must be considered a choice, revealed as preferred over the alternative of retaining the value of the dowry and the daughter remaining unmarried. This indicates that there exist what I would call 'gains from marriage' for the girl and her natal family, which are at least equal to the value of the dowry given. Furthermore, if the marriage market is competitive and there is no hidden information, then it may be stipulated that the 'gains from marriage' for the girl and her family exceed any gains from marriage for the man and/or his family. It is the net difference in gains that the latter appropriates as dowry. A competitive marriage market with no hidden information includes the following characteristics:

- Due to the continuous stream of people entering the market, there are always a large number of prospective grooms seeking brides and vice versa.

- The participants from either sex in the market are all of similar quality and eligibility.

- The participants do not collude and connive with each other to raise their value artificially. That is, dowry is not the result of some form of 'male conspiracy' on the part of the grooms.

- No participant can lie about his/her true worth.

- Any bride, when considering a groom, is perfectly aware of the presence and quality of alternative candidates, and vice versa.

Two alternate theories, offered by Gary Becker (1981) to explain dowry in general, should be briefly mentioned. First, he argues that dowries act as an insurance against divorce, thus serving to protect women's marriage-specific investments such as childbearing. The groom is aware that in deserting or ill-treating the woman, he stands at risk of losing the dowry. In the Indian case, however, the legal non-recognition and the handshake nature of the contract make its recovery uncertain under any circumstances. Therefore the role of dowry as an element of insurance becomes suspect. Becker gives the example of the orthodox Jewish *ketuba* to make his point. A parallel example might be the Muslim institution of *mahr* or *mehr*, which does perform the insurance function more effectively; *mahr*, once given, unquestionably belongs to the wife. However, there appears to be no Hindu tradition of returning a dowry in case of divorce, partly because Hindu law supposedly has no tradition of divorce in the modern sense. Since South Asian societies were polygamous until this century, there was little need to divorce a wife in the event of her being barren, unattractive or physically or mentally incapable. A wife discarded due to 'improper behaviour', or one who initiated a separation, was not considered worthy of sympathy or financial compensation, including return of dowry.

Second, it is argued here that a dowry serves as an inducement for men to enter matrimony with a particular woman if there is a relative scarcity of men in the marriage market. Again, this argument is suspect for India, given that her gender ratio is notoriously anti-female. Though men typically marry younger women, and though the population of India continues to grow at a fairly high rate, the pattern of population growth has greatly exacerbated the gender-ratio imbalance over this century, so that the country's female-male ratio has declined from 972:1000 in 1901 to 927:1000 in 1991 (see Dreze and Sen, 1995 and below). Therefore evidence indicates that if there is a scarcity of one gender in the marriage market, it should be the female. However, combining the state-by-state female-male ratios with data on dowry murders (in lieu of data on dowry incidences), I find no indication that brides are regarded as of greater value (i.e. murdered less frequently) in states that have relatively smaller female to male ratios.

State	Females/1,000 males in 1991	Number of reported dowry deaths 1990
Haryana	865	336
Uttar Pradesh	879	1398
Punjab	882	177
Rajasthan	910	286
Bihar	911	303
West Bengal	917	245
Assam	923	8
Madhya Pradesh	931	556
Maharashtra	934	632
Gujarat	954	58
Karnataka	960	210
Tamil Nadu	974	124
Kerala	1036	4

Source: Column 2, Table 7.1 from Dreze and Sen 1995.

5.4 Economic explanations: Dowry and human capital

Indira Rajaraman (1983) offered an alternate explanation for dowry by imposing the condition that the present value of a woman's domestic productivity is always less than the present value of the cost of her sustenance. This is an argument capable of raising strong objections. A more reasonable version is that the woman's domestic productivity is perceived to be less valuable than her sustenance cost. This is probable enough, given a patrilineal society's penchant for undervaluing women's work. This is in keeping with Uma Narayan's hypothesis that the decreased labour force participation of women causes them to be viewed as economic liabilities, thus implicitly legitimising the demand for a compensation to marry them (Narayan, 1993). Another grave objection to Rajaraman's argument is that due to its rather simplistic form, it fails to explain why an employed woman earning more than her sustenance cost cannot typically command a bride price, but must settle at best for zero dowry (on this see Sambrani and Sambrani, 1983).

Rajaraman's hypothesis nevertheless echoes the one point that much of the literature on this topic consistently agrees upon, namely that incidences of dowry are less frequent and less severe when the woman is gainfully employed (see also Narayan, 1993). Basu (1996) had in her sample a case where the man's parents did not demand a dowry because their prospective daughter-in-law was a doctor, indicating their realisation that the marriage market would not support a demand for marriage payment from a highly qualified professional woman. Thus it must be that a woman with sufficient market power stands to gain relatively less from marriage, so has less incentive to pay dowry.

I argue that differences in gains from marriage for men and women that lead to dowry arise primarily from differences in patterns of acquisition of human capital. The whole process is viewed as being driven by two crucial factors. First, that traditional social norms inhibit the acquisition by women of market-oriented skills. Second, that individual utility, a term which in economic literature means 'well-being' or 'happiness', is derived not only from consumption of material goods but also from a sense of maintaining a 'good name' by following societal dictates – which helps to explain the constraining of individual actions by the force of tradition. Neo-classical economics cannot rationally explain the human capital choices made by a woman (or her family on her behalf) due to its paramount failure to ignore the utility derived from the pleasure of a good name (on this see Becker, 1974). The explanation must fall within the domain of institutional economics, which acknowledges the importance of social and institutional forces alongside market forces (see Mangum, 1988) .

In this context, I define two broad categories of human capital: market-specific human capital, hereafter referred to as MHC, and household-specific human capital, hereafter referred to as HHC. This terminology is borrowed from Robert Pollack (1985). The former category augments productivity in the labour market, and hence strengthens earnings skills. The latter consists of skills that enhance household production and family status. For analytical purposes, I assume that the two types of capital are mutually exclusive in function, in that MHC imparts no household skills and HHC imparts no earning capability. Final commodities which persons consume are a combination of market-purchased goods and householders' time and skill. Decisions to acquire the different types of capital are based on consideration of future consumption, and whether such acquisition has any social repercussions.

I assume that MHC is acquired primarily through formal education and hands-on training in market activities. HHC is acquired through tutelage under senior female household members and active participation in housework, child care, rituals and ceremonies. Furthermore I assume that the acquisition of MHC requires funds, whereas acquisition of HHC more or less costs nothing. In India, it is typical for parents, particularly mothers, to be dependent on their sons in their old age, whereas it is relatively atypical to become dependent on daughters in a similar situation. Accordingly, spending money for a son's MHC may partly be looked upon as a form of investment by parents, which will yield them benefits later in life. In contrast, a daughter's acquisition of MHC is not perceived to yield any significant benefits to her parents (see Dreze and Sen, 1995, chapter 6). Thus, when the funds available to finance their children's MHC acquisition via education and training are limited, the rational choice on the part of parents would be to allocate the greater part of it to their sons. Moreover, girls attempting to acquire MHC in India stand to violate social norms on two counts, relating to the eventual implications of acquiring it, and the methods required to do so.

Traditional Indian society views the acquisition of economic resources by women with a strong antipathy. This is probably due to an inherent conviction in the Indian mind that stability of the family depends on the maintenance of an unequal resource position between man and woman (Agarwal, 1994). The appropriate task of women is by and large considered to be what Papanek (1985) terms 'family status production work', namely supporting the remunerative activities of the male members of the household, enhancing the future earning ability of the (male) children, and enhancing the household's status in the community by displaying skills in appropriate social and religious activities and traditional crafts. A woman is also expected to maintain a deferential mien, as indicative of good breeding. So too much education or education of the 'wrong kind', such as education that grants her the means of economic self-sufficiency, increases the probability that a girl will gain an unseemly amount of independence, violate her traditional role and disrupt familial and societal harmony in the future. Unfortunately, the various educational commissions and committees in the post-independence era have yielded to the need to appease society's conservative elements. Indian female education has been vaunted as a tool for improving the quality of child care and the home environment rather than being treated as a means to attain equal market opportunity and equitable household distribution. It has been emphasised by the National Committee on Women's Education that a woman's role outside the home will always be defined by and subject to 'the demands and exigencies of her role within the house' (Desai and Krishnaraj, 1987: 152). Needless to say, this attitude on the part of policy makers has not served to propagate in the Indian mind-set any desire for promoting the independence of women.

While trepidation over the eventual result of MHC acquisition is inhibiting, even more serious are the obstacles in actually acquiring MHC. As in many traditional patriarchal societies, a family's esteem in India is strongly subjected to the reputation of its women (see Hill and King, 1995). The residues of the *purdah* system remain embedded in Indian societal norms, and the compromising of a daughter's 'honour' in the eyes of the community can bring about a range of social penalties: from shunning by extended kin and acquaintants, to public ridicule and humiliation, to a ritualised ex-communication of the family from their communities. So a daughter's attempts to acquire MHC in the form of education and training, and her early forays into the labour market present serious psychic costs to her family insofar as they involve her commuting or living away from home, keeping late hours, and interacting in relatively non-supervised environments with male overseers, colleagues and clients. The spectre of illicit liaisons, cohabitation, and unsuitable *pratiloma* unions looms large. *Pratiloma* (literally 'against the grain') occurs when a woman gets involved with a man who belongs to a caste or group inferior to her own. Such unions were virtually forbidden in ancient religious texts, and continue to be abhorrent to traditional, upper caste Hindus. In the US context, of course, a different form of *pratiloma* ideology elicits similar feelings, for example towards a white woman marrying a black man in the Southern USA a few decades ago – or liaisons between Asian women and black men. Such cultural constraints frequently goad a woman's family into curtailing her aspirations towards MHC acquisition so as to protect her and, of course, their own reputation. Faced with such obstacles, many girls are forced to forego the maximum amount of MHC they could have acquired and substitute it with HHC.

However, the crucial economic characteristic of HHC is that it cannot be fully utilised in the non-married state. For instance, the single woman is unable to exercise and 'consume' the full benefits of her child care skills, since single motherhood is a non-viable option in India. She is also unable to reap the full benefits of much of her acquired proficiency in household rituals, arts and fancy cookery, all carefully calculated to evoke the appreciation of her affinal family. A striking example in middle class contexts is learning how to sing. In Bengal, for example, a training in classical music, even more so in 'Rabindra Sangeet' (the songs of Rabindranath Tagore) or 'Nazrul Geeti' (the popular songs and poetry of the Bengali poet Nazrul Islam) is considered a highly desirable trait in a bride. Therefore a girl may spend much time and effort – and her parents much money – ensuring that she acquires such skills. But she will rarely be allowed to perform for monetary gain. The skill is purely for the purpose of displaying 'breeding' and for pleasing her future in-laws.

A woman who has made positive accumulations of HHC while in the single state receives two forms of gains from marriage: an increase in consumption due to recouping the full benefits from the acquired HHC, and an increase in consumption due to the existence of 'public goods' within marriage, i.e. goods of which the consumption by one spouse does not detract from the consumption of the other. The latter gain applies equally to men and women with investments only in MHC while the former becomes a gain from marriage exclusive to women from 'tradition-abiding' backgrounds, for which they and their families are willing to make a net payment to acquire a husband. This, I maintain, is the payment which translates into 'dowry'.

5.5 The economic model to explain dowry

I illustrate the phenomenon of willingly giving dowries more explicitly by means of a two-period model. Let the agents be a number of families from similar socio-economic backgrounds, since in arranged marriages the families are typically from the same socio-economic stratum, each family having one son and one daughter. At the beginning of the first period, the parents make the human capital accumulation decisions for their children. There is no further accumulation or depreciation of capital in the second period. At the end of the first period, the young men and women enter the marriage market, marriage contracts are negotiated and decisions regarding dowry are made. Events like dowry murders occur immediately or soon after the marriage, at the beginning of the second period. I make the following simplifying assumptions:

1) There exist no inherent ability differences between the young men and women. All are capable of acquiring a maximum amount of human capital, K^*. This entity K^* consists of non-negative amounts of the two available types of capital, K_m (MHC) and K_h (HHC). Therefore the maximum potential amount of K_m each can acquire, provided they acquire zero K_h, is K^*. The basic economic assumption here is that the two capitals are quantifiable and measurable in units. A unit of K_m has a monetary cost of 'p'. Parents allocate an amount of funds 'M' to cover the costs of K_m acquisition by their children.

2) A person's earning capacity is decided by his/her accumulation of K_m. I assume that K_m commands a real wage rate of 'r' per unit, so that the person's real income is rK_m. There exists a 'final good' C, which is produced by a simple additive combination of real income (i.e. the goods purchased with it) and HHC. That means $C = rK_m + K_h$. This is a simplified representation of the fact that all goods and services one enjoys at home are to varying degrees a combination of market-purchased articles and the time and effort of household

members. After marriage, C becomes a public good between the spouses. This represents the fact that within marriage, most material goods, like a well-kept house, meals, and more abstract things like the joy of 'high-quality' children, and the social status marriage brings, are produced by the combined MHC and HHC of the spouses and are shared by both.

3) $r \geq 1$. Therefore each unit of K_m contributes at least as much towards C as each unit of K_h. I do not debate whether the differences in contributions of the two forms of capital are real or due to societal perceptions. As long as all relevant participants 'buy' that perception, its effect on my model is the same as if it were real.

4) Prior to marriage, parties can utilise only a fraction λ of their acquired K_h towards production of C, $0 < \lambda < 1$. The remaining $(1-\lambda) K_h$ then refers to skills specific to commodities which may only be consumed conditional on marriage.

5) Parents expect a rate of return in the second period from every unit of K_m their son acquires in the first. Since this rate of return usually involves being able to reside in the son's household, a common practice especially for widowed mothers, I assume that this does not actually detract from the rK_m available to the son, i.e. this, too, is a form of public good. Parents expect no future return from the K_m acquired by their daughters. The expected rates of return are identical for all parents belonging to the same socio-economic class.

6) Parents are altruistic – they are concerned about the consumption levels and future utility of their children. However, parents are also selfish insofar as they are concerned with the future rate of returns they can expect from investing in K_m of their children. Parents are also concerned with adhering to norms and behaving in a socially appropriate manner. There exists a level of social approval, S^*, available to all parents at the onset. But as a daughter acquires more and more K_m, the parents apprehend that they are diverting further and further from the socially acceptable course, so that their S^* is steadily declining. Each set of parents assign a specific, positive weight α to S^*, depending on how much value they attach to the societal norms.

7) Each man and woman inherits some amount of wealth, ω, from their parents at the beginning of the second period. Unlike C, ω is not a public or shared good between spouses, but remains under individual control. Marriage payments between a man and woman take the form of transfer of ω from one to the other. By this, I assume that if dowry is paid, it comes out of that part of parental property which was implicitly earmarked for the daughter and would otherwise have gone to her. Note that it then makes no difference whether the final decision-making power regarding dowry giving rests with the parents or the daughter – the end result will be the same.

8) Marriage markets are competitive, and there is perfect information about the ω, K_m and K_h levels of each participant. However, there is imperfect information regarding certain personal characteristics of the individuals in question.

In the first period, the parents decide on their children's human capital accumulation by considering the following factors: First, that K_h will always contribute less towards the final good C than Km. Moreover, a significant part of K_h will remain dormant until the child is married. But the parents will also consider the fact that only a son's K_m accumulation yields them any future returns, and that their daughter's accumulation of K_m will cause their own S* to decline. Hence, it follows logically that parents will allocate the greater part of M towards their son's MHC. The relative difference between the amount of MHC their son and daughter end up with depends on the value placed on S* (i.e. the magnitude of α), and the expected rate of return from the son's K_m. Obviously, the higher the value of α, the smaller the amount of MHC the daughter is allowed to acquire. Both children compensate for the difference between K_m and K^* by acquiring that amount of K_h.

The predictions of the model are that the son will always acquire more K_m than the daughter. It is possible that sons will actually acquire the full potential amount of MHC that is possible, K^*. It is also almost a certainty that a daughter's acquisition will fall short of K^*, unless $M \geq 2pK^*$, and the value of α is sufficiently low. Therefore the daughter's final accumulation of capital will consist of more K_h and less K_m than the son's and she will compensate for the difference by acquiring HHC. Since all families are assumed to be identical except for the value of α, any man in that class will almost certainly have more K_m than any woman of that class.

For the sake of simplicity, I assume now that a marriage contract is negotiated between the ith man and the jth woman, the former having a level of MHC, $K_{mi}*=K*$, the latter having a level of MHC, $K_{mj}*<K*$, and a level of HHC equal to $(K*- K_{mj}*)$. For a case where the man has MHC that is less than $K*$, but greater than the woman's MHC, the reasoning is exactly the same, but the notation is a little more messy. They each have, at the end of the first period, inherited an amount of wealth ω from their parents. The utility of each is expressed as a mathematical function of ω and C, and takes the form $\omega+f(C)$. I should explain that f is an increasing function in C. The linear form of (is adopted solely for simplifying the final results.

Hence, if they do not get married (substituting for C and taking into account that only a fraction λ of HHC is utilisable in the single state), the anticipated second-period utility of the ith man and jth woman are $\omega + f(rK*)$ and $\omega + f(rK_{mj}*+((K*-K_{mj}*)$ respectively. On the other hand, I specify three forms of gain from the event of marriage:

1) For the jth woman, the gain in consumption due to being able to utilise the full amount of $K_{hj}*$, that is, to recover the dormant fraction $(1-\lambda)(K*- K_{mj}*)$.

2) For all the concerned parties, the gain in consumption due to C being a public good between spouses. Therefore after pooling their MHC and HHC, both spouses are able to enjoy a C equalling $rK*+ rK_{mj}*+ (K*- K_{mj}*)$.

3) A final 'residual gain' from marriage, η for men and μ for women. This captures benefits from love, companionship and so forth, and generally indicates how attractive one spouse finds the other. I define this gain to be couple-specific, which is the utility the ith man receives, given the attributes and disposition of the jth woman (η_{ij}), and vice versa (μ_{ji}). The actual value of this residual gain is hidden at the time of the marriage. I say this since most marriages are arranged, and the couple have at best a superficial knowledge of one another. Both parties expect this residual gain to be some fixed, positive amount X.

Given that there are gains from marriage and that the marriage market is competitive, each individual is obliged to make an implicit 'payment' to acquire a spouse, which equals the gain the married state is expected to yield for him or her over the non-married state. The net difference in payment translates into an explicit transfer of assets from one party to another, and is termed 'dowry' or 'bride-price' according to the direction of the transfer. So in order to marry the jth woman, the ith man is willing to pay:

$$M_{ij}= f (rK^*+ rK_{mj}^*+ (K^*- K_{mj}^*)) + X - f (rK^*).$$

In order to marry the man, the woman will pay:

$$W_{ji}= f (rK^*+ rK_{mj}^*+ (K^*- K_{mj}^*)) + X - f (rK_{mj}^* + \lambda (K^*- K_{mj}^*)).$$

Since in this model W_j can never be less than M_i, explicit transfers can occur only from the woman to the man, and are hence categorised as 'dowry'. Thus, the jth woman pays the ith man a dowry D_{ji} of the amount:

$$D_{ji}= W_{ji}-M_{ij}= f(rK^*)-f(rK_{mj}^*+ ((K^*- K_{mj}^*)).$$

It can be seen from this that the smaller the amount of K_{mj}^*, the greater the dowry.

5.6 Analysis of the economic dowry model

The first conclusion derived from this model is that even after the payment of dowry, expected post-marriage utility levels of both parties are higher than their respective single state utilities. The second conclusion is that women who select $K_m = K^*$ will not pay a dowry.

It has already been seen that the crucial factor affecting a woman's accumulation of MHC is the weight α that her parents attach to S^*. From personal observations, I believe that α is affected by the area of India the family resides in, the family's religion and caste, residence in a rural or semi-urban area, living in close proximity to their extended kin, and the level of education of the parents, especially the mother. However, such conjectures must be subjected to empirical testing, and the immediate direction of empirical research suggested by this paper is to rigorously investigate the factors that affect α and thereby affect the level of a daughter's K_{mj}^*.

It is also seen that parents divert funds away from a daughter's MHC acquisition to a son's if they expect to be dependent only on the latter in the future. This suggests that in cases where the parents do not expect to become dependent on their sons in the future, or in social environments where they have an equal chance of becoming dependent on a daughter, parents may be more sympathetic towards a daughter's acquisition of greater MHC.

One basic assumption made in this model is that MHC yields the same real rate of return, r, to both men and women. That is, I am disclaiming the existence of any form of wage discrimination in the Indian labour market. However, a recent study (Duraisamy and Duraisamy, 1996) contradicts this assumption. They found that Indian women with post-secondary schooling earn about 21% less than Indian men, and that about 67-77% of this wage gap may be attributed to discrimination. This has dual implications regarding women's acquisition of MHC. Firstly, parents may think it futile to spend funds on a daughter's MHC, since it will yield low returns to her anyway. Secondly, it means that even a woman with $K_{mj}*=K*$ may have to pay a dowry of the amount f (r_1K*)- f (r_2K*) (where r1 is the real rate of return on the man's K_m and r_2 is the real rate of return on her K_m), because her smaller real income in the unmarried state puts her in a position of receiving a relatively greater gain from marriage. In such a situation, action on the government's part to curb discrimination in the labour market will contribute towards alleviating the dowry problem.

Many believe that the popularising of 'love marriages' as opposed to 'arranged marriages' in India will contribute towards reducing dowry. This idea was suggested by Narayan (1993) and also surfaced during the First Dowry Conference in Harvard but it may be unduly optimistic. Given the heavy emphasis on women's 'reputation' in India, a woman who enters into a pre-marital relationship with a man may well find herself in a situation where she must ultimately marry him because her reputation has been compromised beyond the possibility of someone else marrying her, thus giving a power advantage to the man. Given the latitude men have in India, it is unlikely that he will have similar problems. Again, men may choose to exploit such advantage by extracting a dowry. Love marriages will be the solution only when the societal environment has become sufficiently liberated to allow for failed affairs and relationships that accompany the search for a mate, without detracting from the reputation of either party. However, such liberation will also remove or greatly reduce the societal barriers that presently stand in the way of a woman's MHC acquisition. So the phenomenon of dowry may then become largely obsolete, even in arranged marriages.

5.7 Reasons for the continuation and abuse of dowry

The foremost reason that dowry persists is that the representative woman's family recognise that their preference for following social norms has left their daughter with a single-state utility level inferior to that of the representative man and a greater need to contract a marriage. They view dowry as a reasonable price to 'buy' her that marriage, so that among other things she can recoup the full benefits of her HHC. The evil then lies, first of all, in the social patterns which deny women their right to acquire this potential MHC and make them unduly dependent on marriage for economic sustenance.

The model can now be utilised to shed light on certain unsavoury facts that result directly from the giving of dowry, especially the vulnerability of brides to abuse, and the possibility of dowry murders. I first explain why dowry-giving leaves women more susceptible to abuse and then investigate how the current system can incite men to get rid of their existing wives – inevitably at the beginning of the second period, when both parties have realised the actual values of the residuals μ_{ji} and η_{ij}.

The model has demonstrated that the married state is expected to yield a utility level for women that is higher than their pre-marriage utility, even after the dowry payment. But the crucial characteristic of dowry, because of both the handshake nature of the transaction and the general ignorance of the populace regarding legal provisions, is that it is irrecoverable in the event of dissolution of the marriage. Even without considering the social stigma of being a female divorcée in India, it is seen that the breakdown-point utilities, the utility levels reverted to if the marriage is dissolved (Manser and Brown, 1980) are lower in case of the woman and higher in case of the man than were their respective single state utilities. Evidently, this gives the woman greater incentives to remain within the marriage. If the dowry amount is sufficient to force her breakdown-point consumption below subsistence level, her natal family may coerce her to remain within the marriage so as to avoid the economic burden of supporting her. These factors combine to create a situation where a woman is compelled to tolerate a bad marriage, even one with a realised value of μ_{ji} that is so negative that her actual married utility is less than her pre-marriage utility, just so long as it is higher than her potential utility in the breakdown position. As stated previously, μ_{ji} is the utility the jth woman derives from the characteristics of the ith man.

Hence, if he were alcoholic, abusive or adulterous, the value of μ_{ji} would be negative.

With a little algebra, it can be shown that in the event of dowry being non-recoverable, the woman will tolerate a range of negative values of (μs subject to the limit

$$\mu_{ji} \geq f(rK^*) - f(rK^* + rK_{mj}^* + (K^* - K_{mj}^*)) - D_j,$$

whereas if dowry were recoverable, she would tolerate a range subject to the limit

$$\mu_{ji} \geq f(rK\ ^*) - f(rK^* + rK_{mj}^* + (K^* - K_{mj}^*)).$$

Thus, the greater the value of D_j, the more negative the value of μ_{ji} which she is forced to tolerate. Hence, insofar as dowry is non-recoverable, the payment of it increases the probability of a woman being trapped in a situation of low well-being.

The other issue of concern is dowry's inducement to a man to 'get rid' of his current wife if the expected gains from doing so exceed the gains from continuing to be with her. A man realises that upon killing his wife, he will be faced with three possible consequences. The possibility that he will be convicted for murder and sentenced (with probability of occurrence 'p'), the possibility that he will escape conviction, but not be able to remarry, though he will still retain the first wife's dowry (with probability of occurrence 'q'), and the possibility that he will be able to remarry, complete with a second dowry (with probability of occurrence '1-p-q'). The condition for a dowry-related murder may then be formulated as:

$$(\omega + D_j) + f(rK^* + rK_{mj}^* + (K^* - K_{mj}^*)) + \eta ij < p.0 + q. \{ (\omega + Dj) + f(rK^*) \} + (1-p-q) \{ f(rK^* + rK_{mh}^* + (K^* - K_{mh}^*)) + X + (\omega + D_j + D_h).$$

Where the left hand side (i.e., everything left of the < sign) denotes the utility of remaining with the current wife, the right hand side is the expected utility from murder of the current wife. I assume that if he is convicted, the man's utility drops to zero. If he is unable to re-marry, his utility stays at the breakdown level. If he successfully contracts a second marriage with the hth woman, he acquires a second dowry D_h, such that $D_h = f(rK^*) - f(rK_{mh}^* + \lambda(K^* - K_{mh}^*)) - \sigma$.

In this formula, 'σ' indicates the fact that due to his having become a widower in unnatural circumstances, the expected residual gain from marrying him has declined to X-σ. Thus, even if the second wife has capital accumulation patterns identical to the first wife, the dowry he receives from her will be smaller. It follows that the lower the value of η_{ij} (which denotes his affection for his current wife), the lower the probability of conviction, the higher the value of the previous dowry that he gets to retain, and the higher the value of the second dowry he can hope to acquire, the greater the likelihood of murdering his existing wife.

The hypothesis here is that dowry murders are not so much an outcome of failure on the woman's part to fulfil the contracted payment obligation at the time of marriage – they are precipitated by the man's desire for a further gain in wealth. This hypothesis is supported by Ghadially and Kumar's 1988 case study of 36 dowry deaths, most of which were preceded by dowry demands over and above the marriage agreement.

The abuse that typically precedes such a murder may serve two purposes. It might induce the woman to leave the marriage, thus enabling the man to contract a second marriage without running the risk of being cited for murder. Or he might extort a further payment from her that at least temporarily assuages his desire for greater wealth. However, insofar as wealth transfers are irrevocable, this model predicts that unless the values of 'p' and 'q' are high enough, paying up will only postpone the next bout of attempted extortion and possible murder, not prevent it.

5.8 Prevention of dowry abuse

On the basis of this model, one can recommend certain long-term and short-term policies for combating the custom of dowry and its resultant evils. The eventual goal is the elimination of dowry itself but as this model demonstrates, it can be attained only if the relative gains from marriage for women and men can be equalised. This requires that the systematic under-accumulation of market-oriented human capital by women be stopped, by bringing about a change in people's attitudes regarding the appropriate role of Indian women, removing the stigma from parents' dependency on the daughter as opposed to the son in old age, and fighting the antipathy towards women attaining the resources to achieve economic self-sufficiency. It is necessary first to investigate the factors that increase a family's propensity to abide by traditional norms when deciding upon a daughter's human capital accumulation and then to formulate policies to negate such factors. Sustained action by the government to prevent employment discrimination and wage discrimination against women is also called for.

Clearly, the above is a long-term proposition. It may well take years, if not generations to achieve, for the roots of tradition run deep in India and in the meantime, more women will be victimised by the custom. Given the impossibility of eradicating the custom immediately, a more short-term and urgent objective must be to check the abuse and murders fuelled by dowry. The susceptibility of women to marital abuse is caused not so much by the giving of dowry as by the non-revocable nature of dowry once given. I have argued that one of the prime contributors towards increasing the expected gains from dowry-murders is the fact that the man gets to retain the dowry received from the first wife – whereas the dowry he receives from the second wife would be smaller. If a man did not get to retain the first wife's dowry, then even if the chances of his being apprehended and convicted were low, his gains from murdering her would be relatively small. Thus, it seems logical that dowry deaths could be greatly reduced if it could be ensured that dowry was made recoverable by the bride's family.

It can be argued that the provisions in s. 6 of the *Dowry Prohibition Act*, 1961 in India, to the effect that all 'gifts' given at the time of marriage will immediately proceed to become the bride's property, seeks to ensure precisely that the husband cannot benefit from the dowry. However, I predict poor success for this provision of the Act, for it unconditionally transfers the full amount of dowry to the bride, thus nullifying the entire transaction, i.e. making it pointless from the point of view of the groom's family to demand property. The legal procedure envisaged by section 6 also requires that official records should be made of all 'gifts' given at the time of the marriage. This is likely to meet with strong resistance from the groom's family, and at best lackadaisical support from the bride's, who perceive the groom to have a legitimate claim on dowry as long as he upholds his part of the marriage contract. However, it would be more palatable to all if the groom's claim over the dowry were recognised as being conditional on the marriage contract being upheld, the dowry being reverting by law to the bride or her family upon the marriage contract being terminated by divorce or unnatural death. This would also encourage the bride's family to document the items given as dowry officially, and leave the groom and his family fewer reasons to protest against such documentation.

To draw a somewhat clumsy parallel, the law as it stands is akin to one saying that after a customer makes a purchase from a shopkeeper, the shopkeeper must then return the payment to the customer. The method I suggest is akin to one where a customer who is dissatisfied with her purchase is permitted to return it to the store and receive a full refund. I would recommend an honest admission on the part of policy-makers that the *Dowry Prohibition Act* in India has been a failure, because it was passed prematurely in a country where dowry is still a rational outcome of the social environment, and the woman's own family perceives it to benefit her. Until this social environment can be altered, it may be advantageous to women to admit the legal existence of dowry, and to direct all efforts towards ensuring that it serves as a marriage-quality insurance for the bride. In other words, it appears that in the current situation dowry should serve as surety that a woman will receive satisfactory treatment within marriage and that, should she choose to leave the marriage, the full value of dowry will revert to her. Upon her unnatural death, it will revert to her natal family or be held in trust for her children, ensuring that her erstwhile husband and his kin do not retain any control over it. Such clauses will strengthen a woman's breakdown position. They will also strongly discourage men from abuse or murder, since the expected gains from either course will be substantially reduced. The force of law, then, should be re-directed towards ensuring that the full value of dowry given is legally registered, and towards facilitating the process for ensuring its recovery by the woman or her kin in case of termination of the marriage. If we cannot eliminate dowry in the near future, then let it at least be moulded to protect the interests of the woman.

The original paper contained a detailed appendix with mathematical derivations, which was deleted from this chapter. The full formulae are available from the author upon request.

Chapter 6

Legal strategies for curbing the dowry problem

Werner Menski

For the First International Conference in 1995 I prepared a paper (see chapter 3 above) which was not explicitly focused on legal analysis. I started from the position that dowry is an immensely complex subject about which we seem to know far too little. My observations about the literature in the field related to the prominence of gender-focused debates in the dowry literature and the manifold distractions from the 'real' issue of dowry deaths which this entailed.

I also suggested that dowry violence is a matter of exploiting unequal power relationships in a family, in a way which leaves 'the other' no space to bargain or, ultimately, to live. Proposing that one can view dowry violence as a severe form of bullying and as evidence of lack of individual self-control when it comes to negotiating the financial transactions relating to marriage, my paper emphasised that an analysis which focuses merely on the groom's side and the role of the wife-takers in creating dowry violence overlooks the central and potentially pernicious role of the bride's side. In the last chapter, Bisakha Sen specifically addressed the subject from the perspective of the bride's family, confirming what many of us suspected, namely that women's families are motivated by solid self-interest when they agree on dowry transactions.

Here I begin by summing up some of the points which came out of the 1995 Conference, putting the spotlight on the woman's family rather than the man's. This is certainly not a male chauvinist counter-attack but, in the light of the 1995 discussions, an approach that promises to be more fruitful than the usual, simplistic male-bashing rhetoric of dowry debates. It is obvious that the dowry problem is situated at the interface of male/ female relations. It is much more than a straightforward gender issue, has powerful economic and status dimensions, as well as psychological elements, which no sensible debate can overlook. We have learnt that it is far too simple to proclaim that dowry should be abolished. At the same time, the First International Conference on Dowry left no doubt that dowry-related violence does need to be curbed, and no debate is needed about the fact that the gruesome dowry murders must be controlled on strict terms. The legal dimensions of the dowry problem become highly relevant and this chapter provides a brief overview of the South Asian anti-dowry laws and then examines how the relevant Indian statute law on dowry prohibition has developed over time. This analysis involves of necessity also a detailed study of the reported case law.

There is a growing body of literature of more recent vintage on dowry problems, including dowry murders. As documented in this book, the bibliography on dowry grows rapidly. Much of the new writing continues to come from South Asia, is produced by women, and has a socio-anthropological and activist focus. This literature seems to suggest that in the outwardly male-dominated, patriarchal structures of South Asian societies almost anywhere in the world, women have become the victims of dowry greed and the casualties of daily atrocities. There is no doubt that dowry murders target women, that they continue every day and that a great deal needs to be done before this cruel practice is eradicated. But what are the key elements for bringing the dowry problem under control? This is where the agendas of individual contributors to the current debate diverge so widely that the overall picture remains quite confusing.

6.1 Who is to blame for dowry-related violence?

The social and economic rationalisations in favour of giving dowries, so impressively documented and analysed by Bisakha Sen in chapter 5 and in chapter 9 by Jagbir Jhutti for Britain, suggest that the giving of dowries would not be easy to stop, since the people involved have what appear to them to be sound reasons for continuing the custom. But what are we really tackling, the giving of dowries, the demanding of dowries, the escalation of costs when it comes to getting married, or the atrocious violence against women in the name of dowry? And in all of this, what is the role of legal control mechanisms? We shall see below that Indian law has been as confused about the answers to these questions as are the contributors to the current dowry debates.

We have begun to see more clearly that it is to a large extent the modern consumerist greed of certain individuals and families, rather than simply 'tradition', which leads to dowry murders and suicides. Dowry abuse is clearly not evenly spread through South Asian societies in the subcontinent and abroad. While dowry as an instrument of extortion did not appear to exist in ancient Hindu society, it seems that the ancient pattern of endowing one's daughter with all kinds of goods on the occasion of her transfer to the husband's family has been 'hijacked' by modern consumerist designs. Knowing that there is a deeply entrenched cultural pattern according to which women are endowed with (mainly movable) property on marriage, it has been easy to abuse that originally sensible and positive process. However, the discussions have been somewhat confused, partly because this ancient process itself, the tradition of giving a daughter goods on marriage, predominantly for use in her new home, has been challenged as an unequal deal for women in a patriarchal set-up. It is portrayed as unfair that the boys get immovable property as inheritance, while the girls get only the scraps in movable form.

My argument, and to some extent the tenor of the first Dowry Conference, has been that dowry transfers of the traditional kind have been abused in two distinct ways. Firstly, from the boy's side, it has been relatively easy to give signals that the bride should come endowed with certain specified items, much beyond the realm of the personally useful and practically needed range of household goods and personal effects that a new wife would normally bring with her. Thus, whether expressly specified and demanded or implicitly expected, the inflation of dowry has been partly driven by the male side, the wife-takers, exploiting their ritually and often socially superior position through the process of marriage, to extract as much as possible from those who are already, as Bisakha Sen might put it, in giving mode. Along the same lines, a groom's family could argue that if the daughter-in-law wanted a good house to live in, and a car to be driven around in (or to drive herself), plus other necessities or luxuries, she (or her family) should ensure the provision of such facilities, and the accompanying status, by bringing it all along into the marriage.

There is probably little disagreement that such chains of justifying arguments for dowry are a major reason for the dowry problems which we have been debating. However, the 1995 Dowry Conference found that this was only half the story, if not less. There will be no real dowry problem (and no dead body at the end of the day) when everyone agrees to give and take only what is expected. A contract between two families to play the status game of marriage to maximum advantage, whether explicit or implicit, does not end in disaster if everyone does their bit. In concrete terms, this means that when the expectations of the boy's side are realistic and end basically with the marriage festivities, there is unlikely to be dowry-related trouble later. Problems are pre-programmed, however, if the demands continue after the marriage or if, as often happens, new demands are suddenly raised during the marriage ceremonies.

The Conferences held so far made it clear that the process of getting married cannot be looked at from only one perspective. Having examined the approach from the standpoint of the groom's family, we omit important elements of the interaction of the wife-takers with the bride's side. In other words, the behaviour of the bride's side conditions at least some of the reactions of the groom's side – the two are interrelated in extremely complex ways. In view of Bisakha Sen's research about the calculated self-interest of the bride's side in offering a dowry, one should probably emphasise that awareness on the groom's side that the bride's side is willing to 'invest' in the dowry could well lead to a further inflation of dowries. It would be useful to explore that line of thinking further in future research. There is no guarantee, of course, that such knowledge will be used for the right purpose.

Thus – and this was a finding which did not particularly please many Conference participants at first – a large portion of the blame for the escalation of dowry violence appears to fall on the girl's side. In the traditional model, when parents endowed their daughter with jewellery, dresses, utensils, household goods and other possessions on the occasion of marriage, there may have been no element of sweetening the transaction, just genuine concern for their daughter's welfare. There may have been more to this transaction, but the ancient texts might not reveal it. Today however, as seems to be public knowledge – now confirmed by the complex economic calculations in Bisakha Sen's chapter – many parents are using the strategy of 'dowry sweetener' to attract the best possible bridegroom for their daughter. This, in traditional hypergamous status games, is an old chess move which tends to work well. Through the marriage alliance, the girl's family buys itself status, which is then likely to reflect well on the whole social group, clan or even caste. Social anthropologists have written a good deal on the subject; the pattern is well-known. Today, when intercaste marriage is less circumscribed than it used to be, and when many more marriageable women have 'undesirable' characteristics in traditional conceptual terms, i.e. they are too old, too educated, perhaps too outspoken, and perhaps also too spoilt by doting parents, 'dowry sweeteners' are used to entice a man into marriage with a woman who might be perceived, by both sides, as less than ideal. While much could be said also about less than ideal men, the concerns about women are what matters here. I would even suggest that this is not a new pattern: the dark-skinned, overweight, not very beautiful bride would probably be well aware that her parents have to bargain with her future family – as a write-up about a dowry case in the *Hindustan Times* of 11 August 1996 confirmed and many other cases would support. The decisive factor for a decision in favour of a particular bride may be – and I emphasise *may be* – that as well as the woman the family gains something else. Again, if there is a consensual understanding about this between the families and the spouses, there will probably not be a dowry problem at any time. As we found again and again, even high-level exchanges of presents and property on the occasion of a marriage need not lead to dowry problems. We also learned that not all Indians, or South Asians anywhere, were involved in dowry transactions of the kind which lead to gruesome murders or suicides

Where, however, parents of girls have to make up their minds about the extent of investment in a daughter's dowry, there are two important decisions they might make which can lead more or less directly to a dowry murder.

Firstly, they might agree to an obviously unreasonable demand from the boy's side. In this situation, we know that many families sensibly call off the marriage negotiations altogether. However, a family desperate to 'catch' this particular groom, or simply to get rid of their daughter, may agree to unreasonable demands. If this is a one-off demand, which is then met, the matter may still be amicably resolved and perhaps no dowry problem will arise. But more often than not, it appears, the boy's side will feel encouraged towards making further demands. As the negotiations progress, and especially once the marriage rituals have actually started, and afterwards, the girl's side finds that it has allowed itself to be trapped. To pull out during the middle of marriage rituals, for example, would involve huge loss of face, and the loss of the groom, so it becomes preferable to go along, often under duress, with even the most unreasonable and humiliating demands. One reads such details, often years later, in divorce petitions where the allegations fly wildly – and extremely openly – when either side seeks to prove cruelty or another ground under Indian law (insanity and sexual infidelity are other favourites) to sever the marriage. Such pleadings may make depressing reading, but at least the woman is alive and can argue her case!

Evidence increasingly confirms that the second major reason why young wives get killed is because their parents promised the other side too much and then cannot pay up. The more we study this area of the law and its social field, the more this is revealed as a key reason for dowry murders, the trigger which unleashes violence on the woman because her parents did not fulfil 'their side' of the marital contract. So it is often the girl's family which is to blame as much as the boy's. It would have been their duty to pull out of the negotiations when they realised that the other side was becoming too greedy, more interested in consumer items or ready cash than in their daughter. Still worse, it would have been their duty not to offer any 'dowry sweeteners' and so incite the other side to expect and demand more and more. It appears that some families offer huge dowry sums up front for the less than perfect daughter's desirable match. There are also indications that it is seen as more meritorious to give of one's own free will than to be forced to do so.

This approach to explaining the causes of the dowry problem still highlights the fact that patriarchy is to blame and that the attitudinal complex in Indian society which demands that women must be married, by hook or by crook, is an important element in disadvantaging women in the dowry drama. However, gender disadvantaging is not the only factor. Since the participants are status-conscious middle class families, concerns about the unmarried daughter are combined with status-seeking and status-affirmation on the occasion of marriage, so relegating the economic and social welfare of one's daughter after status concerns of a more impersonal nature.

This seems to be precisely what was opposed by ancient Indian tradition which hinted that the best marriage arrangement is that in which the bride herself is the main, indeed the only, consideration. This was the case in the classic *Brahma* form of marriage, which needs to be freshly explored as an ideal 'dowry-free' model. All other forms of marriage, according to such stereotypical and yet expressive classifications, are inferior. Today's parents of less than perfect daughters, therefore, by offering the carrot of economic incentives to the wife-takers, violate not only ancient ideals about the key roles and expectations of the Hindu bride, but also act in distinctly modern fashion by placing consumerist and status-focused concerns above the welfare of their own daughter, using obviously economic incentives to achieve their own socio-economic goals. It could be said that, rather than assisting the daughter to get married and thus fulfilling familial obligations towards her, such families are using her as a means for further status acquisition and consolidation.

The key to solving the dowry dilemma may thus lie in the realm of the bride's family rather than the groom's. Looking at the literature and the legal discourse, however, there are few indications so far of writers, commentators and judges being aware of this. It has been far too convenient to wrap dowry discourses into feminist, anti-patriarchal slogans and to blame one sector of society (the male world) as though at the point of marriage it was possible to isolate that world from everything else. If marriage as a complex process is viewed as a complicated interaction between the spheres of the male and the female, the male world and the female world, any gender war scenario makes no sense at all. If the wife-givers of today are the wife-takers of tomorrow, as indeed they mostly are, their respective roles and their intricate reversals do not allow for instant switching of basic moral assumptions. For example, I do not believe – and I do not see in social reality – that a family will demand dowry for their son's wedding and then not give dowry on the occasion of their daughter's marriage. Since it is more often the case that the daughter marries first, a family which agrees to give in to dowry demands on that occasion will most likely demand a substantial dowry when their son gets married. But if their daughter got married 'without dowry', the son will then not expect to find a wife whose family will offer him or his family lavish dowry articles. If they did, a sensible young man (and, of course, his family) would probably be suspicious: is this a less than desirable woman who needs to come with a 'sweetener'? I am sorry to be so cynical, but having read masses of divorce cases from India in which dowry and other financial arrangements were an issue, I can see that it is often obvious from the start – to the outsider and those with the benefit of hindsight – that certain arrangements could not possibly have fostered a happy married life together.

So it is increasingly clear that the various arguments about how to eradicate the dowry problem do not lead to straightforward solutions, nor is it easy to apportion blame. Social and economic forces being somewhat favourable to dowry arrangements, what can a modern state's legal system do to counteract the problem? More specifically, can the law reasonably expect to abolish dowry transactions, or should the focus of attention rather be towards the control of dowry-related violence?

6.2 Dowry and the law: Where do we stand today?

When we came together in the Dowry Conferences to discuss strategies for combating dowry-related violence and dowry murders in India and elsewhere, the common view, including my own, was that legal strategies had proved virtually ineffective. The Indian anti-dowry law itself, in the form of the *Dowry Prohibition Act*, 1961 was widely dismissed as a toothless paper tiger. The various and important amendments to the 1961 Act during the 1980s had either been ignored or criticised and dismissed as inadequate. The prevailing view was that cases on dowry-related violence did not even reach the Indian courts, and it was stated with some vigour in many debates that there were no convictions whatever for dowry murder in India. The few cases that did receive a judicial hearing were said to be confirming the worst fears of those critical of the Indian legal establishment and its pro-male biases.

It is my observation now that few researchers on dowry have had the time or facilities to study the available legal material in depth. What we have been given so far are superficial assessments and opinionated per-sonal views from activists and other concerned individuals, rather than solid legal assessments. Thus, the need to research the South Asian anti-dowry laws in more depth became still more evident. This chapter is one result of a sustained effort to make sense of the current Indian anti-dowry law and its effectiveness. Given that there is now a sizeable reported case law on dowry from the Indian courts, the main question we must ask is whether there has been any meaningful impact of such legal intervention. In other words, could it be claimed that the legal strategies for curbing the dowry problems in India have been in any way successful? Concerning the role of law within the various state-sponsored efforts to control dowry murders in India, it should be possible to come to a more solid finding than a few years ago about progress in legal intervention. Reading case reports, it quickly becomes evident that the superior Indian courts did very little about the dowry problem before the mid-1980s. However, the Indian Supreme Court has since begun to jail dowry murderers, in some instances awarding the death penalty. Indian press reports began to refer to the growing number of mothers-in-law languishing in jails for killing a daughter-in-law. Something has evidently been happening in this field which the academic literature has not yet picked up.

When I argue here that Indian statute law on dowry has now reached a point where hardly any further reforms are needed, and where the highest judiciary now appears to be fully sensitised to the gruesome realities of daily dowry killings, my aim is not to produce a pro-establishment view. Rather, this chapter reinforces the message that dowry is indeed a grave social issue and not primarily a legal problem. The courts, and the entire legal machinery, can only do so much. Dowry violence remains a serious illness of society, which ultimately can only be healed through self-controlled action on the part of people as members of society (as I argue here in chapter 3.5). The law may have a role to play but, as always, legal intervention has limits. Judges can – and now do – send dowry murderers to jail for life, but the murders will only stop if people in society reflect on what they are doing and 'bring compassion (*daya*) back into life', as one of my local Gujarati shopkeepers said when I told him about the plan to compile this book.

Turning now specifically to a focus on the legal perspective, I begin by providing a brief overview of the various South Asian anti-dowry laws before proceeding to the examination of the reported case law from India and ask more specifically what recent legal developments there show us about the potential role of the law in controlling dowry-related problems of violence and murder. There are a variety of relevant strands and debates around dowry which interlock. It also seems useful to examine the scope for further legislative reform, particularly as far as the giving of dowry is concerned.

6.3 Legal dimensions of dowry control in South Asia

My literature survey in chapter 3 and the debates during the First International Conference, in particular, showed that several tried and tested arguments for the abolition of the so-called 'dowry problem' have failed or proved ineffective. More specifically, it was found that the attempted legal controls – the abolition or prohibition of dowry – had not been successful. As a socio-legal researcher, I have never been surprised about this, because any official state law has definite limits in the face of opposition from society and its unofficial laws. In the present case, these include practices that are positively prohibited by state law, such as the giving and taking of dowries. The criminalisation of such practices by state law could not be fully effective save in a police state where every infringement of the law was reported. That would surely be too high a price to pay for controlling one problem and it would create many others, as is shown in chapter 7.

My main argument in this brief section is that the Indian dowry control law is still very young and needs time to develop 'bite' more effectively. Even though the *Dowry Prohibition Act* came into force in 1961, there were no reported cases under it until well into the 1970s. It is only during the mid-1980s that several important amendments were made to the original Act, which then became activated. Only during the late 1980s and early 1990s has the initial trickle of reported cases grown to a little stream, whose muddied waters have not been clarified by detailed, serious analysis. So it is hardly surprising that the analysis of the anti-dowry laws has remained so unsatisfactory. It has simply been too early to assess the limited impact of the law in detail and, as I said, other agendas have prevailed.

In the past few years, we have begun to see significant changes in the application of the Indian anti-dowry law, confirmation of a clear judicial strategy, particularly at the highest level, of toughening up against dowry bullies and murderers of newly married women. Undoubtedly, much more remains to be done, but a beginning has been made. Still, in view of continuing evidence of dowry murders all over India, year after year, and growing trends of so-called dowry murders also in Pakistan and Bangladesh, the law manifestly is not active enough, is not doing the right things, or is perhaps not an appropriate tool to put a stop to dowry-related murders and violence.

Rather than engaging in ritualised rhetoric criticism, which unfortunately seems a hallmark of much of the existing writing, it will be useful to analyse what the statute law actually provides and then focus on the Indian case law and its effects so far. I begin with a brief overview of the entire South Asian legal scenario on anti-dowry legislation.

The first major piece of national legislation in India which sought to outlaw and abolish dowry transactions is the *Dowry Prohibition Act* of 1961. In India's federal set-up, this Act now has a large number of state amendments, but it suffices for our purpose to focus on the main Act and its subsequent important amendments in 1983, 1984, 1985 and 1986. The close sequence of these amendments reflects a desperate attempt by Indian law makers to control a growing social evil, and to be seen to be doing something against the growing mass of dowry murders perpetrated during the 1980s. Since 1986, there has been no further legislative activity in this field and the emphasis in anti-dowry legal activity has shifted to the Indian courts, especially the Supreme Court, and the various NGOs concerned with women's rights. The judicial involvement shows a clear progression from male collusion and siding with the procedural tricks of lawyers during the early 1980s (see section 6.5 below) to increasingly outspoken criticism of the dowry evil, reflected in a growing number of decisions which seek to help women who have in some way become dowry victims. To the extent that judges can become the moral apostles of humane interaction, they have grasped this nettle and no longer see their role exclusively as the wielders of the punishing rod for dowry murderers.

In Pakistan, significantly, the need to legislate against growing abuses has also been felt. Consolidated research on the Pakistani and Bangladeshi experience is urgently needed. So far there is a marked absence of academic writing in this difficult field. It is certainly not correct to argue, as many Muslims try to do, that the Islamic system of payments from the groom to the bride (the *mahr* or 'dower', as it should correctly be called, rather than 'dowry') excludes the possibility of dowry payments. In fact, the two systems unhappily co-exist in many cases, and South Asian Muslim societies are in no way immune from abuses of the dowry syndrome. The relevant enactments in Pakistan are the *Dowry and Bridal Gifts (Restriction) Act*, 1976 plus Rules made under that Act, and the *Dowry and Bridal Gifts (Restriction) (Amendment) Ordinance*, 1980.

There is as yet no published specialised research on these statutes, but there is a considerable, and growing, list of decided and reported cases (Balchin, 1994).

As recently as 1997, Pakistan has taken further interesting steps to control the inflated expenditure on marriage celebrations by passing the *Marriages (Prohibition of Wasteful Expenses) Act*, 1997 which surprisingly had instant socio-economic effects, almost putting many large hotels and wedding halls, as well as groups of highly specialised musicians and other entertainers, out of business. Many families seem to have breathed a sigh of relief and seized the chance to spend less on marriages, so the Act is actually being observed in practice by many, although not quite to the letter. Interestingly, the Act itself allows for the feeding of guests in private homes, so one can still impress one's guests in many ways. But the Act appears to have effectively stopped the huge wasteful dinner parties in often lavish five star surroundings. An instant repercussion, I was told, which definitely remains to be researched, has been that the groom's side may now expect the actual savings from the prohibited lavish dinners to be transformed into higher dowry payments!

Pakistan also experiences bride-burning cases, but so far on a lesser scale than India, and apparently only in certain localities, namely in Panjab, which is intriguing since Indian Panjabis lead the league tables of dowry murderers. In Pakistan, the standard explanation for the death of young women by burning has been alleged 'accidents' caused by substandard cooking equipment. This has given rise to strange pleadings about faulty kerosene cookers, called 'stove blast' cases. The only prominent reported case on this matter so far is *The State v. SSP Lahore*, PLD 1991 Lahore 224, in which the High Court of Lahore exploded the myth of 'stove blasts' as a convenient smokescreen and used strong language to condemn the murder of women in this way. However, little further action appears to have been taken. I have been told recently by several observers that in Lahore, burnt women are still brought to certain hospitals every day. The most recent indications have been that this practice may be spreading to Karachi, where it was once unheard of. Research on this problem is urgently needed, for it looks to me more like a cruel method of divorcing a woman who is perceived as unsatisfactory than an explicitly dowry-related phenomenon.

Bangladesh has quietly copied the entire Indian anti-dowry legislation, including subsequent amendments during the 1980s, but has not followed all provisions in detail, especially not the legal provision that any dowry given in violation of the law shall belong to the bride alone. The relevant enactments for Bangladesh are the *Dowry Prohibition Act*, 1980, the *Dowry Prohibition (Amendment) Ordinance*, 1982 and the *Dowry Prohibition (Amendment) Ordinance*, 1986. While in Pakistan the emphasis of control has been on lavish spending for marriage celebrations, which has increasingly (and quite effectively) been portrayed as contrary to Islam, Bangladeshis experience many problems with dowry extortions, much increased because of Gulf-induced prosperity in certain middle class circles (Ahmed, 1993). Rather than killings by fire, the prominent feature in Bangladesh appears to be the murder of wives by poison or knife attack (Monsoor, 1994). Again, more research is needed, since the problems appear to be growing.

6.4 The Indian statute law on dowry prohibition

The original *Dowry Prohibition Act* of 1961 was, by common consent and obvious evidence (there were no reported cases under the Act until *Thomas* 1975 KLT 386, actually a Christian case) a total failure, a dead letter, or a paper tiger. The Act states in its 'Object' section what its purpose was supposed to be. The legislators clearly saw dowry as a social problem, and the role of this new law was perceived as an educative measure. The section stated:

> The object of this Bill is to prohibit the evil practice of giving and taking of dowry. This question has been engaging the attention of the Government for some time past, and one of the methods by which this problem, which is essentially a social one, was sought to be tackled was by the conferment of improved property rights on women by the Hindu Succession Act, 1956. It is, however, felt that a law which makes the practice punishable and at the same time ensures that any dowry, if given, does enure for the benefit of the wife will go a long way to educating public opinion and to the eradication of this evil. There has also been a persistent demand for such a law both in and out of Parliament. Hence the present Bill. It, however, takes care to exclude presents in the form of clothes, ornaments, etc. which are customary at marriages, provided the value

thereof does not exceed Rs. 2.000/-. Such a provision appears to be necessary to make the law workable.

By its own admission, this law indicates that there is a 'long way' to go to eradicating dowry. Such candid statements recognise at once that the law maker never envisaged that this enactment would be followed to the letter. This is typical of much of modern South Asian legislation, but we in the Western world have problems interpreting this. These kinds of law are not necessarily indications of lawlessness. Rather, it is recognised in the countries of South Asia that the state's laws serve different purposes to much of Western law. Thus, it is equally typical that the state law considers the consequences of its own rejection and violation, and even provides for it in explicit terms. In the present case, s. 6 of the 1961 Act lays down that any dowry shall be for the benefit of the wife or her heirs, thus anticipating that dowries will continue to be given, in violation of the letter of the anti-dowry law. But the matter does not stop there: the law also takes the next logical step and provides for cases in which the particular rule of s. 6 is violated. The approach taken at this stage of double violation of the law reflects classic criminal law strategy, stipulating discretionary punishments of imprisonment up to six months and/or a fine of up to Rs. 5,000. This is a classic case of social engineering through law and illustrates the educative function of law.

There is not a word in the statements quoted above of dowry-related violence to women, nor of dowry murders. Did such evidence not exist in the 1960s, or is it purposely not mentioned? It is difficult to find a clear answer. Further, the explicit reference to existing forms of financial transactions on the occasion of marriages and the desire not to outlaw the practice altogether, indicate acute awareness on the part of the law makers about the positive social aspects of making presents on such auspicious occasions. What this law seeks to combat, therefore, is not the institution of dowry in the sense of giving presents to the bride on the occasion of her marriage, but the excesses of dowry practices. However, it is not specified where precisely these excesses are located.

Apart from granting property rights in any dowry to the woman or her heirs, the 1961 Act defines dowry in s. 2 as 'any property or valuable security given or agreed to be given either directly or indirectly.....at or before or after the marriage *as consideration for the marriage*' (my emphasis), while sections 3 and 4 of the Act specify the penalties for giving, taking or demanding dowry. These were originally fairly low. S. 3 of the original Act provided:

3. Penalty for the giving and taking of dowry.-
If any person, after the commencement of this Act, gives or takes or abets the giving or taking of dowry, he shall be punishable with imprisonment which may extend to six months, or with fine which may extend to five thousand rupees, or with both.

Section 4 of the original Act also criminalised the demanding of dowry and read as follows:

4. Penalty for demanding dowry.-
If any person, after the commencement of this Act, demands, directly or indirectly, from the parents or guardian of a bride or bridegroom, as the case may be, any dowry, he shall be punishable with imprisonment which may extend to six months, or with a fine which may extend to five thousand rupees, or with both:

Provided that no court shall take cognizance of any offence under this section except with the previous sanction of the State Government or of such officer as the State Government may, by general or special order, specify in this behalf.

While section 5 also provided that 'any agreement for the giving or taking of dowry shall be void', section 7 deals with cognizance of offences and section 8 of the 1961 Act made the offence non-cognizable, bailable and non-compoundable, indicating a softly-softly approach to the criminalisation of dowry offences. Of particular relevance to the analysis of dowry-related violence is s. 6 of the Act, which provided as follows:

6. Dowry to be for the benefit of the wife or her heirs.-
(1) Where any dowry is received by any person other than the woman in connection with whose marriage it is given, that person shall transfer it to the woman –

(a) if the dowry was received before marriage, within one year after the date of marriage; or

(b) if the dowry was received at the time of or after the marriage, within one year after the date of its receipt; or

(c) if the dowry was received when the woman was a minor within one year after she has attained the age of eighteen years; and pending such transfer, shall hold it in trust for the benefit of the woman.

(2) If any person fails to transfer any property as required by sub-section (1) and within the time limited therefore, he shall be punishable with imprisonment which may extend to six months, or with fine which may extend to five thousand rupees, or with both; but such punishment shall not absolve the person from his obligation to transfer the property as required by sub-section (1).

(3) Where the woman entitled to any property under sub-section (1) dies before receiving it, the heirs of the woman shall be entitled to claim it from the person holding it for the time being.

(4) Nothing contained in this section shall affect the provisions of section 3 or section 4.

Here in s. 6(3), we have for the first time clear indications of legislative awareness of dowry-related murders or suicides. By providing that the heirs of the dead woman should be entitled to claim whatever dowry was due to her, the law again envisages abuse of legal rules and makes provisions for the resulting eventualities. It will be interesting to research further to what extent awareness of dowry murders was already a feature during the 1960s.

The dowry problem itself was not a high-profile legal topic then, but it was not absent from the agenda. In a leading textbook on Hindu family law (Derrett, 1970: 306), we find the following comment on one particular dowry problem, the non-return of property given in engagement contracts which then do not proceed to a full marriage:

The dowry system was recognised as an abuse as far back as eight centuries ago, and states have attempted to abolish or regulate it here and there in India ever since. It is accepted as an evil by all payers of dowries, especially since the amount is not stabilised at law as is the *mahr* of a Muslim bride (a somewhat different matter). Parliament has prohibited the demanding and paying of dowries, but the statute (of 1961) is not frequently adverted to, except in cases where families, agreeing to a betrothal and receiving part of the consideration, refuse subsequently to return the money and ornaments when the proposed marriage falls through, on the ground that the contract was an illegal one.

When Professor Derrett wrote this, there was not yet a single reported dowry case in Indian law. Nothing seemed to happen, and it took a long time for amendments to the 1961 Act to be introduced. Because of the absence of case law for almost 20 years, which was mainly blamed on the fact that both the givers and the takers of dowry were criminalised by the Act, there has been a strong call for making only the demanding and taking of dowry an offence. The main argument was that having made both sides culpable, putting them *in pari delicto*, had prevented the wife givers from starting any legal action, since they themselves were also guilty under the law. The obvious remedy would have been to de-criminalise the giving of dowry, but this step has – for several reasons – never been taken. In my view, this persistence in criminalising the givers of dowry along with the takers reflects elite (and legal) awareness of the fact that the bride's side is indeed guilty of connivance in dowry atrocities. In view of growing evidence (see chapter 5, by Sen) about the evident culpability of the wife givers, one should maybe argue for stricter legal supervision of the bride's side rather than their exculpation altogether. I am aware that this amounts to an argument for maintaining the legal *status quo*, but if one amended the law to decriminalise the giving of dowry, how would one prevent the bride's side from continuing to play status games while endangering the life of the woman concerned? As we shall see below, this is not the only relevant consideration preventing direct legal intervention.

The first amendments to the anti-dowry laws in the 1980s related to criminal law issues and focused on violence against women during the first seven years of marriage. This is an implied admission on the part of the law makers that dowry-related violence had become a severe problem by the early 1980s, when the first dowry cases went to the superior Indian courts and it became apparent that the legal machinery was full of loopholes. The *Criminal Law (Second Amendment) Act*, 1983 strengthened relevant provisions of three major Acts on criminal law and evidence and imported a more precise definition of 'cruelty' in this context. The 1983 Act introduced a new section 498-A into the *Indian Penal Code*, 1860, providing as follows:

498-A. Husband or relative of a husband of a women subjecting her to cruelty.–

Whoever, being the husband or the relative of the husband of a woman, subjects such woman to cruelty shall be punished with imprisonment for a term which may extend to three years and shall also be liable to fine.

Explanation: – For the purposes of this section, 'cruelty' means –

(a) any wilful conduct which is of such nature as is likely to drive the woman to commit suicide or to cause grave injury or danger to life, limb or health (whether mental or physical) of the woman; or

(b) harassment of the woman where such harassment is with a view to coercing her or any person related to her to meet any unlawful demand for any property or valuable security or is on account of failure by her or any person related to her to meet such demand.

Other amendments through the same Act of 1983 focus on procedure and evidence. They were designed to empower law enforcement agencies to gain evidence of dowry murders, in explicit language which reflects clear awareness of the need for urgent action. Significantly, a new sub-section was also introduced in s. 113 of the *Indian Evidence Act*, 1872, to the effect that a presumption of dowry death is raised if a married woman dies within seven years of the marriage. The new section 113-A reads as follows:

113-A. Presumption as to abetment of suicide by a married woman.–

When the question is whether the commission of suicide by a woman had been abetted by her husband or any relative of her husband and it is shown that she had committed suicide within a period of seven years from the date of her marriage and that her husband or such relative of her husband had subjected her to cruelty the court may presume, having regard to all the other circumstances of the case, that such suicide had been abetted by her husband or by such relative of the husband.

Explanation. – For the purposes of this section, 'cruelty' shall have the same meaning as in S. 498-A of the Indian Penal Code (45 of 1860).

We know today that this did not go far enough, but this was an impressive attempt to strengthen the prosecution's hand in cases where there was evidence of dowry extortion and even murder.

More specifically, the *Dowry Prohibition (Amendment) Act*, 1984 sought to follow up some of the suggested improvements. By this time, the early case law on dowry-related questions (see section 6.5 below) had thrown up tricky definitional problems and had made it obvious that the legal definition of dowry in the 1961 Act was inadequate. In 1984, therefore, it was perceived as a matter of priority to modify and tighten the unsatisfactory definition of 'dowry' in section 2. The definition phrase quoted and highlighted above, treating dowry quite widely as 'consideration for the marriage', was now rephrased to read that dowry is 'any property or valuable security given or agreed to be given... *in connection with the marriage*' (italics provided). This was supposed to be a still wider definition, which would basically cover any transaction which could in any way be related to the marriage. It appears that this did help the Indian courts, which were meanwhile taking a more serious view of dowry offences, to cast the definitional net of dowry wider than had been possible before.

Another significant change in the *Dowry Prohibition (Amendment) Act*, 1984 are the higher penalties for violation of the law. In this respect, s. 3 of the 1961 Act was amended to become s. 3(1), and the old wording was replaced by tougher rules. The new s. 3 of the 1961 Act now read:

3. Penalty for the giving and taking of dowry –

(1) If any person, after the commencement of this Act, gives or takes or abets the giving or taking of dowry, he shall be punishable with imprisonment for a term which shall not be less than six months, but which may extend to two years, and with fine which may extend to ten thousand rupees or the amount of the value of such dowry, whichever is more:

Provided that the Court may, for adequate and special reasons to be recorded in the judgment, impose a sentence of imprisonment for a term less than six months.

(2) Nothing in sub-section (1) shall apply to, or in relation to, -

(a) presents which are given at the time of a marriage to the bride (without any demand having been made in that behalf):

Provided that such presents are entered in a list maintained in accordance with the rules made under this Act;

(b) presents which are given at the time of a marriage to the bridegroom (without any demand having been made in that behalf);

Provided that such presents are entered in a list maintainable in accordance with the rules under this Act.

Provided further that where such presents are made by or on behalf of the bride or any person related to the bride, such presents are of a customary nature and the value thereof is not excessive having regard to the financial status of the person by whom, or on whose behalf, such presents are given.

This re-structured section shows a tougher criminal law approach in cases of *mala fide* transactions and extortions in the name of dowry. Again, however, the concern of the law not to disturb genuine economic transfer and exchange mechanisms on the occasion of marriage is evidenced by the new rules in the proviso to s. 3(1), to the effect that courts can award less than six months imprisonment, but only for adequate and special reasons to be recorded or mentioned in the judgment. Although we see a definite toughening up, allowing the courts to become really strict when necessary, the amendments of 1984 are tempered by provisions in s. 3(2) which explicitly allow for the genuine and pressure-free customary giving of presents to either side. The wording of these saving provisions shows that they implicitly allow for the continuation of *bona fide* financial transactions on the occasion of marriage among elite groups, protecting these elites from criminal prosecutions. One can be in two minds about whether this is a good law, but if the law's main aim was to catch the dowry bully and murderer, rather than to prescribe to all members of society that they must not give more than absolutely necessary to women in marriage, this seems a rather sensible legal provision. We must note, then, that the modern Indian law does not prohibit dowry as such, it merely seeks to criminalise abuses of the dowry system and extortion in the name of dowry.

This brings us back to why the law prohibits also the giving of dowry, rather than just demanding and taking. It appears that the saving provisions discussed above were inserted in 1984 because of growing awareness that dowry disputes are not necessarily over money alone but about status and esteem in society, so that litigation which accused certain persons of dowry offences could easily be abused for ulterior purposes. Continuing to outlaw dowry for both sides, thus, seems to be a legal strategy of dispute avoidance, taking the wind out of either party's sails, just in case they are tempted to use the courts as a forum for washing dirty linen in public.

The *Dowry Prohibition (Amendment) Act*, 1984 also amended s. 4 of the 1961 Act (as quoted above) and increased the penalties in line with those found in s. 3(1) of the Act, as cited above. Thus, under s. 4 of the Act, too, the new position was that any person who demands any dowry 'shall be punishable with imprisonment for a term which shall not be less than six months, but which may extend to two years and with fine which may extend to ten thousand rupees'. Here again, a proviso was added to the effect that in certain circumstances, to be specified by the court in the judgment, a sentence of imprisonment of less than six months may be given.

The 1984 Amendment Act also sought to tighten the rule system concerning the transfer of any dowry property to the woman concerned. In the re-worded s. 6 of the 1961 Act (cited above), it was now provided in s. 6(1) that the transfer of any dowry received should be made to the woman within three months rather than one year. Further, the penalties for non-transfer of the dowry in the stipulated time, as detailed in s. 6(2) and cited above, were increased to a punishment of 'imprisonment for a term which shall not be less than six months, but which may extend to two years or with fine which may extend to ten thousand rupees or with both'. Finally, a new sub-section 3A was added to the original sub-section 3. It reads as follows:

(3A) Where a person convicted under sub-section (2) for failure to transfer any property as required by sub-section (1) has not, before his conviction under that sub-section, transferred such property to the woman entitled thereto or, as the case may be, her heirs, the Court shall, in addition to awarding punishment under that sub-section, direct, by order in writing, that such person shall transfer the property to such woman or, as the case may be, her heirs within such period as may be specified in the order, and if such person fails to comply with the direction within the period so specified, an amount equal to the value of the property may be recovered from him as if it were a fine imposed by such Court and paid to such woman or, as the case may be, her heirs.

This provision reinforces the impression that the amended anti-dowry law clearly signals its intention to become tough on violators of the legal rules. In this case, as we shall see with reference to decided cases, in particular *Pratibha Rani v. Sushil Kumar,* AIR 1985 SC 628, the statute appears to counter the stereotypical perception of North Indian patriarchal traditions to the effect that women are owned by men, so their property will be owned by men, too. For a new bride, the problem would be that since she is treated as property of the husband's joint family, everything she brings with her will also be perceived in this way.

Probably in reflection of public interest strategies concerning easier access to justice (see now Menski, 1996), relaxed rules on *locus standi* for complainants in cases of dowry problems were also introduced by the 1984 Act. This amendment is found in the re-worded s. 7 of the Act, which now reads:

7. Cognizance of offences –

(1) Notwithstanding anything contained in the Code of Criminal Procedure, 1973, –

(a) no court inferior to that of a Metropolitan Magistrate or a Judicial Magistrate of the first class shall try any offence under this Act;

(b) no court shall take cognizance of an offence under this Act except upon –

(i) its own knowledge or a police report of the facts which constitute such offence, or

(ii) a complaint by the person aggrieved by the offence or a parent or other relative of such person, or by any recognized welfare institution or organisation;

....

Explanation. – For the purposes of this sub-section, 'recognized welfare institution or organisation' means a social welfare institution or organisation recognized in this behalf by the Central or State Government.

Offences under the 1961 Act were now also made cognizable through amending s. 8 of the 1961 Act in that respect, but such offences remained bailable and non-compoundable under s. 8(2) of the Act. The provisions in s. 9 of the Act about the framing of Rules under the Act emphasise, significantly, the need for 'the better co-ordination of policy and action with respect to the administration of this Act'. This reinforces the impression that by the mid-1980s, the need for tackling the growing dowry-related forms of violence had become a subject of public policy concern.

Closely linked to the 1984 amendments, new rules concerning registration of dowry transactions were further specified in 1985. These rules were introduced to improve the evidentiary position of dowry complainants, since husbands and their families would frequently argue that specific items of contested ownership had been given to them rather than the woman. The *Dowry Prohibition (Maintenance of Lists of Presents to the Bride and Bridegroom) Rules*, 1985 clearly lay down that lists of presents are to be kept by both sides and are to be signed. This legal provision appears to be inspired by Pakistani methods of listing gifts, as found in the *Dowry and Bridal Gifts (Restriction) Rules* of 1976 which have been quite effective in curbing excesses of vulgar display of wealth, at least according to some respondents. The Indian rules do not comment on the undesirability of displaying presents but focus instead on technical rules of evidence to ensure that prosecution cases become stronger and less time-consuming.

The Rules came into effect on 2 October 1985. Their main substantive provisions are found in rule 2, which reads as follows:

2. Rules in accordance with which lists of presents are to be maintained. –

(1) The list of presents which are given at the time of the marriage to the bride shall be maintained by the bride.

(2) The list of presents which are given at the time of the marriage to the bridegroom shall be maintained by the bridegroom.

(3) Every list of presents referred to [in] sub-rule (1) or sub-rule (2),

(a) shall be prepared at the time of the marriage or as soon as possible after the marriage;

(b) shall be in writing;

(c) shall contain,

(i) a brief description of each present;

(ii) the approximate value of the present;

(iii) the name of the person who has given the present; and

(iv) where the person giving the present is related to the bride or bridegroom, a description of such relationship;

(d) shall be signed by both the bride and the bridegroom.

Explanation 1. – Where the bride is unable to sign, she may affix her thumb-impression in lieu of her signature after having the list read out to her and obtaining the signature, on the list, of the person who has so read out the particulars contained in the list.

Explanation 2. – Where the bridegroom is unable to sign, he may affix his thumb-impression in lieu of his signature after having the list read out to him and obtaining the signature, on the list, of the person who has so read out the particulars contained in the list.

(4) The bride or the bridegroom may, if she or he so desires, obtain on either or both of the lists referred in sub-rule (1) or sub-rule (2) the signature or signatures of any relation or relations of the bride or the bridegroom or of any other person or persons present at the time of the marriage.

These Rules, by making explicit reference to illiterate spouses, seem to indicate that dowry-related problems of evidence may occur in all social groups, not just among the elite. I know from personal experience that the maintenance of such lists had been a customary practice in some communities even before the introduction of the 1985 Rules. The original purpose of such lists was to have a record, for the purposes of the family, of what gifts were given by whom on auspicious occasions such as marriages. Since this might be gifts of cash, the level of such gift-giving could be monitored (significantly by the women of the household), so that when it was the family's turn to reciprocate, they would know how much to give. A study of such traditional interactions and their current shape would also help to throw some light on the extent of the inflation of gift-giving on the occasion of marriages today. To what extent the 1985 Rules have actually been used in practice, and as evidence in litigation, remains to be researched.

Finally, the *Dowry Prohibition (Amendment) Act*, 1986 introduced further important changes in the criminal and evidence laws of the country. This Act represents a further toughening up in that a number of small amendments fine-tune the legal dowry prohibition mechanisms. In the revised definition of 'dowry' in s. 2 of the Act, there is now clearer recognition that dowry may be given or demanded at any time after the marriage. Thus, the revised definition of dowry, and the current wording of the relevant part of that section, is now that dowry means 'any property or valuable security given or agreed to be given either directly or indirectly... at or before or *any time* after the marriage as consideration for the marriage' (my emphasis). This small amendment explicitly recognises that dowry demands may be made months or even years after the marriage, so this new definition is yet more careful to cast its net as widely as possible.

Significantly, the criminalisation of dowry has also been further extended, in that the maximum jail sentence under s. 3 of the amended 1961 Act is now five years (rather than two) and the maximum fine is now Rs. 15,000 (rather than Rs. 10,000) or the value of the dowry, whichever is higher. The 1986 Amendment Act also introduced a new s. 4A, which bans dowry advertisements, makes dowry offences non-bailable, and s. 8B introduced Dowry Prohibition Officers, a new social work profession already tried in various states before the amendment of the Central Act. I am not aware of any research on their effectiveness to date and this would be a challenging topic to investigate.

In s. 6 of the 1961 Act, which regulates how dowry is to be transferred to the woman herself (see the original text cited above), various new provisions have been made to strengthen the control mechanisms. These indicate two forms of toughening up. First, a minimum penalty of Rs. 5,000 for non-transfer of any dowry given has now been specified, with a maximum fine of Rs. 10,000 as before. Further, in several sub-sections of s. 6, the new law specifies explicitly that where a woman has died within seven years of her marriage as a result of dowry-related violence and has no children, her property shall be transferred to her parents. This new law obviously seeks to get the message across that dowry murderers will not benefit financially, since the dowry belongs to the bride and her natal family rather than the groom's family. This strictly reinforces the messages of the earlier legal provisions.

In addition, a new s. 304B was introduced into the *Indian Penal Code* of 1860, dealing with dowry death. This provides:

304B. Dowry death. –

(1) Where the death of a woman is caused by any burns or bodily injury or occurs otherwise than under normal circumstances within seven years of her marriage and it is shown that soon before her death she was subjected to cruelty or harassment by her husband or any relative of her husband for, or in connection with, any demand for dowry, such death shall be called 'dowry death', and such husband or relative shall be deemed to have caused her death.

Explanation. – For the purposes of this sub-section, 'dowry' shall have the same meaning as in S. 2 of the Dowry Prohibition Act, 1961.

(2) Whoever commits dowry death shall be punished with imprisonment for a term which shall not be less than seven years but which may extend to imprisonment for life.

These various amendments, in their combined strength, have given the Indian legal system and particularly the judiciary enormously powerful weapons to punish any violations of the dowry prohibition law. It is no surprise, therefore, that for the last ten years further calls for legislative amendments have scarcely arisen. We have already referred to the call for decriminalising the giving of dowry and have seen that there may be several reasons why the giving of dowry has remained a crime under the 1961 Act.

To sum up, the Indian statute law on dowry prohibition is now in place, and it is tough and menacing. What matters in practice is firstly, whether society will take any notice of this law and secondly, how the Indian judges will deal with prosecutions and with the offenders and their excuses for killing or driving a woman to suicide. It appears that the daily occurrence of dowry murders and the increasing prominence of dowry murder cases and dowry-related violence has at last shaken the judiciary into a form of activism not unlike that found in the much more publicity-conscious public law sphere. The anti-dowry law is of course not exclusively a matter of the private sphere, nor of the personal law of the parties, so it is not surprising that a certain measure of legal activism can be observed when we turn to a detailed analysis of the judicial treatment of dowry-related violence.

6.5 The Indian case law on dowry

We have noted the virtual absence for many years of case law under the *Dowry Prohibition Act* of 1961. This has been much commented on, but how much can one say about a void? The main explanations focused on the fact that the provisions of the Act itself were not strong enough to curb the abuses. Khalid J, in *Thomas* 1975 KLT 386, at p. 387, complained that '[A] well-intentioned piece of legislation has not achieved its object at all... though enacted to prevent a malady, [it] has only aggravated the same'.

By the early 1980s, a trickle of cases on dowry appeared in the Indian law reports. In many of these, tricky defence lawyers got away with pleading all kinds of reasons why their clients should not be found guilty of an offence under the 1961 Act. In *Daulat Mansingh Aher,* 1980 CriLJ 1171, the accused did not succeed in pleading that dowry demands by letter were not dowry demands and he also had his instant application for grant of leave to the Supreme Court dismissed. However, there are some appalling early cases. Successful tricks are reported in *Inder Sain v. The State*, 1981 CriLJ 1116, while the wife in *Kiran Kapoor*, AIR 1982 Delhi 543, was slapped on the wrist for complaining that her husband and his family demanded more dowry. Worst of all, the atrocious case of *Vinod Kumar*, AIR 1982 P&H 372 FB, confirmed the patriarchal inclinations of North Indian judges by, in effect, holding that women are owned by men.

By 1983, the Indian superior courts were getting busy with dowry issues and a set of three cases resulted in a Supreme Court verdict which significantly improved the definition of dowry and, it seems, led directly to the *Dowry Prohibition (Amendment) Act*, 1984. In *Shankarrao Abasaheb Pawar*, 1983 CriLJ 269, the Bombay High Court had still shown a remarkable lack of activist inclination, holding that an unful-filled demand for dowry was not an offence under the 1961 Act. How-ever, in *Lajpat Rai Sehgal*, 1983 CriLJ 888, where the wife had died of burns, it was held on the facts that partly unfulfilled demands were still demands, and the husband's appeal against conviction was thrown out. This divergence of views at High Court level needed to be sorted out at once. The Supreme Court, in the appeal case arising from *Shankarrao* above, a case reported as *L. V. Jadhav*, AIR 1983 SC 1219, overturned the Bombay High Court's clearly unsatisfactory verdict and signalled judicial toughening up on the question of how 'dowry' was to be defined and how wide the courts were willing to cast the definitional net.

Mixed messages continued to be given by the Supreme Court at this time, as evidenced in two fascinating cases. *Pratibha Rani*, AIR 1985 SC 628, was a woman's case on female property rights (*stridhanam*) and is widely seen today as a key precedent that helped (and helps) Hindu or Sikh women to establish their property rights against men. This case contains extremely strong criticism of the Punjab & Haryana High Court's handling of *Vinod Kumar*, AIR 1982 P&H 372 FB, and reaffirmed the importance of s. 6 of the *Dowry Prohibition Act* in the context of women's ownership of property. The *Pratibha Rani* case has also been successfully used in several cases in British courts concerning the property rights of South Asian women.

On the other hand, a deceptively brief case on the human rights of convicted dowry murderers could be taken to suggest that the human rights of the present and future victims of dowry murders are less important than those of their killers. The case report of *Attorney General of India v. Lachma Devi*, AIR 1986 SC 467, is so brief that it does not make much sense without the help of several press clips published at the time. The contentious issue in that case was whether the public execution of dowry murderers, as decreed by the Rajasthan High Court, could be stopped by the Supreme Court on grounds of violation of the human rights of the convicted prisoners on death row. The Rajasthan High Court had passed an order for execution of death sentence by public hanging in a stadium in Jaipur after giving widespread publicity. The court had clearly wanted to set a public example of extremely tough treatment of dowry murderers to educate the public about the evils of the dowry system and had therefore proposed to have the murderous mother-in-law and the husband of the victim punished by hanging in public. This was struck down as a violation of Article 21 of the Indian Constitution regarding the right to life. The court's brief order reads as follows:

> The direction for execution of the death sentence by public hanging is, to our mind, unconstitutional and we may make it clear that if any Jail Manual were to provide public hanging, we would declare it to be violative of Art. 21 of the Constitution. It is undoubtedly true that the crime of which the accused have been found to be guilty... is barbaric and a disgrace and shame on any civilised society which no society should tolerate; but a barbaric crime does not have to be visited with a barbaric penalty such as public hanging.

By 1988, many Indian courts, and certainly the Supreme Court, began to take a much stricter approach to dowry offenders. Making dowry demands became a ground for divorce under the *Hindu Marriage Act* of 1955, fitted under the wide umbrella of cruelty. The leading case on this is *Shobha Rani*, AIR 1988 SC 121 and [1988] 1 SCC 105, followed for example in *Rajani* 1989(1) KLT 234. On the other hand, if a husband made dowry demands and threw the wife out of the house if she or her family did not comply with such demands, he could not claim breakdown of the marriage, because he would be taking advantage of his own wrong. The explicit application of the 'own wrong rule' in *Ashok Kumar*, AIR 1989 Del 121, seems to show that the High Courts of North India have now also become more sensitised to dowry issues.

More recent cases have been sending an increasingly unambiguous judicial message to dowry murderers and men who drive their wives to suicide, to the effect that the punishments will be severe and that the courts will be unwilling to tolerate all prevarications. Already in 1986, in a bride-burning case, where neighbours had unsuccessfully sought to rescue the woman and the Delhi High Court – almost unbelievably – had acquitted the accused, two judges of the Indian Supreme Court reversed that decision and sentenced the husband and other members of the family to life imprisonment. The case of *State (Delhi Administration)*, AIR 1986 SC 250, was also a landmark decision on the difficult question of how to treat the dying declarations of the victim. In some cases of suicide rather than murder, the evidential position was less clear, as in *Wazir Chand*, AIR 1989 SC 378, where dowry demands were made, but it could not be established with certainty that the accused had murdered the woman rather than driven her to suicide.

In other reported cases during the early 1990s, the Supreme Court has explicitly awarded deterrent punishments of life sentences to murderous mothers-in-law. This is documented in *Paniben*, 1992 [2] SCC 474, where the young woman's dying declarations were fully accepted. The husband, father-in-law and sister-in-law were convicted of dowry murder in *State of U.P.*, 1992 [2] SCC 86, where again a High Court had acquitted the accused. A husband who had prevented neighbours from rescuing his burning wife was convicted of dowry murder in *Ganeshlal*, 1992 [3] SCC 106. In this case, the husband appealed against the life sentence imposed by the High Court but had this verdict confirmed by the Supreme Court.

It seems that other family members of this husband were lucky to get away because the husband acted so very obviously to further his evil design.

In another significant case, *State of U.P.*, 1992 [3] SCC 300, a husband had been acquitted of a dowry murder, committed in 1971, by a High Court decision of 1979. It is a clear sign of judicial activism that this case was then brought before judges of the Supreme Court after all that time. The Supreme Court brushed aside all suggestions that this old matter should not be taken up again and sentenced the accused to life imprisonment. The court left no doubt about its opinion that non-action would amount to perpetration of injustice. Not a word of *dharma*, nor wordy references to public interest litigation, but one cannot emphasise enough that ten years earlier, such a decision would have been unthinkable.

More recent cases, especially in 1996 and 1997, indicate clearly that the Indian judges have become alarmed about the extent of the dowry problems. In *State of Himachal Pradesh v. Nikku Ram*, AIR 1996 SC 67, Mr. Justice Hansaria started his judgement as follows, at p. 67:

> Dowry, dowry and dowry. This is the painful repetition which confronts, and at times haunts, many parents of a girl child in this holy land of ours where, in good old days the belief was: ...(where woman is worshipped, there is abode of God). We have mentioned about dowry thrice, because this demand is made on three occasions: (i) before marriage; (ii) at the time of marriage; and (iii) after the marriage. Greed being limitless, the demands become insatiable in many cases, followed by torture on the girl, leading to either suicide in some or murder in some.

This judgement, at p. 67, characterises the *Dowry Prohibition Act*, 1961 as 'this soft statute' and provides a brief summary of the various legislative attempts to tighten the anti-dowry law. In the case in hand, the question was whether the accused persons had committed offences relating to abetment of suicide. Significantly, the Sessions Court as well as the High Court had found no reason to convict the respondents, but the state administration had insisted on appealing to the highest forum, itself remarkable evidence of growing social activism. The facts were that the couple had got married in February 1985 and after five or six months the husband, his mother and a sister-in-law started taunting the wife for not bringing enough dowry. When the demands for several consumer items were not met, the young wife was subjected to cruel treatment, including attacks with a sickle. One day in June 1988, she could bear this treatment no longer and swallowed naphthalene balls, which proved fatal. Letters by the deceased to her father and other evidence, including the sickle, came to light but 'the defence was one of complete denial' (p. 68).

The Supreme Court noted that the offence of dowry deaths 'is in steep rise' (p. 68) and proceeded to examine the evidence afresh. It was held that the mother-in-law, by now over 80 years old, should not be put into jail. Instead, she was fined Rs. 3,000 to be paid within two months, and to be made over to the parents of the deceased.

In its judgement, the court also took notice of the fact that the sessions judge had relied on the case of *Inder Sain v. The State*, 1981 CriLJ 1116, which we criticised above as one of the early negative cases. The lower court had relied on this case to hold that any transactions of dowry after the marriage did not fall under the definition of 'dowry'. So here the tightened definitions of dowry under the amended Act of 1961 are assisting activist judges in convicting dowry murderers while the unsatisfactory earlier case law is still being used by litigation tricksters to get dowry murderers off the hook. The learned judge in this case took great care to go through the amended provisions in detail, virtually lecturing the lawyers on how to apply the law. However, because of lack of evidence of the demands made, it was held that the prosecution had failed to establish a case on these counts.

Of course, this case can be criticised as lacking an aggressive prosecution strategy. But one must not forget that the case was taken up by the Supreme Court eight years after the death of the woman, that the mother-in-law was extremely old, and it appears that the prosecution lawyers simply did not work diligently enough to document the dowry demands that were undoubtedly made. So despite a presumption in favour of dowry death, the respondents were acquitted on those counts and only the vicious sickle-wielding mother-in-law was convicted.

In *S. Gopal Reddy v. State of Andhra Pradesh*, AIR 1996 SC 2184, the younger of two brothers appealed to the Supreme Court against his conviction for offences under s. 4 of the *Dowry Prohibition Act*, 1961. The older brother had already lost his appeal to the Supreme Court and had been held guilty of such offences. The background facts were that the brothers had been negotiating with a lawyer who had four daughters, for the marriage of his eldest daughter, to be married to the younger brother. During these negotiations, various demands of dowry were made, and were subsequently increased in letters, 'dowry talks', and during and after some form of engagement ceremony or *varapuja*. The facts of the case, laid out in detail in this case report, represent a model lesson for the parents of marriageable girls in how not to negotiate. Inevitably, the parties fell out and a prosecution was launched against the two brothers for demanding dowry.

Dr. A. S. Anand J, in the Supreme Court, commented at p. 2186 that 'the curse of dowry has been raising its ugly head every now and then but the evil has been flourishing beyond imaginable proportions' and relied on the helpful case of *L. V. Jadhav v. Shankar Rao Abasaheb Pawar*, AIR 1983 SC 1219, to the effect that the 1961 Act must be liberally construed.

The present case turned on the judicial interpretation of s. 4 of the *Dowry Prohibition Act*, 1961. It was held at p. 2187:

> Under Section 4 of the Act, mere demand of 'dowry' is sufficient to bring home the offence to an accused. Thus, any 'demand' of money, property or valuable security made from the bride or her parents or other relatives by the bridegroom or his parents or other relatives or vice-versa would fall within the mischief of 'dowry' under the Act where such demand is not properly referable to any legally recognised claim and is relatable only to the consideration of marriage. Marriage in this context would include a proposed marriage also more particularly where the non-fulfilment of the 'demand of dowry' leads to the ugly consequence of the marriage not taking place at all. The expression 'dowry' under the Act must be interpreted in the sense which the statute wishes to attribute to it.

It was further held at p. 2188:

> The Act is a piece of social legislation which aims to check the growing menace of the social evil of dowry and it makes punishable not only the actual receiving of dowry but also the very demand made before or at the time or after the marriage where such demand is referable to the consideration of marriage. Dowry as a quid pro quo for marriage is prohibited and not the giving of traditional presents to the bride or the bridegroom by friends or relatives. Thus, voluntary presents given at or before or after the marriage to the bride or the bridegroom, as the case may be, of a traditional nature, which are not

given as a consideration for marriage but out of love, affection or regard, would not fall within the mischief of the expression 'dowry' made punishable under the Act.

While Dr. Anand J was therefore not going to take a narrow view of the matter, he expanded on the social aspects of the dowry problem and sought to find a balance between social activism and judicial impartiality, saying at p. 2189:

The alarming increase in cases relating to harassment, torture, abetted suicides and dowry deaths of young innocent brides has always sent shock waves to the civilized society but unfortunately the evil has continued unabated. Awakening of the collective conscious-ness is the need of the day. Change of heart and attitude is needed. A wider social movement not only of educating women of their rights but also of the men folk to respect and recognise the basic human values is essentially needed to bury this pernicious social evil. The role of the courts, under the circumstances, assumes a great impor-tance. The Courts are expected to deal with such cases in a realistic manner so as to further the object of the legislation. However, the Courts must not lose sight of the fact that the Act, though a piece of social legislation, is a penal statute. One of the cardinal rules of interpretation in such cases is that a penal statute must be strictly con-strued. The Courts have, thus, to be watchful to see that emotions or sentiments are not allowed to influence their judgment, one way or the other and that they do not ignore the golden thread passing through criminal jurisprudence that an accused is presumed to be innocent till proved guilty and that the guilt of an accused must be established beyond a reasonable doubt. They must carefully assess the evidence and not allow either suspicion or surmise or conjectures to take the place of proof in their zeal to stamp out the evil from the society while at the same time not adopting the easy course of letting technicalities or minor discrepancies in the evidence result in acquit-ting an accused. They must critically analyse the evidence and decide the case in a realistic manner.

Examining the facts of the case in detail, the learned judge ultimately came to the conclusion that the appellant could not be found guilty of the offence of demanding dowry, since, as stated at p. 2193,

The evidence on record does not establish beyond a reasonable doubt that any demand of dowry ...was made by the appellant. *Maybe* the appellant was in agreement with his elder brother regarding 'demand' of 'dowry' but convictions cannot be based on such assumptions without the offence being proved beyond a reasonable doubt. The courts below appear to have allowed emotions and sentiments, rather than legally admissible and trustworthy evidence, to influence their judgment.

The young man was therefore let off, but the husband's conviction stood. We shall see below that several such cases have come to the higher courts and that careful analysis of the evidence is required to make sure that innocent family members are not criminalised in the clamour for retribution for dowry murders.

State of U.P. v. Ramesh Prasad Misra, AIR 1996 SC 2766, concerns the horrendous bedroom murder of a young married woman of 19 who was two months pregnant, after only five months of marriage to a young lawyer. It had been argued in defence that this murder had been committed by a stranger, but the husband's story was not believed and he had been sentenced to death by the Sessions Court in 1985, while his mother had been sentenced to rigorous imprisonment for several years. However, the Allahabad High Court had acquitted mother and son in 1988, hence this appeal by the State against the acquittal.

The cause of death had been established as asphyxia due to strangulation. Since the body had subsequently been burnt, this was a case of post-mortem burns. The entire prosecution case for murder rested on circumstantial evidence. There were prosecution witnesses, neighbours, who were also lawyers, but they all turned hostile to the prosecution, confirming the difficulties of bringing social control mechanisms into the court room. The Supreme Court judgment is scathing in its criticism of this elaborate collusion to cover up a dowry-related murder at pp. 2767-2768:

It is most distressing to note that practising advocates...with a view to exculpate the first respondent from the clutches of the law, have, without any compunction, spoken falsehood and have no regard for truth betraying their duty of being responsible law officers who are expected to uphold truth and nothing but truth.

The husband sought to establish an alibi, claiming that his wife had been murdered by someone else in the middle of the night and in the couple's bedroom. However, his entire story was inconsistent and the two Supreme Court judges hearing this case leave no doubt of their negative opinion of the High Court judgement (p. 2769):

> It is rather most unfortunate that the learned Judges of the High Court dealt with the matter very casually and did not apply their mind to the crucial circumstantial evidence in this case. They merely superficially read the evidence of hostile witnesses... and held that from their evidence the presence of the accused in the house was excluded... The evidence of... father and sister of the deceased who spoke about the motive, was excluded... It is difficult to appreciate this line of reasoning.

The father and sister of the murdered woman had stated clearly in evidence that she had been harassed because certain dowry items (a sofa, a motor-cycle and some other goods) had not been forthcoming, but the judges had chosen to ignore such tell-tale signs of dowry-related murder altogether. Yet they had uncritically accepted the rather improbable story of the husband that his young wife had been murdered in their bedroom at midnight by a stranger, while he was away. The husband's version also involved casting aspersions on the moral standing of his wife, a frequently used strategy to deflect judicial attention from the real issue before the court.

The Supreme Court came to the conclusion that the husband alone had committed the offence, but upheld the acquittal of the mother-in-law. How the Supreme Court then handled the conviction of the husband is extremely interesting. It was held, at pp. 2769-2770:

> In view of the long passage of time from the date of the commission of the offence till date, we are of the view that it is not a case warranting restoration of death sentence and confirmation thereof as imposed by the learned Sessions Judge...
>
> Accordingly, we set aside the acquittal of the first respondent in respect of all the three charges and restore the conviction of the first respondent for an offence of murder... However, the sentence of death... is converted into RI for life.

Significantly, the Supreme Court judges also recorded openly critical words about the miscarriage of justice at High Court level and went so far as naming the judges involved in this case. It was held, at pp. 2769-2770, that:

... the learned Judges of the High Court betrayed their duty of final court of fact, to subject the evidence to close and critical scrutiny. They either have no knowledge of the elementary principles of criminal law or adopted casual approach towards a serious crime like the present one. In other [sic] case, miscarriage of justice is the inevitable result at their hands in criminal cases.

We request the learned Chief Justice of the Allahabad High Court to bring this judgment to the notice of learned Judges, B. N. Katju and Bajpai JJ if they have not already retired with a view to see that the learned judges would be more careful in future in deciding criminal matters assigned to them so that miscarriage of justice would not result.

It appears that both judges named here retired during 1989, Mr. Justice B. N. Katju actually as Acting Chief Justice of the Allahabad High Court. These, then, were not inexperienced junior judges, who made a regrettable mistake, but so-called pillars of society who colluded with a group of lawyers to protect one of their kind from just retribution for the murder of his young wife, who evidently died because her father could not afford to produce the additional dowry items demanded.

In *Mulak Raj v. State of Haryana*, AIR 1996 SC 2868, we find a classic case of unfulfilled dowry demands leading straight to the death of a young woman who had argued that 'the system of giving and taking dowry should be abolished' (p. 2869). This young woman had, as S. B. Majmudar J put it, 'lost her life on the altar of dowry demands' (p. 2868) after only two months of marriage in 1977. Four accused persons, the father-in-law, the husband, and two women of the family, had been acquitted by the trial court but had been sentenced by the High Court to life imprisonment. They appealed against this sentence to the Supreme Court, claiming that the young woman had committed suicide.

Already before the marriage ceremony, the husband's family had apparently demanded certain extra goods, notably a refrigerator and a television, which had not been given by the girl's father. After the marriage, she experienced harassment and confided in her sister and several other people.

It is significant that the father-in-law wanted to cremate her dead body quickly, but he was forced by the dead woman's father to go to the police station – where he reported that she had committed suicide. On investigation, the police registered a case of homicide, but nothing further happened for a long time and nobody was arrested, until the dead woman's father lodged a private complaint. This case illustrates the tardy processes of non-implementation of the anti-dowry law at local level. Indeed, the Supreme Court observed, at p. 2872, that 'the police appeared to have adopted a lukewarm attitude'.

The Sessions Court had found that the prosecution was not able to establish beyond reasonable doubt that the deceased had been murdered and had acquitted the accused. However, the High Court had sentenced the accused to life imprisonment. The rival contentions before the Supreme Court included detailed and 'clinching' (p. 2873) medical evidence, to the effect that this was a case of homicidal death and subsequent burning of the body.

But who had murdered this young woman? There was evidence before the court of the husband's dissatisfaction with the financial arrangements during the marriage and the dowry offered. The Court castigated the unsatisfactory actions of the police who appeared to have 'developed cold feet' (p. 2873) and had allegedly been bribed by the accused. It was found, at p. 2874, that the High Court had been justified in holding that 'the prosecution has established by satisfactory evidence that there was a strong motive for the accused to threaten the deceased and to pester her by demanding dowry article, having not received refrigerator and television from her father'.

However, the question of who had killed this young woman could not be answered with certainty because of the lack of proper police investigation from the start and the subsequent weakness of the prosecution case. *Mulak Raj* therefore illustrates that the Indian Supreme Court, in such a situation, upholds the principle of innocence of the accused until proven guilty and, in consequence, had to acquit the accused. S. B. Majmudar J held, at pp. 2876-2877:

All these questions remain unanswered on the unsatisfactory state of evidence led by the prosecution. As we have noted earlier the basic flaw in the case lies in the lukewarm and cursory investigation initiated by the police after registering the offence... Result was that prosecution case became lame from the very beginning and, therefore, it must be visited with the logical consequence of failure to bring home the offence of murder to the accused who may at the most remain under the cloud of a strong suspicion of having liquidated Krishna Kumari in their household on that fateful morning. However strong the suspicion may [be], it cannot take the place of proof. The High Court seems to have been swayed [sic] away by the unfortunate and untimely homicidal death of a young girl in the household of her father-in-law and husband on the altar of dowry demand. However, it is impossible on the state of evidence on record to bring home the offence... beyond the shadow of reasonable doubt to any of the accused. The High Court with respect seems to have almost rendered a moral conviction against the accused rather than a legal one... All the accused are given benefit of doubt.

Similarly, in *State of Haryana v. Rajinder Singh*, AIR 1996 SC 2978, where a young woman's body had been recovered from a well and the accused persons had been acquitted by the High Court, an appeal to the Supreme Court seeking conviction for dowry-related murder was thrown out. It was claimed in defence that the woman had fallen into the well while drawing water. However, the well had been fitted with a pump and there was much evidence of injuries to her body which were caused by severe beating with a stick. The prosecution therefore claimed that the woman had been murdered and subsequently thrown into the well.

Here it appears that the natal family of the deceased woman failed to assert the dowry nexus and therefore weakened the prosecution case. The Supreme Court did not take an activist stance and placed, in my view, far too much reliance on a statement by the deceased's brother that there had been no ill-will between the families. Thus, the acquittal was confirmed and this dowry-related murder remains unpunished.

In *Prem Singh v. State of Punjab*, AIR 1997 SC 221, a dowry-related death due to poisoning had occurred in 1985 in a Sikh family, after seven and a half months of marriage. Allegedly, the deceased had complained of harassment because her father had not given a certain type of motor cycle in dowry. The defence version was that the woman had committed suicide by swallowing poison. The woman's husband and brother-in-law had been sentenced to life imprisonment by the trial court, and the High Court had confirmed the sentences. On appeal before the Supreme Court, it was held, at p. 223:

> In the present case, motive is a vital issue and evidence adduced by the prosecution in that behalf is not satisfactory and there are certain inherent improbabilities which were overlooked by the Courts below.

One can see where this leads: here is another recent case where insufficient evidence precludes a safe conviction for dowry-related murder, and the result has to be an acquittal, with the accused being given the benefit of the doubt. It was held, at p. 224, that:

> Having regard to the facts and circumstances of the case, we are of the considered view that prosecution has failed to prove beyond reasonable doubt that Surinder Kaur met with a homicidal death. The defence plea of suicide cannot be ruled out.

However, such somewhat unsatisfactory conclusions are not always a smokescreen for Supreme Court inactivity – it does depend on the facts and circumstances of the case. *Godabarish Mishra v. Kuntala Mishra*, AIR 1997 SC 286, involves a mother-in-law, a midwife, who strangulated her daughter-in-law after an operation, while the young woman was still in a state of drowsiness. She immediately reported the death as suicide, but the circumstantial evidence clearly indicated that suicide by self-strangulation was highly unlikely and that the mother-in-law was the only person who could be responsible for the young woman's death. It was further found that this was a dowry-related death, since a sum of Rs.8,000 had been demanded as dowry from the deceased's father, but he had paid only Rs.6,000, after much pressure. The evidence of harassment being established, and in view of the medical expert opinions, the mother-in-law was sentenced to life imprisonment.

In *Kumbhar Dhirajlal Mohanlal v. State of Gujarat*, AIR 1997 SC 1531, we find a recent case of dying declaration by a burnt woman. The appellant husband had been sentenced to life imprisonment for murdering his wife and appealed to the Supreme Court. Three months after their marriage, the husband had apparently set his 18 year old wife alight during a quarrel and she had sustained severe burns and had died the next day after making three separate dying declarations in hospital. The husband claimed, typically, that she had been the victim of a cooking accident while preparing breakfast.

The trial judge had acquitted the husband on the ground that it had not been shown beyond reasonable doubt that he was responsible for the death of his burnt wife. The High Court of Gujarat, however, reversed the order of acquittal and relied instead on the dying declarations of the wife as conclusive evidence of the husband's culpability. In the Supreme Court, too, the fact that the husband himself had sustained burn injuries did not work in his favour. In dismissing the husband's appeal, it was held, at p. 1534:

> Even if we proceed on the assumption that the appellant sustained the injuries while extinguishing the fire still it would not lead to the inference that the fire was accidental for the dying declaration itself indicates that he received those injuries after he had set her on fire. As rightly pointed out by the High Court, a shrewd person may adopt this tactics of first setting his wife on fire and then make a show to extinguish [the] fire and thereafter remain by her side. The High Court was equally justified in remarking that in this case the appellant almost succeeded in making out his defence but unfortunately for him the wife was able to speak and make [a] statement disclosing the entire facts.

Several other cases from the Supreme Court were reported in 1997. In *Baldev Krishan v. State of Haryana*, AIR 1997 SC 1666, Pratibha, a young mother of a son, had been killed in 1992 by burning in her kitchen. There was strong evidence of taunts about her insufficient dowry as well as her own defect of a squint. In the Supreme Court, S. P. Kurdukar J flatly refused to accept the family's version of how well they treated their daughter-in-law and found much evidence of persistent dowry harassment. It was held at pp. 1669-1670:

> There are ways and ways to express the demand of dowry. One adopted by the appellants could be said to be a sophisticated one without using the word 'dowry'...There is no manner of doubt that the appellants had given most humiliating treatment not only to Pratibha but also to Rekha Rani... to the extent of calling the parents of Pratibha as bastards and telling her that they should have found out a suitable match for their daughter having a squint.

Given such overwhelming evidence of motive, coupled with the unquestionable fact of death due to burns in her own kitchen, the fact that her clothes smelled of kerosene, and the false explanations for the death offered by the accused, it was held that the accused in-laws were liable to be convicted for murder and that their conviction would not be bad. The defence lawyers had clearly tried to argue, in various ways, that the benefit of doubt should be given to the accused, but this strategy did not work in the present case.

In *Sham Lal v. State of Haryana*, AIR 1997 SC 1873, however, we find another case in which there was held to be insufficient evidence to convict the accused. The wife had died of burns in 1987 and the husband, his father and his grandmother had been charged with murdering her. While the Sessions Court had acquitted the grandmother, the High Court had also acquitted the husband's father, and the husband now appealed against his conviction to the Supreme Court. The factual matrix is stated at p. 1874:

> There seems to be no dispute on the fact that Neelam Rani died of burns on 17-6-1987. The prosecution case in brief is that appellant was persecuting her with the demand for more dowry and at last set her ablaze for not quenching his greed for dowry. On the other hand the stand of the appellant... was that by frustration, as she could not give birth to a child and as she could not adjust in the village life with the appellant, she committed suicide by burning herself.

The judges then proceeded to examine the case in detail and refused to accept that a presumption of dowry-related murder should be upheld. This was done in a very technical manner and it may be of interest to discuss this here, given the unsatisfactory result of this case. Remarkably, an accident was ruled out (p. 1874), so the question remained whether this was a dowry-related murder or a suicide. The judges proceeded to ask themselves whether a presumption of dowry-related murder could be maintained. It was said, at p. 1874:

> The primary requirements for finding the appellant guilty of the offence under Section 304-B I.P.C. are that death of the deceased was caused by burns within seven years of her marriage and that 'soon before her death' she was subjected to cruelty or harassment by the appellant for or in connection with any demand for dowry.

Having found that the death occurred within seven years of the marriage and that it was a death by burning, the only other element to establish a presumption of dowry death was that 'soon before her death' such a woman was harassed for dowry. It was held, in this regard, at p. 1875:

It is imperative, for invoking the aforesaid legal presumption, to prove that 'soon before her death' she was subjected to such cruelty or harassment. Here, what the prosecution achieved in proving at the most was that there was persisting dispute between the two sides regarding the dowry paid or to be paid, both in kind and in cash, and on account of the failure to meet the demand for dowry. Neelam Rani was taken by her parents to their house about one and a half years before her death. Further evidence is that an attempt was made to patch up between the two sides for which a panchayat was held in which it was resolved that she would go back to the nuptial home pursuant to which she was taken by the husband to his house. This happened about ten to fifteen days prior to the occurrence in this case. There is nothing on record to show that she was either treated with cruelty or harassed with the demand for dowry during the period between her having been taken to the parental home and her tragic end.

It was therefore decided, at p. 1875:

In the absence of any such evidence it is not permissible to take recourse to the legal presumption....The corollary of the aforesaid finding is that appellant cannot be convicted of the offence under Section 304-B, I.P.C. But this would not save him from the offence under Section 498-A of the I.P.C., for which there is overwhelming evidence...

Using an argument which I have not seen before in any reported case, this rather technical reasoning was employed to virtually acquit the husband, though he was found guilty of his wife's murder under s. 498-A of the *Indian Penal Code*, which carries a maximum penalty of rigorous imprisonment for three years only, rather than life imprisonment. This is a deeply unsatisfactory case, also because it might encourage families to plan evidence of dowry harassment much more carefully than before to avoid convictions for dowry murder under the tougher provisions of section 304-B of the *Indian Penal Code*, 1860, as amended by the anti-dowry law.

Mangat Rai v. State of Punjab, AIR 1997 SC 2838, involved a medical doctor who poisoned his young wife, mother of a small baby boy, and had been convicted of her murder by all courts concerned. In final appeal to the Supreme Court, it was confirmed that the chain of circumstantial evidence in this case was complete and that his guilt had been proved beyond reasonable doubt. S. B. Majmudar J expressed his criticism of the defence in strong words, at p. 2841: 'The entire defence version to say the least was preposterous and violated all basic norms of probabilities and was an affront to common sense.' It was obvious that in this case the husband's claims for more dowry had been rejected by the wife's family. We read, at p. 2841:

> The appellant was not happy with the dowry brought by Madhu Bala at the time of marriage and had motive to get rid of Madhu Bala who instead of forcing her parents to give articles demanded by the accused, had sent her relations to prevail upon him to withdraw the demand and accused also had given promise of treating her properly in future.

Faced with a situation in which he knew he could not squeeze anything more out of his wife's family, the husband simply resorted to cold-blooded murder. It is very satisfying to see that the Supreme Court did not hesitate to uphold the husband's conviction and dismissed his appeal.

State of Maharashtra v. Ashok Chotelal Shukla, AIR 1997 SC 3111, is an interesting case because of the peculiar facts, which are drawn out in great detail in the case report. They are certainly not unusual facts but it is educative to see in such detail how the parents of a daughter handle dowry negotiations when it is so evident that the son-in-law is only interested in money.

Vibha, the daughter of an uneducated man who had become a rich businessman, was given in marriage in 1981 to the son of a police officer. A dowry of Rs. 150,000 had been demanded and Vibha's father had agreed to pay Rs. 100,000 as dowry, inclusive of jewellery, utensils and clothes. Thereafter, however, her father had paid many sums of money on demand from the son-in-law, for all kinds of purposes. When Vibha delivered a female child in 1982, her husband's family did not at all care about the child, who had to be brought up by her maternal grandparents. The wife continued to experience harassment from the husband and other family members and he set her on fire in June 1984. Before she succumbed to her injuries, Vibha was apparently able to tell her sister and her father that her husband had burnt her, but her dying declarations were not given much weight on procedural grounds. Having examined the case, Nanavati J said, at p. 3118:

It is very unfortunate that a young girl without any fault of her [own] lost her life. It is also a matter of shame that the respondent did not treat his wife properly because her father was not willing to give more money and for that reason on one occasion he had driven her out of his house and also because she had given birth to a female child. The facts and circumstances which can be accepted as proved no doubt create a strong suspicion that on the fateful day the respondent had, after some quarrel, poured kerosene over her and put her to flames. But this is a case of circumstantial evidence...

Ultimately, the Supreme Court found in this case that it was not safe to assume that the husband had been responsible for the death of his wife. It was held, at p. 3119, that 'the prosecution has failed to establish beyond reasonable doubt that Vibha committed suicide because of ill treatment or cruelty by the respondent. The view taken cannot be regarded as unreasonable'. The husband's acquittal was therefore confirmed and we are left with the allegation that this was a case of suicide of a desperate wife and mother whose call for help ended in her death by burning. This does not appear to be a satisfactory outcome in a case so manifestly based on dowry extortions and utter greed and one must wonder whether the fact that the husband's father was a high-ranking police officer has anything to do with it.

Mahesh Mahto v. State of Bihar, AIR 1997 SC 3567, is an appeal against conviction by the younger brother of a husband who killed his wife and had thrown her body into a local river, from where it was recovered. The men had been jointly sentenced by the High Court of Patna, the husband to life imprisonment, the younger brother to seven years of rigorous imprisonment. Apparently, the husband had been dissatisfied with the nature of some marriage gifts in 1983. He had demanded a scooter but had received only a cycle.

In view of medical evidence, there was never any doubt that this was a case of homicidal death. While the murderous husband had been refused leave to appeal to the Supreme Court, the position of his younger brother, who was only 18 years old, was re-assessed by the court and it was found, at p. 3568:

> There is no evidence on the record to substantiate the prosecution case that the appellant was causing any harassment or assaulting Meera Devi. The Courts below have totally overlooked this fact and had erroneously held the appellant guilty for the murder of Meera Devi... We are of the considered view that the prosecution has failed to prove beyond reasonable doubt the complicity of the appellant in committing the murder of Meera Devi.

As a result, the young man was not totally acquitted, but his sentence was reduced to the period of imprisonment already undergone. In this case, therefore, the Supreme Court sought to find a balance between severe treatment of the murderer (the husband) and extending benefit of doubt to an accomplice, here the husband's younger brother, whose precise role was not clarified and who was in many ways dependent on his older brother. In the context of a jurisdiction where policemen are known to be harsh on low-caste, rural people, this judgment may therefore be seen as an attempt to restore justice, i.e. releasing an innocent family member who had been accused of a crime by implication, rather than condoning a dowry-related murder.

Two cases reported during 1998 have so far come to my notice. *State of Tamil Nadu v. P. Muniappan*, AIR 1998 SC 504 is again a State's appeal against acquittal of a man who was charged with murdering his wife, in this case from South India. The parties, both college professors, married in 1976 and the husband subsequently insisted on the wife resigning her job and being simply a housewife. He also made repeated demands for dowry in the shape of household articles. When the wife did not agree with these demands, the husband filed a suit for divorce in 1978. The wife responded by expressing her anxiety that she live with her husband. The couple then lived together on and off, but on 2nd July 1982 her body was found hanging in the kitchen.

The High Court of Madras believed the husband's story that this was a case of suicide and acquitted the husband of any charges. The Supreme Court took a more vigorous approach to investigating the element of dowry harassment in the case. We read at pp. 508-509:

According to the High Court, the mental and physical torture endured by Nagammal in the hands of her husband made her desperate to put an end to her life. The said inference is wholly unreasonable and un-warranted... The high court has completely overlooked the letters written by Nagammal which prove clearly that Nagammal was not such a weak-minded person to commit suicide on a sudden provoca-tion of which we have no evidence whatever. The evidence makes out clearly that Nagammal had a strong mental frame and was keen on living with her husband. The sequence of events does not lead to any inference that something happened during the night which made her commit suicide immediately.

Investigating the matter further, the Supreme Court considered in detail the circumstantial evidence of this case, concluding that 'the entire circumstantial evidence points to homicide only, and the medical evidence is not to the contrary. Thus we have no doubt that the death of Nagammal was homicidal only' (p. 509). As a result, the Supreme Court restored the order of the trial court and the husband was forthwith taken into custody for life imprisonment.

The most recent case report from India available in London at the time of writing is *Pawan Kumar v. State of Haryana*, AIR 1998 SC 958. This decision by A. P. Misra J starts, at p. 960, with a social comment on the dowry problem which immediately highlights the dilemma for the judi-ciary in terms of benefit of doubt:

For more than a century, in spite of tall words of respect for women, there has been an onslaught on their liberties through 'bride burning' and 'dowry deaths'. This has caused anxiety to the legislators, judi-ciary and law enforcing agencies, who have attempted to resurrect them from this social choke. There have been series of legislation in this regard, without much effect. This led to the passing of Dowry Prohibition Act in 1961. In spite of this, large number of 'brides burning' and dowry deaths continued. To meet this stringent measures were brought in the Indian Penal Code and the Evidence Act through amendments. It seems, sections of society are still pursu-ing this chronic action to fulfil their greedy desires. In spite of strin-gent legislation, such persons are still indulging in these unlawful activities, not because of any shortcomings in law but under the protective principle of criminal jurisprudence of benefit of doubt.

Often, innocent persons are also trapped or brought in with ulterior motives. This places an arduous duty on the Court to separate such individuals from the offenders Hence the Courts have to deal with such cases with circumvention, sift through the evidence with caution, scrutinise the circumstances with utmost care. The present matter is one such where similar questions have been raised, including questions of interpretation of the stringent laws.

In this case, the husband of the deceased wife and his parents had been convicted by the trial court and had been sentenced to long prison sentences, which were in essence upheld by the High Court, hence the appeal to the Supreme Court. The couple had been married in 1985 and within a few days dowry demands and harassment were evident. We read at p. 960:

> According to the prosecution case, within a few days of the marriage Urmil returned home and complained regarding demands of dowry for a refrigerator, scooter etc. by appellants. These demands were reiterated on subsequent visits. On account of non-fulfilment of these demands, the deceased was allegedly tortured and harassed.These alleged actions ultimately contributed towards a suicidal death. It is not in dispute that she died of burn injuries on 18th May, 1987.

It had been argued by the lawyer for the appellants that mere mention of fridge and scooter did not amount to a demand for dowry, so this could not be a case of dowry-related murder. In response, the learned judge cited the relevant provisions of the *Dowry Prohibition Act* of 1961 and several other criminal law provisions. At p. 962 he stated:

> The aforesaid 1961 Act was enacted to provide an effective check to dowry deaths which were continuing despite the then prevailing laws. The object of the Bill was to prohibit the evil practice of giving and taking of dowry. This objective was not achieved hence drastic amendments were brought in by amending various provisions of the said Act and the related provisions under the Indian Penal Code and the Evidence Act... Various other amendments were brought in bringing more stringent provisions in the aforesaid 1961 Act in order to stem the onslaught on the life of a married woman.

Next, the judge's attention turned to the question of benefit of doubt for the accused. It was held, at pp. 962-963:

The concept of benefit of doubt has an important role to play but within the confines of the stringency of laws. Since the cause of death to a married woman was to occur not in normal circumstances but as a 'dowry death', for which the evidence was not to (too) easily available, as it is mostly confined to within four walls of a house, namely husband's house where all likely accused reside. Hence the aforesaid amendments brought in the concept of deemed 'dowry death' by the husband or the relatives, as the case may be. This deeming clause has a role to play and cannot be taken lightly and ignored to shield an accused, otherwise the very purpose of the amendment will be lost. Of course, the prosecution has to prove the ultimate essential ingredients beyond all reasonable doubt after raising the initial presumption of 'deemed dowry death'.

In terms of statutory interpretation, it was then stated, at p. 963, that the Court must adopt that construction which suppresses the mischief and advances the remedy, thus calling for a renewed effort in making sure that dowry murderers were duly prosecuted by the law. It was held, at p. 693:

Applying this principle, it is clear that the earlier law was not sufficient to check dowry deaths hence aforesaid stringent provisions were brought in, so that persons committing such inhuman crimes on married women should not escape, as evidence of a direct nature is not readily available except of the circumstantial kind. Hence it is that interpretation which suppresses the mischief, subserves the objective and advances the remedy, which would be acceptable. Objective is that men committing such crimes should not escape punishment. Hence stringent provisions were brought in by shifting the burden on to the accused by bringing in the deemed clause. As aforesaid, the definition of 'dowry' was amended with effect from 19th November, 1986, to include a period even after the marriage.

Strongly refuting the argument that in the present case there had not been a demand for dowry, it was held, at pp. 963-964:

In cases of dowry deaths and suicides, circumstantial evidence plays an important role and inferences can be drawn on the basis of such evidence. That could be either direct or indirect. It is significant that Section 4 of the 1961 Act, was also amended by means of Act 63 of 1984, under which it is an offence to demand dowry directly or indirectly from the parents or other relatives or guardian of a bride. The word 'agreement' referred to in Section 2 has to be inferred on the facts and circumstances of each case. The interpretation that the appellant seeks, that conviction can only be if there is agreement for dowry, is misconceived. This would be contrary to the mandate and object of the Act. 'Dowry' definition is to be interpreted with the other provisions of the Act including Section 3, which refers to giving or taking dowry and Section 4 which deals with penalty for demanding dowry, under the 1961 Act and the Indian Penal Code. This makes it clear that even demand of dowry on other ingredients being satisfied is punishable. This leads to the inference, when persistent demands for TV and scooter are made from the bride after marriage or from her parents, it would constitute to be in connection with the marriage and it would be a case of demand of dowry within the meaning of Section 304-B, IPC. It is not always necessary that there be any agreement for dowry.

This authoritative restatement on the ambit of the definition of dowry must be seen as helpful and indicates, we nust hope, an activist approach of the Indian Supreme Court towards the prosecution of dowry-related offences in future. In the present case, A. P. Misra J took the view that there was a demand of scooter and fridge a few days after the marriage, which clearly fell within the definition of 'dowry demand'.

Asking whether there was any evidence of cruelty or harassment of the deceased by her husband and his family soon before her death, the judge reiterated the well-known principle that cruelty or harassment did not have to be physical. There was ample evidence of this, as stated at p. 964:

We find, in the present case, on account of not satisfying the demand of the aforesaid goods, right from the next day, she was repeatedly taunted, maltreated and mentally tortured by being called ugly etc. A girl dreams of great days ahead with hope and aspiration when entering into a marriage, and if from the very next day the husband starts taunting for not bringing dowry and calling her ugly, there cannot be greater mental torture, harassment or cruelty for any bride. There was a quarrel a day before her death. This by itself, in our considered opinion, would constitute to be a wilful act to be a cruelty both within the meaning of Section 498-A and Section 304-B, IPC.

It is interesting, especially if we compare this to *Mulak Raj v. State of Haryana*, AIR 1996 SC 2868 and *Sham Lal v. State of Haryana*, AIR 1997 SC 1873, discussed above, that the judge in *Pawan Kumar* vigorously assails the defence argument that there was no cruelty to the victim 'soon before her death'. Not only was there evidence of many quarrels between husband and wife, but in this case the wife had sought shelter with her sister and was most reluctant to join her husband again when he came to pick her up. In fact, she may have had a foreboding of her cruel end, since she told her sister (as cited at p. 964) that 'it would be difficult now to see her face in the future' – and she was killed the next day. Significantly, in the Supreme Court Misra J emphasised that in view of the statutory presumption of dowry death, the onus of proof lies on the accused to prove that the woman's death was not on account of dowry-related problems and he found that, in the present case, the husband had not discharged that burden of proof. This shifting of the burden of proof is undoubtedly a key element in tightening procedure in such cases.

There is also an activist element in the Court's approach to the question of benefit of doubt. We have seen how in several cases in 1996 and 1997 the use of this technique has led to non-punishment or reduced sentences for dowry murderers. In the present case, Misra J indicated, at p. 965, that benefit of doubt to the accused would be available only if there was supportive evidence on the record. However, there was no such evidence for the husband in this case. It was held, however, that no convincing evidence had been provided that the deceased had been subjected to cruelty by her parents-in-law. Hence, the benefit of doubt was extended to the parents-in-law and they were acquitted, while the husband's sentence of seven years' rigorous imprisonment was confirmed.

In the above cases we find very clear indications that judges in the Indian Supreme Court have become more sensitised to the problems of dowry-related murder cases, but this does not necessarily translate into convictions for an offence under the *Dowry Prohibition Act*, 1961 or related legislation. There is a thin line here between male collusion with the prosecuted offenders under the guise of such technical key elements as standard of proof and 'benefit of doubt', and an allegedly more 'emotional' approach which takes the presumption of guilt in dowry-related murder cases just that much further. It is also noticeable that in several cases discussed above, the Supreme Court has become more sophisticated in making distinctions between different members of the murderous family, rather than tarring everyone in the household with the same brush. This is certainly a positive development, given the frequent allegations that South Asian law enforcement agencies find it easy to criminalise members of the more marginal sections of the community. The case of the young brother-in-law in *Mahesh Mahto v. State of Bihar*, AIR 1997 SC 3567, a village youth who was acquitted on appeal, illustrates this new-found and appropriate caution. On the other hand, lingering doubts remain over whether the perpetrators of dowry murder are always brought to book.

There is some evidence of a trend to bring constitutional law provisions into the picture when dowry death cases come before the court, although the recent cases discussed here largely concentrated on matters of circumstantial, medical and criminal evidence. Jethmalani (1995: 30) reported that already in *Neelam Varma and others v. Union of India*, a Supreme Court writ petition of 1983, seven dowry victims and two women's organisations had moved the Supreme Court of India, alleging that their rights under Articles 21 and 14 of the Constitution of India had been violated. These are the right to life and the right to equality before the law. The petitioners submitted that the police authorities had not complied with their statutory obligations under the criminal laws and under the Constitution, by refusing to register their complaints regarding dowry harassment, thereby not carrying out the necessary investigation enjoined upon them under the Criminal Procedure Code. It was contended that the right to life included the right to live with human dignity. In several cases pertaining to dowry death similar pleas have been advanced by women's organisations. This method has enabled women to raise public consciousness through social action litigation, to lobby for changes in the dowry law and to obtain direct supervision of the highest court in view of manipulation by unscrupulous police officers and dishonest accused. At the end of the day, though, as the recent cases clearly confirm, conviction in dowry-related murder cases depends on the strength of evidence, otherwise the risk of extending the benefit of doubt remains.

The growing Indian case law thus indicates that the Supreme Court has become more alert to issues concerning dowry murder and that the High Courts, too, are now accepting their responsibility in punishing dowry killings. The Kerala High Court, ever vigilant in protecting women, produced an excellent judgement which considered in detail the appropriate procedures to be followed in cases of suspected dowry deaths. The judicial order made in *State of Kerala*, 1994 [2] KLT 700, is a fine model of procedural structuring, designed to save judicial time and to have maximum effect on the ground.

While most of the cases above also involve some judicial critique of social practices, most judges have been reluctant, it seems, to make explicit comments about how they think the growing menace of dowry can be controlled. As Saini (1983: 147) argued, the classic approach of the law has been to rely on punishment, as though this would, by itself, provide the solution to social problems. In one case, however, *Ashok Kumar v. State of Rajasthan*, AIR 1990 SC 2134, Mr. Justice R. M. Sahai of the Supreme Court launched into a lecture on the desirability of social ostracism to curtail what he called the 'increasing malady of bride burning' (p. 2136). Significantly, the learned judge also confirmed, in no uncertain terms, that the poor never seem to resort to that kind of crime. Such critique, and the focus on neighbourhood vigilance and social ostracism, echoes very closely what activist writers have been saying (see e.g. Kishwar, 1990).

Although the courts can busy themselves with putting dowry murderers behind bars forever, what counts is whether the new toughness of the law will actually act as a deterrent. I can provide no answer and more research is needed. But I can report that there is now some progress in the way in which the law and its personnel react to the growing tide of dowry murders in India – although I do not wish to create the impression that all Indian cases of dowry-related violence and murder are now being pursued and legally prosecuted. One major problem of implementation, as Manjaree Chowdhary confirms in chapter 7, remains that neither police officers nor the lower judiciary appear to be taking much notice of the need for vigilance and activism in this area. Some of the recent cases discussed above bring this out clearly, but it is good to see that the Supreme Court has, at least in some cases, commented on lack of active search for evidence in relation to dowry murders. It remains true to say that the vast majority of dowry murders still never reach the judicial fora and somehow remain a matter for society. Even in cases where women have evidently been murdered for reasons relating to dowry, there is no assurance that the case will involve any kind of law enforcement or judicial personnel.

Unlike judicial fora in Britain (and, we must assume, in the USA and Canada), the Indian and other South Asian courts have a good understanding of what dowry problems involve. Whether judges will act on such social understanding for the benefit of the victims of dowry-related violence is, as we have seen, a different matter. After all, judges are themselves members of society, and their offspring will be among the most attractive marriage partners in terms of status, if not wealth. I would argue that this itself may partly explain why South Asian judges have finally taken more explicit cognisance of the fact that South Asian women continue to be murdered for dowry. At least it is no longer correct in 1998 to assert that the higher Indian judiciary, which itself remains a male-dominated elite, plays chauvinistic collusion games with women's lives in the complicated scenario of the dowry prohibition law and refuses to listen to those who want retribution for dowry murders.

Thus there is some progress in tackling the dowry problem, but it is clearly not going far enough in tackling the roots of the dowry problems (see already Saini, 1983). Still, the South Asian jurisdictions are, at least in this respect, well ahead of Western jurisdictions, in which the law is officially colour-blind and culture-neutral, and where personnel of the law are not even aware of the true extent of the grave problem of dowry-related violence among South Asians.

Chapter 7

Miles to go: An assessment of the enforcement hurdles in the implementation of the anti-dowry law in India

Manjaree Chowdhary

Even after fifty years of independence, perpetuation of gender inequality and female deprivation poses a major hurdle to India in her quest for the democratic ideals of social and economic justice. More than ever before, the Indian woman finds herself a helpless victim of the dowry system, an integral part of domestic violence. The practice of dowry in contemporary Indian society is no longer a benevolent concept but has assumed a gruesome and appalling magnitude, being largely responsible for serious wife abuse, resulting in the brutal and untimely death of many women.

There has been a general consensus amongst government and intelligentsia on the urgency for legal remedies to combat and control it. Consequently the *Dowry Prohibition Act*, 1961 was enacted. This Act has since been variously amended and armed to deal more effectively with the menace of dowry. It remains, however, a matter of grave concern that despite evidence of increasing dowry-related atrocities – and of legal measures for dealing with them – prosecutions remain few and far between. For effective legal control, it is necessary to assess a combination of causative factors creating impediments in the enforcement strategies so that policies can be formulated to target these specific areas.

This chapter seeks to analyse possible enforcement hurdles to effectively implementing the legal measures to check the increasing dowry crimes. The various lacunae have been identified at different levels, beginning with the legal provisions themselves, followed by the law enforcing agencies, particularly the police, the administrative machinery and the judiciary. Finally, the social attitudes in which the problem has its roots are examined. In conclusion, measures are suggested for better adherence to laws, in the hope of making a small contribution in saving Indian womanhood from further social indignity and cruelty.

7.1 Legal provisions

The *Dowry Prohibition Act*, 1961 (hereafter referred to as the Act) has been incessantly debated, criticised and generally dismissed as being sadly wanting. The Act was initially riddled with inherent shortcomings which impeded successful implementation. Subsequent amendments to the Act with concomitant changes in the criminal law, however, have endeavoured to create a more comprehensive legal framework. Despite an apparently favourable law, statistics continue to reveal increased dowry-related violence and dowry deaths. Two major defects in the existing provisions which have been repeatedly overlooked in all amendments, were and are still responsible for the poor response to the law, and especially the appallingly small number of prosecutions.

The first major defect is in the explanation which exempts 'voluntary and customary gifts of love and affection' given by the bride's family to her or her husband from the definition of dowry, while the Act prohibits demands of dowry by extortionate means. This provides a convenient loophole for all parties, leading to the present situation where huge dowries continue to be exchanged but are never admitted, since most people prefer to claim that gifts were 'voluntarily' given and that no demands were made. The definition further assumes that such presents should be of a customary nature and the value of such presents should not be excessive, and should take account of the financial status of the person by whom or on whose behalf such presents are given. Such leeway allows for subjective interpretations. Custom varies according to caste, community and region. What may be viewed as customary gifts in the boy's family may not be so considered in the girl's. A similar analogy can be applied to what is excessive. Vanita (1984a: 29-30) has rightly condemned this section of the Act as merely strengthening the existing social hypocrisy and legalising this form of extortion, holding that should prosecution ensue, decisions will be made arbitrarily by each judge, leaving scope for individual bias and contradictory decisions.

The other major loophole requiring urgent redressal is that both giver and taker of dowry are treated as offenders under the Act. Diwan and Diwan (1995: 24) rightly remark that it is indeed a unique law which considers both the committer of the act and the person against whom the act is committed as offenders. The giver is more sinned against than sinning, since the act of giving is circumscribed by social compulsions. As it is, the girl's parents would hesitate in prosecuting her in-laws for fear of jeopardising her domestic happiness. The added risk of being liable to equal punishment as givers of dowry is an even stronger deterrent. It is difficult to perceive punitive measures succeeding when the victim is punished along with the offender (Diwan and Diwan, 1995 : 24). While providing stringent measures for reclaiming dowry by the woman or her heirs, the Act seriously damages their effect by subordinating them to the supremacy of the definition of dowry, thereby placing the woman in a complex dilemma of risking punitive measures against her family if she demands her dowry back. Should she decide to spare them, she loses her dowry, as she would have to accept that what was given were merely voluntary gifts and not 'dowry' (Vanita, 1984a: 31). Such self-contradictions send negative signals, deterring effective recourse to law. Relevant changes in the Act would potentially enhance the existing comprehensive legal framework to ensure greater prosecution. However, to judge the appropriateness of legal strategies in isolation would indeed be an exercise in futility, a digression from other factors contributing to their lack of enforcement.

7.2 The enforcement agencies

While appropriate legislation is an important step towards providing protection against dowry-related violence, law reform alone does not guarantee implementation (Connors, 1994: 187). Indeed, the implementation of anti-dowry provisions in India has been disappointing, hampered greatly by the attitude and operation of enforcement agencies: the police, the administrative machinery and the judiciary.

The role of the police is more central in this context than existing research has so far acknowledged. By emphasising the criminal nature of dowry-related violence, the legislature itself has recognised the central role of the police in responding to it. Legal strategies encourage police intervention at various levels, placing upon them a heavy responsibility for effective and unbiased enforcement. In practice, however, the situation is grim. The paradoxical picture of governmental activism on the one hand and general police apathy on the other finds reflection in the establishment and functioning of Crime Against Women Cells (hereafter referred to as the Cells). Formulated as specialised fora to deal with dowry complaints, *inter alia,* they are run by staff inadequately trained in the dynamics of domestic violence and available legal alternatives and services. Understandably such Cells have assumed a mediatory role, seeking to affect reconciliation rather than pursuing the matter under prescribed criminal law. The absence of gender sensitisation may result in dangerous assumptions regarding the inferior status of women, which are carried over to the place of work. Thus a woman who is trying to make a complaint about dowry harassment finds herself unwillingly dragged into a process of negotiations which she neither wants nor understands, receiving virtually no information or advice different from what her family or society would have given her. In cases of reconciliation the 'follow up' procedure is the least efficient part of the process. Summons for effective monitoring are either not sent or, if they are and couples do report back, they are summarily dismissed without allowing the woman a chance to voice her opinion (Vanita, 1987: 15-16).

The police frequently hesitate to intervene in what is perceived as a family matter. It is only after intense pressure from the aggrieved party or social organisations that a case is registered, which in the event of a dowry death is usually registered as a suicide, changed only after much persuasion into murder (Jha and Pujari, 1996: 280). This follows a lapse in ordinary procedural duties of providing the complainant a copy of the First Information Report (FIR) informing her of her legal rights and further judicial procedure (Vanita, 1987: 17).

The Indian criminal justice system is evidence-based and requires adequate incriminating material for prosecution. Instances often indicate that the police may be guilty of collusion and gross misconduct. Relevant evidence may be completely ignored or tampered with so that it fails to build a good case admissible in law, defeating the ends of justice (see 'Appeal to Supreme Court...'1984: 41-42). Courts have often lamented the callous and almost prejudiced stance of the investigating officers, reprimanding them for exonerating culprits despite clear evidence of their guilt. The reported cases of *Lichhmadevi v. State of Rajasthan*, AIR 1987 SC 1785, and *Joint Women's Programme v. State of Rajasthan*, AIR 1987 SC 2060, exemplify these problems. Police malfunctioning and apathy has taken many forms; among them undue influence in recording dying declarations, delay in sending the body for post-mortem, intimidation of prime witnesses and exploitation of the legal ignorance of both parties to extort money as a price to build a good case in their favour. Mrs. Justice Sarojni Saxena of the Punjab and Haryana High Court stated in a personal interview, that there would be a conviction in almost ninety per cent of cases if the police refrained from introducing their own facts while building evidence.

Along with the corruption, deliberate lapses of duty and the pre-conceived mind-set of the police, frequent transfers of the functionaries add to the piecemeal preparation of the case. As the case file goes through the many hands, the seriousness of the situation is lost on the officers, permitting a thoughtless and disinterested mechanical approach. All such factors combine to make it difficult to generate a fair and just approach from a machinery turned corrupt, apathetic and gender-biased, causing disillusionment among the victims, preventing them from reporting violence in the home and so reinforcing the fact that such violence so often goes unreported.

The role of the administrative machinery in the implementation of the anti-dowry law is equally to be found wanting. As administrative agents, government doctors, prosecutors and Dowry Prohibition Officers play an integral role in the enforcement process of the legal provisions pertaining to dowry. Practice reveals that agents of this tardy administrative machinery are increasingly guilty of professional misconduct.

Studies have shown that doctors, too, can fall prey to greed and become manipulative. Collusion with the interested party is not unusual. It is quite common for wrong fitness certificates to be given to fabricate dying declarations in favour of the accused (Jha and Pujari, 1996: 235-236). Postmortem reports are similarly skewed. Vital evidence is thus destroyed, killing the prosecution even before the case has begun. Counsellors, both public and private, commonly exhibit a mercenary attitude that cuts across professional obligation and, instead of protecting the interests of the client, extends to colluding with the defence for personal gain. Moreover, the propensity to shun dowry cases as being unprofitable leaves victims with little hope of achieving justice, even after withstanding untold pressures not to approach the court.

The Act as amended by the *Dowry Prohibition (Amendment) Act*, 1986 envisaged the appointment of Dowry Prohibition Officers under a new section 8B of the Act. Such officers were to be assisted by an advisory body of social workers to promote better legal awareness and provide effective enforcement machinery. It is an entirely different matter that hardly any such appointments of Dowry Prohibition Officers have been made and where they do exist, are there only in name and make no effective contribution. The state of Maharashtra is an apt example, where in spite of six dowry vigilance committees, 471 dowry deaths were recorded in 1995, second only to Uttar Pradesh (National Crime Records Bureau, 1995: 228).

7.3 The role of the judiciary

Although an increase in the number of dowry death cases is evident, only a tiny proportion are reported, of which fewer still reach trial and judgement. Statistics compiled by the National Crime Records Bureau (1995: 125) reveal that as many as 87.1 per cent of the dowry death cases remained pending in the courts as compared to the disposal rate of 12.9 per cent in the year 1995. This may be due partly to the lengthy and archaic judicial procedure. More alarming is the extremely low rate of conviction. The acquittal or discharge in cases of cruelty by the husband or his relatives amounted to 75.8 per cent (National Crime Records Bureau, 1995: 125).

What ails the Indian judiciary, preventing it from performing its duty as protector of justice? On being asked about possible explanations, a sample of judicial magistrates and judges interviewed opined that the courts were at the mercy of the evidence placed before them. Faulty and fabricated evidence or a complete lack of it, circumstantial evidence which might prove to be inadequate, lack of proof and corroborative evidence, prime witnesses turning hostile and hesitating to depose, plus the self-contradictory nature of the legal provisions, were cited as major difficulties faced by the court in arriving at a fair and just verdict.

Apart from procedural inadequacies, the attitude of the judiciary towards gender equality which stems from the values of the patriarchal society of which they are a part, may be seen as an important component in preventing a truly impartial appraisal of dowry offences and crimes against women. Our submission is based on reported cases, the list of which is very small. Structural shortcomings in the legislation can be cited as a probable excuse for a narrow interpretation of legal strategies as reflected in the early cases of *Thomas*, 1975 KLT 386; *Daulat*, 1980 CriLJ 1171; *Inder Sain*, 1981 CriLJ 1116 and *Shankarrao*, 1983 CriLJ 269, but the judicial sanction to the arbitrary use of procedural trickery to dissuade dowry victims from approaching the courts is too evident to be overlooked. Lotika Sarkar (1985: 499) rightly remarks that 'judicial commitment to social justice and declaration of the need to promote gender justice often brings in conflict with the years of unquestioned principles of male dominance and women's inferior status'. The *Vinod Kumar* case, reported at AIR 1982 P&H 372, exemplified this approach, for it virtually held that women are owned by men. This case shows that when it comes to protecting the male right over the matrimonial home and men's control over their wives' possessions, social justice can easily be forgotten. Fortunately, that case was overruled in *Pratibha Rani v. Sushil Kumar*, AIR 1985 SC 628 and is therefore no longer good law.

At present, the amended Act provides a reasonable if not foolproof mechanism for dealing with dowry offenders. Social awareness has with time evoked a perceptible shift in judicial perspective, towards greater legal and social consciousness, as is evident in more recent judgements convicting dowry offenders. The significant pronouncement in *Pratibha Rani v. Sushil Kumar*, AIR 1985 SC 628, established the right of the woman over her own property (*stridhan*), including the dowry. Again in *Surinder Kumar v. State*, AIR 1987 SC 386, *State v. Laxman*, AIR 1986 SC 250, *Brij Lal v. Prem Chand*, AIR 1989 SC 1661, *Paniben* (1992) 2 SCC 474 and *Ganeshlal v. State of Maharashtra* (1992) 3 SCC 106, to mention only the most important cases of the late 1980s and early 1990s, the apex court is seen playing a dynamic role in expounding law and clarifying legal norms so that culprits do not escape because of the inadequacies and procedural technicalities of law. Such judgements, though encouraging, only comprise a very small percentage of the total cases coming to trial. Evidence is still predominantly in favour of acquittal.

A closer look at the above cases, moreover, reveals that convictions were made at the level of the Supreme Court, the last and final court of appeal, often reversing orders of acquittal granted by the trial or the High Court. This display of gender sensitisation and judicial activism has unfortunately not percolated down to the subordinate courts, raising serious questions about arbitrary and blatantly biased judicial strategies still commonly operating. A majority of the dowry victims belong to the middle and lower middle income groups, so have no financial resources to pursue the case beyond the trial court or, at most, the High Court (Jha and Pujari 1996: 224-225). A lengthy and tedious court process extending for two or three years from the filing of the complaint to the actual trial, at the end of which the accused is set free on flimsy grounds, leaves the girl (if indeed she is still alive) and/or her family mentally exhausted, financially depleted and disillusioned with a system that functions on a narrow prejudiced level rather than being based on norms of justice and fair play. Clearly, then, despite the positive beginning made by the Supreme Court, the legal subjectivity of the subordinate courts coupled with the apathy of the police and the inefficiency of the administrative machinery make it immensely difficult to sustain a charge of dowry murder in the courts.

7.4 Social attitudes

The dowry system and dowry-related violence are issues which can not be addressed in isolation. Any discussion of the subject must be placed within the socio-economic and cultural framework of the complex Indian society, if effective answers are to be found to the unabated dowry crimes and lack of commensurate prosecution under law. A paucity of scientific research on the role of social attitudes in condoning and indeed perpetuating dowry-related violence permits explanations based on mere conjecture and conventional wisdom. However, there is a need to guard against generalisations, for the existence and form of dowry atrocities is as varied as the regional, community and caste variations.

Dowry crimes may be linked to socially structured and highly distorted traditional expectations about dowry giving, engineered to foster the inferior status of the woman. Strong societal and religious dictates continue to demand the marriage of a girl to a man of appropriate caste and class, subjecting her family to grave censure and disgrace if they fail to perform this religio-cultural duty. As Bisakha Sen's research, discussed in chapter 5, also confirms, most parents are not opposed to giving a dowry to their daughter, seeing it essentially as the maximum price a family is willing to pay to 'settle' her in matrimony and also to safeguard their social standing, creating in the process a dangerous asymmetry between the two parties to the transaction. Associated with this belief is the general consensus that divorce and separation are a disaster for women, who should go to great lengths to avoid them. Consequently a violation of customary transactions (since no dowry problem arises when there is agreement about reciprocal transactions) by the groom and his kin exploiting their assumed position of strength to amass more wealth, as shown by Menski in chapter 3, resulting in the harassment or even ousting of the bride from the matrimonial home for unfulfilled demands, elicits a stereotypical parental response. They either acquiesce to the unreasonable demands or condone such violence, in the belief that marriage is a 'private affair' that does not welcome interference by the bride's family. The girl may also genuinely lack support because of financial constraints (Jha and Pujari, 1996: 228).

In fact, the natal family's attitude towards recurring dowry-related violence is seen largely to determine whether the girl would opt out of a bad marriage and seek legal recourse to bring dowry offenders to book. Sample studies indicate that all the women who refused to return to violent husbands were those whose families concurred in the decision. All those who returned to continuing violence which could ultimately result in a dowry death were women whose parents were willing to humiliate themselves and concede to the unreasonable demands of the husband, if he would only agree to take her back (Vanita, 1987: 15). A woman finds herself under pressure from her family to return to a violent marriage and adjust to the ways of her 'real' home, reinforcing the concept that her natal home is no longer her home. Negotiations are usually kept within the family for fear of social disgrace or even deference to the husband. Such matters would be reported to the authority as the last resort, only to be met with indifference, as we have seen. Rejection from all quarters may tend to produce feelings of self-blame and unwantedness, causing the victim to commit suicide in a vain hope of regaining control (Jha and Pujari, 1996: 272).

In cases where the victim or her family muster the courage to break free of social parameters to seek justice under the law, they find themselves forsaken by an apathetic society. The victim's immediate neighbours and other local residents are an important source of information which has great bearing on her decision to report the crime. Existing literature indicates that dowry disputes are generally accepted as a 'family affair' requiring no neighbourly intervention. There is enough misconception that such violence exists because the girl might have provoked it. Neighbours desist from reporting anything for fear of losing the goodwill of their immediate neighbours, going to the lengths of sanctioning another dowry-based marriage for the same murderer (Jha and Pujari, 1996: 279). A rigid mind-set operates to override social duty, adding to the long list of odds against prosecution.

The educational and economical disadvantages imposed on women have been seen as adding to their vulnerability against violence, impairing their capacity to exercise their rights. However, to assume that education and economic independence alone would encourage a woman to prosecute dowry offenders is to underestimate the hold of social traditions on an individual (Rani, 1984: 16). Young women, though more willing to rebel against an unjust system that devalues them, are still generally compelled to put up with continual atrocities because of deeply ingrained subservience to customs and mortifying fear of the stigma of single existence in an inflexible and dogmatic society (Grover, 1990: 13).

Consequently, without a fundamental attitudinal change in society, law and its enforcing agencies by themselves cannot overcome the obstacles to the effective enforcement of the legal system. The issue of escalating dowry crimes in India, without a commensurate prosecution under law, continues to defy easy solutions, making a critical study of the subject much more complex and demanding.

7.5 The need for a multi-dimensional approach

Given the varied location of the enforcement hurdles, achieving effective legal control would necessitate a multi-dimensional approach incorporating measures that operate simultaneously at different levels to create a more conducive environment for legal action. Some of the suggestions for better enforcement made here have found mention at various points in the existing literature on the subject. The purpose of endorsing them is to emphasise the pressing need to initiate quick action for better implementation of existing laws to ensure fair legal processes and speedy justice for a visibly distressed womanhood. It is imperative that a system that adopts a legal approach to deal with a social evil should frame laws which express the views of the community about an offence as grave as bride-burning. Assuming that Indian society does not underwrite such a practice, I argue here that a need still exists to rectify glaring self-contradictory provisions in the Act that continue to reflect the ambivalent social perceptions of a patriarchal society, thereby instilling much-needed faith in victims about the viability of a legal system that does not act to reinforce male control.

To bring about a consistency of legal response, with appropriate penalty for the accused and justice to the victim, the police and associated administrative agencies need to be trained in the dynamics of a specialised crime and diligent in the performance of public duty, to ensure fair and efficient investigating procedures and the gender sensitisation essential to deal with crimes against women. The recurrent demand for exclusive family courts for the speedy disposal of dowry cases may prove to be counterproductive. Giving judges arbitrary powers could convert the court into an extended family, legalising the private and more diffused pressures the victim faces (Vanita, 1984b: 46). It would be more effective to restructure archaic legislation governing judicial procedure and carefully monitor the working of the judges, holding them personally responsible for inordinate delay. Under the circumstances, the role of judges assumes greater importance in interpreting legal strategies. India has been witness to a recent spate of legal activism shown by its Supreme Court in dealing with dowry cases (described in chapter 6.5). What is needed now is their effective dissemination to the lower rungs of the judiciary, to jolt them out of their legal subjectivity and motivate them to move beyond procedural technicalities to adopt a more realistic approach in dispensing justice.

Clearly, the tardy enforcement of dowry provisions is linked to the inferior status of the woman and crimes associated with her in a male-dominated society. It is likely, therefore, that without a major attitudinal shift in the perceived role and status of women, all other efforts would prove futile. The lawmakers, the police and the judiciary reflect the prejudiced assumptions of an indifferent society of which they are a part. A start has been made by social organisations and anti-dowry activists

(Kishwar, 1990: 13) who have persistently addressed the vital question of social control and morality when they argue for greater neighbourhood control and surveillance, effective family support systems and inculcation of basic human morals. The government has carried it forward by educating public opinion through legislation, information campaigns and education. The continued increase in dowry crimes heightens the need to reinforce and expedite efforts towards securing educational and economic independence of women, creating gainful employment opportunities, making cheap and purposeful legal aid available and providing secure social support and services to victims. There remains, however, the urgent task of inter-relating and integrating such measures into a comprehensive programme aimed at removing the obstacles to better enforcement of legal provisions which will promote justice for Indian women in private and public life.

Chapter 8

Dowry and hypergamy among the Gujaratis in Britain

Rohit Barot

This chapter* examines the dowry phenomenon among the South Asians of Gujarati background in Britain. After drawing a brief distinction between dowry and bridewealth, it offers a theoretical exposition of dowry as an element of *jati* hypergamy and gender relations. Both are embedded in caste and class relations and in wider economic and political contexts and institutions. Dowry practices among the Gujarati population in Britain confirm that dowry and hypergamy do occur among British South Asians. It is argued that some understanding of inter-generational differences is required to explain social changes which are affecting dowry transactions in the context of South Asian hypergamous marriage relationships.

8.1 Bridewealth and dowry in context

Both dowry and bridewealth (or brideprice) involve the transmission of property at marriage (see Goody and Tambiah, 1973). Following Goody's seminal contribution on the topic, dowry and bridewealth can be readily distinguished. A transaction involving dowry occurs when the bride's family transfers property to the bridegroom and his family whereas bridewealth occurs when the bridegroom and his family transfer property to the groom's family. As Enrica Garzilli (1996) notes, dowry is an ancient element in almost all South Asian cultures, but the problem of brides as victims of homicide is a recent phenomenon.

We cannot treat dowry or bridewealth in isolation from the networks of kinship and affinity to which they belong. In turn, these networks constitute broader realms of social relations. In his study of Anavil Brahmins of South Gujarat, van der Veen (1972) provided an excellent example of the embodiment of hypergamy and dowry in a wider set of economic and political relations. Tambiah (1973b: 64) also observed that 'bridewealth and dowry have different potentialities in the way they can link up with the politico-economic institutions of the society where they are found'. Such observations raise the question of the relationship between wider institutional structures and the practice of dowry, and the extent to which ideological configurations of patriarchy and gender influence dowry practices and dowry murders. The explanations of dowry, and of violence and abuse associated with the giving of dowries, would require complex analysis of the varied factors which influence the nature of the dowry transaction and its aftermath. Only then can practical measures for the elimination of conditions which foster dowry be determined.

8.2 Dowry murders in India

According to Srinivas (1989b), an understanding of hypergamy and caste is essential for analysis of the dowry problem. Besides other forms of hierarchical relations (see Dumont, 1970; Kolenda, 1976), hypergamy expresses asymmetrical gender relations between families within a particular sub-caste (jati) where the bride and bridegivers are regarded as inherently inferior to the groom and bride receivers. In other words, a woman marries a man who belongs to a higher order and this defines the lower status of an incoming woman in the family. Central to the dowry system is the transfer of gifts which the bride brings to the family of the groom. These material goods, in the form of ornaments, items of clothing and so, constitute her dowry. Srinivas (1989b: 100-101) makes a further distinction between pre-modern and modern dowry. The notions around giving away a virgin daughter (*kanyadan*) and of women's property (*stridhanam*) were related to certain traditional exchanges. The colonial and post-colonial transformation of India, the increasing penetration of the cash nexus, market relations, various forms of consumerism, including the current economic liberalisation, along with the tendency of the aspiring lower castes to emulate higher castes (see Srinivas, 1989b: 109-111) have made great impact on what the author calls 'modern dowry'.

Nowadays, the bridegroom's family can demand large amounts of money, wedding expenses and a whole range of consumer goods. These demands put pressure on the bride's family. Often, these pressures do not cease after the bride's family have submitted to the demand for various goods at the time of the marriage. The pressure on the bride to bring more cash and gifts often continues for an extended period. In many instances the bride is exposed to harassment, intimidation, violence and death, as recent accounts illustrate in detail (Kumari, 1989; Ghadially and Kumar, 1988, Liddle and Joshi, 1986; Moore, 1997). Equally, there are contributions which document resistance to dowry (Kumar, 1993a) and proposals to create conditions which will give women greater power to protect themselves from threats to their life and limb (Rajan, 1993a).

What is most striking today is that both dowry and dowry murders persist and even increase. Himendra Thakur has reported the distribution of dowry deaths in India. His tables (see Preface), based on figures from the National Crimes Bureau, Home Ministry, Government of India, shows that in 1994 1,977 women were murdered for dowry in Uttar Pradesh, 519 in Maharashtra, 396 in Andhra Pradesh, 354 in Madhya Pradesh, 349 in West Bengal, 298 in Rajasthan, 296 in Bihar, and a smaller number in other states. According to the same set of statistics, between 1987 and 1994, 11,118 women lost their lives as a consequence of dowry murders in Uttar Pradesh alone (see Tables 1 and 2 in the Preface).

Dowry transactions also occur in Pakistan and Bangladesh and among the Pakistani and Bangladeshi – as well as Indian – communities in Britain. Dr. Iftikhar Malik (Bath University) has informed me that in Pakistan, deaths of women caused by burning are referred to as 'stove deaths'. There, too, the family's claim that the woman died accidentally is often untrue. This callous destruction of human life and violence against women in various parts of South Asia is a persistent evil. It is nothing less than a gross violation of the fundamental human right to life.

8.3 British South Asians and dowry

In social anthropological accounts of South Asian groups in Britain, scholars have constantly argued that people from India, Pakistan and Bangladesh have generally tended to reproduce their caste and sectarian communities underpinned, by their regional and linguistic identities.

These accounts also assert that these groups have recreated their religious organisations as a major focal point of their social solidarity, collective organisation and political mobilisation (Desai, 1963; Helweg, 1979; Anwar, 1979; Bhachu, 1985; Barot, 1987; Shaw, 1988; Jackson and Nesbitt, 1993; Ballard, 1994; Nye, 1995). A logical extension of this argument is that in reproducing their caste and sectarian communities, Indians, Pakistanis and Bangladeshis re-create a cardinal structure that helps to preserve the identities of particular groups. This is the principle of endogamy, according to which all marriages should occur within the community of one's affiliation and not outside it. As David Pocock (1957: 289-300) demonstrated for East Africa, South Asians living outside the context of the subcontinent cannot fully reproduce the reality of the *jati* social system to which they belong in their natal societies. Similarly, the South Asian groups living in Britain lack the social surrounding to the institutions which make up social formation in South Asia. In other words, even in reproducing their institutions in Britain or anywhere else outside the subcontinent, South Asians invariably face social changes.

Of critical importance is the distinction between endogamy which is national and that which is trans-national. Trans-national endogamy encompasses the entire social group irrespective of territorial location of its members. In contrast, endogamy which is national is restricted to search for spouses within the national society. South Asian groups may exercise both national and trans-national choices, depending on their circumstances. For instance, it is not uncommon for South Asian families to argue that they should marry their sons and daughters in the UK only, on grounds that young people born and brought up in the UK are more likely to be compatible than a couple in which one spouse is from South Asia. Some families will advance strong arguments in favour of selecting spouses from South Asia for a whole host of reasons. One common assertion is that brides from South Asia are better behaved than their counterparts in the UK and better home-makers.

The fact that the UK-based South Asian families are often materially better off may have an important bearing on traditional gender relations. For instance, Bangladeshi families who 'import' a groom from 'back home' may require the groom's family to transfer property to their daughter's name, almost as collateral lest the groom decide to end the marriage in Britain. Bangladeshi men marrying wives from Bangladesh demand no less expensive gifts. We need to understand these transnational relationships and transactions and the degree to which they lead to positive or negative outcomes. Whether or not these marriages create new patterns of asymmetrical relationship between British South Asians and their kin and affines in Asia is a chapter unto itself that needs further research and documentation.

I am told that in British Pakistani communities, the parents of grooms do not hesitate to demand dowry even in the context of parallel cousin and cross-cousin marriages. Information I have from Bangladeshi respondents also points to incidents of dowry demand and high expenditure on weddings. Here I concentrate on South Asians from a Gujarati background.

8.4 Practice of dowry among British Gujaratis

The Gujarati population in Britain consists of a variety of Hindu, Muslim, Jain, Parsi and Christian groups. Gujarati Muslims (Sunni or Shia, among the latter Ismailis, Ithna Asharis and Daudi Bohras), Jains or Parsis do not observe hypergamy, so do not have a convention of giving between unequal parties. However, the belief in the general superiority of the groom's family appears to be a common feature of most South Asian groups in Britain and has some bearing on the transactions made when families arrange marriages. The Gujarati Hindu population consists of a range of *jati* groups, and a small number of Brahmins. There are groups such as Vaniyas, Lohanas, Patels (who need to be distinguished in different categories) who might have generally occupied middle-ranking positions in their native habitat. There are also Gujjars, Suthars and Mochis, whom some Gujarati Hindus may still regard as of lower caste (*nichi jatna*). Such perceptions are likelier among the primary generation of Gujaratis than for secondary and subsequent generations for whom *jati*, in some instances at least, may be of little consequence beyond the knowledge of belonging to their own endogamous group and associations within it. Be that as it may, such groups are now well-organised and continue to mobilise themselves so as to maximise their economic and social advantages. Undoubtedly, marriage arrangements play a role in this context, too.

Information on dowry that has been collected for this chapter mainly concerns the Gujarati Hindu Lohanas and the Patidars, often referred to as the Patel community. However, not all Patels are Patidars. For instance, Patels who come from different parts of Gujarat form different caste communities. The Leva Kanbi Patels of Kutch district, for example, constitute a separate group unrelated to the Patidar community. The Lohanas and the Patidars have relatively similar histories of migration and settlement in the UK via different parts of East and Central Africa. What H. S. Morris (1968: 25-44) called 'communal crystallisation' to describe the formation of different Asian communities in Uganda, is a process that has been reproduced in the UK in the last 35 to 40 years. In their UK residence, self-employment has been the hallmark of both the Lohanas and the Patels and they have used small shopkeeping and family labour to accumulate resources and to branch out in successful medium-sized businesses. The relative prosperity of both communities is not insignificant. Their British settlement and economic success have consequences for the marriage of their sons and daughters. Giving dowry and maintaining hypergamous relationships in Britain is one part of this story. Social change among all South Asian communities, especially intergenerational change, has opened up possibilities of some resistance to demands for dowry and hypergamous marriages. This topic is further explored later in this chapter.

Before discussing dowry among the Lohanas and Patels, it is worth clarifying the relationship between dowry and hypergamy, which are not always synonymous. In South Asian cases, hypergamy involves dowry but not all cases of dowry involve hypergamy. The custom of mutual gift exchanges (*paheramni* gifts) and large expenditure on one's daughter's marriage equals dowry without deployment of explicitly defined hypergamy. Among the Charottar Patels, dowry is categorically linked to hypergamy and the search for a groom of a higher social rank is an observable phenomenon. Therefore the examples below illustrate dowry on its own as well as dowry that is linked to an internal system of ranking among the Charottar Patels. Both examples illustrate that dowry is alive and well among the Gujarati Hindus. It is also a source of great anxiety and distress, especially for the families (and not only for the women) who have to make specific financial plans to ensure that there will be large funds available to meet marriage expenses.

8.5 Dowry among the Lohanas

Organised under their own *jati* associations, Lohanas are one of the largest Hindu communities in the UK. Having been successful merchants and traders in East African countries, even after their forced migration from Uganda, they have established for themselves a basis for wealth creation through both employment and self-employment that now includes several successful international trading houses. The Madhvani family who revitalised the sugar industry in Uganda is an example of Lohana enterprise that earns them a place in the records as one of Britain's 200 richest Asian families.

Lohanas require their sons and daughters to marry within their own *jati* community and the arrangement of marriage may involve both traditional negotiations and an element of personal choice for British-born young spouses. The social organisation of the jati incorporates both endogamy and rules of exogamy. Exogamy is generally expressed by surname (*atak*) which roughly defines agnatic kin (Barot, 1975: 70-80). The basic rule is that you do not marry someone who has the same surname as yourself. As a social category, *atak* is not hierarchical and Lohanas do not regard some *atak* names as superior to others. In the arrangement of marriages, wife givers again do not have the same status as wife receivers and women have to play a subordinate role. Lohana families comply with direct and indirect social pressures for lavish weddings and presents which may constitute a substantial dowry, although the Lohanas may dissociate this gift giving from the English word 'dowry' and use a simple Gujarati expression to describe it.

Individual Lohanas I spoke to emphasised the cost factor more than the community pressures and especially the sense of discomfort and powerlessness which some young women may experience as their marital future is planned. A Lohana father whose daughter recently married highlighted the cost dimension. London is the most expensive British city for South Asian weddings. To hire a hall large enough to accommodate the bride's and groom's extended families may cost thousands of pounds. Depending on location and size, the hiring charges for a single day vary from about £2,500 to £4,500, although the costs may go down outside London. Indian families who hire Webbington Hotel in Somerset, for example, pay nearer to £3,000 for a hall that will accommodate between 500 to 1000 guests. Catering charges are high, depending on the kind of menu that is chosen. A Bristol-based Lohana caterer charges £5 for each platter of various foods (*thali*), so for an average gathering of about 500 guests, charges for food alone can cost £2,000 to £2,500. Most families employ the services of a professional photographer and video service, which can cost up to £2,000.

The most important item is jewellery, which the bride's parents are expected to provide. The bride's family may spend a substantial amount on 22 carat gold ornaments. In areas like Wembley and Southall, where many Indian families have settled, jewellers have exquisite shops which do thriving trade as families spend thousands of pounds to collect ornaments for the occasion. Clothing for the marriages is hardly less expensive. In order to shop as cheaply as possible, now it is quite common for the bride's parents to fly out to Mumbai or Delhi to do all the shopping. Some people have told me that the cost of a trip overseas can pay for itself, given the savings one can make in India. One father said that 'you can buy two dresses in India for the price of one in Leicester or London'. On the basis of his personal observations, he concluded that ordinary families with husband and wife working could spend up to £25,000 on a wedding. Those in more successful businesses spend even more. Expenditures of £40,000 to £60,000 are not uncommon. Such costly weddings, and the display of splendour and consumerism associated with them, supposedly enhance the status of the family in the community. Posh and expensive weddings make a statement about the family and their ability to splash out on gifts and entertainment for their relatives and friends. In the limited time I had for this investigation, it was difficult to find out whether women reacted differently from men. It is unlikely that they would have diverged greatly from the wishes of their menfolk.

If one expects liberal university education among the young to undermine lavish dowries and expensive gifts, this hypothesis is certainly not supported by the facts. For many young Asians seem to have no desire to end expensive practices which parents may find unbearable.

8.6 Dowry and hypergamy among British Patidars

Patidars, commonly known as Patels, are one of the major Gujarati-speaking communities in Britain. One major group comes from Charottar district and shares a history of migration and settlement in the UK with other South Asian groups. As David Pocock (1972: 126-152) has explained in considerable detail, Patidars have marriage circles. Each circle consists of a cluster of villages and identifies itself by the number of villages to which it belongs. These circles express a principle of hierarchy and hypergamy contained within them. Accordingly, parents of brides from lower circles attempt to marry their daughter to grooms from a higher circle. In order to gain acceptance in a higher marriage circle, parents of the bride have to pay a dowry commonly known as *paithan*. It is well known that *paithan* has recently tended to involve considerable expenditure for the parents of the bride. In the Indian context, the institution of *paithan* has been oppressive and has led to misery and tragedy for many families, and unfair and unjust treatment for young women regarded as a burden. The Patels I spoke to claim that the system is changing and breaking down in India as a consequence of educational and cultural change. Only further research can show to what extent that is so.

From my personal contacts and observations in Uganda throughout the 1960s, it was evident that the Patidar marriages there involved *paithan*. Many families with more than two daughters found the practice deeply disturbing, but were generally required to comply with customary demands. From East African countries and from other colonial possessions like Aden, the Patidars began to migrate to the United Kingdom. As for their settlement in the UK, we have Harald Tambs-Lyche's short monograph of London Patidars that largely concentrates on their strategies of accumulation (Tambs-Lyche, 1980). As his concern was mainly with migration and settlement, his observations on the social system of London Patidars are limited.

The British Patidar community has thrived also in shopkeeping and trade since the 1970s, to a point that 'Patel' has become virtually synonymous with ownership of a corner shop. Today the Patidar community in Britain consists of a number of highly organised groups which continue to define membership and affiliation in terms of marriage circles consisting of a collection of villages. These groups have a modern associational structure and often own property for the use of their members and they also provide a range of supportive services. Individuals from the Patidar community to whom I spoke identify the following hierarchical hypergamous marriage circles among the British Patidars:

Chha gamvala (6 village circle)
Panch gamvala (5 village circle)
Bavis gamvala (22 village circle)
Satyavis gamvala (27 village circle)

The logic of hypergamy would dictate that a bride's family from the 27 village circle, the lowest rank, should seek a groom from a higher ranking group, with men from the 6 village circle at the top of this hierarchical arrangement. Traditionally, the lower village family would have to pay a *paithan* in order to secure a groom from a higher village circle.

As the associations established on the basis of these circles are so well-consolidated, it is fair to assume that there is a desire to perpetuate such rules of hypergamy. Responses to questions about the arrangement of marriages invoke a reaction that points both to the persistence of traditional practice and increasing social change between generations. Further research is required to establish clearly the degree to which reproduction of these circles helps to perpetuate dowry.

I have been told that the practice of demanding *paithan* from a bride's family persists in Britain and that there is considerable pressure to ensure that the marriage that has been arranged is properly conducted. As all generations of South Asians are exposed to the dominant British paradigm of equality and individual freedom, crassly extortionist demands for *paithan* are less common than before. However, once the engagement has been fixed, it is not uncommon for the groom's family to make additional demands for *paithan*.

In one example quoted to me, the groom's family began to advance their demands after the engagement. The young man was a pharmacist and his potential wife was also a university graduate. When the bride learnt that the groom's family demanded that her parents should set him up in business, she reacted strongly and withdrew from the engagement and marriage altogether. She is reported to have uttered some 'rude' words about the Patidar marriage, adding that she would happily marry an Indian from outside the Patidar community. While this example highlights the kind of defiance that may be emerging, it is fair to say that the bride's family still remain under pressure to provide a substantial amount of property upon marriage and to throw a lavish wedding, costing anything from £20,000 to £50,000 and more for the very rich. Demands for expensive household items, a deposit for a house, provision of furniture or a new motor car are not uncommon.

8. 7 British Gujaratis, dowry and social change

From the kind of evidence I have been able to collect, it is obvious that the custom of dowry and its oppressive monetisation has not declined among the British Gujarati Hindus. Hindus themselves may shun the English word 'dowry', as it has acquired strong negative associations in the public domain. However, among the Lohanas and Charottar Patidars, the institution of dowry does persist. The evidence also indicates that the bride's parents are under great pressure to provide expensive gifts, and this is likely to affect the young bride and her brothers and sisters. Personal observations confirm that Lohana families which lack economic resources to organise a 'good' wedding could find their daughters totally excluded from the prospects of getting married. However, the stigma associated with an unmarried daughter sitting at home is still sufficiently strong to induce parents to make every possible effort to arrange marriages for their daughters. In 1984, Pat Healy reported the suicide of three daughters in Britain who decided to take their lives rather than burden their mother with having to find husbands for them after their father, Balak Chand Adi, had left their home (Healy, 1984). Although not directly related to dowry, this illustrates the seriousness with which families view marriage as a crucial rite of passage. In the Patidar community, where a bride's parents have higher walls of hypergamy to climb, the degree of distress and humiliation can be very disturbing indeed, affecting not only the welfare of brides but also of other siblings, especially young girls. The kind of helplessness and despair that families may face certainly calls for proper research.

As Kalwant Bhopal (1997) noted in her recent investigation, women who have higher professional education can avoid marriages which require their families to provide a dowry. My own preliminary research indicates that social change influences the social organisation of marriages in South Asian communities. Among the Lohanas and Patels, several respondents have pointed out that some, but not all, young members of their community openly oppose the system of dowry as marriages of personal choice increase within the wider South Asian community and lead to inter-caste, inter-religious, inter-regional and inter-ethnic marriages. However, rules of endogamy continue to influence a vast number of marriages in all South Asian communities. Where parents provide gifts to their daughter and her husband, as well as members of the respective families, out of their own willingness to give, such acts may be perfectly acceptable. However, when the groom and his family begin to make unreasonable, unethical and extortionist demands for property and money, dowry transforms itself into an evil that must be eradicated.

Ultimately, dowry is an expression of unequal power between men and women. Does this inequality fully explain dowry and dowry murders in India and the persistence of dowry among South Asians in Britain? Modernisation and socio-economic changes which have transformed the profile of many communities have a crucial impact on the persistence of dowry. Better education, changes in gender relations and better opportunities for women to influence their own lives are essential pre-conditions for ending the oppressive and unjust aspects of the institution of dowry.

* This is a revised version of the paper produced for the Third Dowry Conference in London. I would especially like to thank Dr. Vibhuti Patel (Mumbai) for providing me with material on the question of dowry in India. I am also grateful to Kunj Kalyani (Wembley), Sudershna Brahmbhatt (Hemel Hempstead), Harshad Nanjiani (Toronto), Badr Dahya (London), Abdul Gani (Bristol), Meena Tanna (Bristol), Rajni Jobanputra (Bristol), Niranjana Desai (Harrow), Raj Kocher (Bristol), Ambalal Patel (Bristol), Chiman Patel (London), Mohanbhai Varambhia (London), Yogesh Patel (London) and the Bangladesh Association of Bristol for their helpful comments on marriages and dowry in different Hindu and Muslim communities in Britain.

Chapter 9

Dowry among Sikhs in Britain

Jagbir Jhutti

Amongst the Sikh community in India and Britain, the dowry given to a daughter is composed of two distinct parts: bridal gifts, which are normally referred to as *daj* (dowry), and affinal gifts, which are gifts for the groom and his family. These gifts, whether presented to the bride or to the groom and/or his family, are given by the bride's parents – even though Sikh religion preaches against this practice. When the religion was established, it was hoped that it would be free of Hindu social divisions concerning caste and Hindu customs such as *daj* (dowry) and *sati* (widow burning). The giving of dowry was one custom that the Sikh Gurus wanted abandoned. Guru Ram Das, for example, claimed that the best *daj* a father can give his daughter is the gift of the Lord's name, and that the display of gifts is false, vain and hypocritical. The Sikh *Rehat Maryada* (1971) states that a dowry should not be given, and the Namdhari Sikhs explicitly ban all dowries. However, the Sikh Gurus and the religious text have not succeeded in achieving a dowry-less society and most Sikh marriages are accompanied by a transfer of varying amounts of property from the bride's family to that of the groom. The practice of dowry giving has been maintained, if not reinforced, by the Sikh community in both India and Britain.

This chapter is based on fieldwork, which shows that various types of dowry and marriage-related expenses have become customary elements of the process of solemnising a marriage among British Sikhs today. While not explicitly emphasising that these customs lead to social problems and to dowry-related violence, the chapter examines to what extent British Sikhs, young and old, participate in dowry transfers at the time of marriage.

9.1 The dowry (*daj*) and changes in practice

The *daj* is compiled solely by the bride's parents and the gifts are normally of three types: clothes and personal accessories, jewellery and household goods. Items that most British-born Sikh brides receive may comprise the following:

(a) Clothes, shoes and handbags, which can be Western and/or Indian. The amount given is always an odd number. Western outfits, handbags and shoes for home and work, Indian outfits (shawls, *saris, salwar kamiz* and *lenghas*) for daily and occasional wear. Most are accompanied by Indian shoes and handbag, in plain or embroidered silk, which match each outfit.

(b) Cosmetics, perfume and jewellery. Gold and silver jewellery will be mainly from Indian jewellers. Artificial gold and silver jewellery may be bought from Indian jewellers or British shops and department stores.

(c) Household goods, such as kitchen utensils, pots and pans and cutlery. Typically two dinner and tea sets, one for everyday use and one for occasions. Bed linen and towels, furniture, such as a bed, cupboards, sofa, coffee and dining suite. Washing machine, television, video, stereo, vacuum cleaner, iron, kettle and hairdryer are standard items in the list.

Although new items have been added to the gifts given to the bride and groom since migration – a car, a house, deposit on a house or a lump sum of money, the major components have remained much the same. But there are some changes that reflect the bride's Western upbringing. For example, most parents give daughters fewer casual *salwar kamiz* suits for everyday use and fewer expensive *salwar kamiz* suits or *saris*, knowing that their daughters will not wear Asian clothes all the time. They are also aware that there is no point buying too many expensive clothes before the wedding because they will most probably go out of fashion, since clothes are usually bought months in advance of the wedding. And the daughter might prefer to buy new outfits for certain events, so as to be in fashion. The reduction in Asian clothes has been matched by an increase in the amount of Western clothes given, for both home and work. One young woman who married in 1989 told me:

Mum and dad gave me twenty-one suits; six *saris* and four shawls. I didn't get any English outfits. I bought them after my wedding. Since my wedding I have worn all my shawls, seven suits, and one *sari*. All the clothes that I haven't worn are in a suitcase, which is in the loft. I know I won't wear them because the styles have changed, but most importantly because I won't fit into them. When I go to India I will take them with me and give them to charity. When my sister got married in October 1996, my parents didn't give her many Indian clothes, most of the clothes she was given were British. A lot of my relatives, aware that their daughters are not going to wear Asian clothes all the time, are doing this now.

Another, who got married in 1995, told me:

I got eleven suits, ten *saris*, five shawls and fifteen English outfits. Six of the suits were for everyday wear, and the other five were for occasional wear. I told mum and dad that there was no point giving me a lot of Indian clothes because I wouldn't wear all of them. They didn't listen. I haven't worn all the Asian clothes that were given to me. It's most likely that I won't, because they are out of fashion now. I have worn all the English clothes they gave me.

A twenty-nine year old lawyer, who got married in 1990, told me:

When mum and dad were buying me clothes I told them not to buy too many Indian clothes because I knew I wouldn't wear them. I told them to get me English outfits for work and for home instead. At first they said 'no' but they eventually came round when my uncle spoke to them. My uncle, speaking from experience, told them that it was better to give me clothes that I wanted, and knew that I would wear. He told them how he had given his daughter a thirty-one item dowry, which only included Indian clothes, and how since she's been married she has only worn six suits, two shawls and not one *sari*. He also told my father how his daughter, when she was invited to a party or a wedding, didn't always wear the clothes that he had given her but bought new ones, because according to her, her clothes were out of fashion. Like all Asian women, my cousin wanted to be seen in the latest designs, and when she's worn an outfit once it is unlikely that she will wear it again. No wonder the Asian clothing industry is doing so well. They gave me a fifty-one item dowry. It contains eleven *salwar kamiz* suits, five *saris*, five shawls, and thirty English outfits: fifteen of these were for work, and the other fifteen were to wear at home. I think my parents are glad that they listened to my uncle because they avoided wasting money. They only see me in an Indian outfit when I am invited to a party or a wedding, or when I visit, or have relatives over. They have also learnt how, when I have worn a suit once, I avoid wearing it again. Like most Asian women I don't want to be seen in the same suit twice. After the first six months of marriage I had worn all my Indian clothes once, so I started buying new ones.

A father told me:

I didn't want to give my daughter English clothes, but my wife told me that if we spent a thousand pounds or more on Asian clothes the money would go to waste because our daughter wouldn't wear them, which is true. I eventually agreed, and most of the clothes she took with her were English. She only took eleven *salwar kamiz* suits, five *saris*, ten shawls, and twenty-five English outfits, i.e. trousers, jeans, dresses, skirts and blouses. She's worn everything we gave her.

One mother said:

There is no point giving a daughter a lot of Asian clothes because she won't wear them. They may be carried away by the moment wanting this and that, but at the end of the day they will not wear everything. They are more likely to wear English clothes than Asian.

Another mother told me:

When I was married, I was given eleven suits, six *saris* and four shawls. I never had a say in what I was given. My mother chose all my clothes. I had worn everything that I was given within the first year, and I didn't buy any new clothes that year. I wore an outfit on several different occasions. I didn't wear a suit once and then never again, like my daughters. When I was buying clothes for my daughters, I got them what they wanted, Indian and English. Since they have been married, they have only worn a few of the Asian outfits that they were given, and the outfits they have worn they have only worn once. When I asked them why they were buying new clothes and not wearing the clothes that I had given them, they told me that they were out of fashion. When I hear of relatives buying their daughters a lot of Asian clothes I want to say something, but my husband tells me to watch and listen, and not say anything. I don't say anything because people will think that I am jealous, or that I don't want the best for their daughters.

So although less Asian outfits are included, more clothes are given in all, mainly of Western style. There has also been an escalation in the amount of real and artificial gold and silver jewellery given to a daughter and many parents also give Western costume jewellery. The amount of household gifts has also increased. However, while household gifts were accepted by the second and third generation in the late 1980s, these are less welcome today. As one girl put it:

> What is the point of giving your daughter a cooker, a washing machine, television, microwave etc. when she is going to live with her in-laws? Most people have all these things.

This is true, and most of the time a daughter's gifts are put away in the loft, an empty room or even a warehouse until she and her husband move into their own house. Although most parents believe that a daughter should receive household gifts even if she is living with her in-laws, there are some second and third-generation Sikhs in Britain who believe that such gifts are only appropriate if the daughter is moving into her own home immediately. Otherwise, parents should give their daughter cash, which she can use when she moves out of her in-law's home. However, most parents are reluctant to do this because they feel that they have to give the traditional three-component dowry even if their daughter is going to be living with her in-laws, lest people ridicule them for not giving their daughter a proper dowry. One young woman, who was married in April 1995, told me:

> My dowry included everything that I would need to set up my own home. I received a stereo, television, gas cooker, washing machine, tumbler dryer, food blender, electric kettle and a vacuum cleaner.
>
> I received three different sets of bed linen; two duvets and four pillows; a bed,bedroom cupboards and a dressing table. I also got a laundry basket and three complete towel sets.
>
> I also received a dining table; a three-piece sofa, coffee table and lamp. For the kitchen I got everything: a dining and a tea set, and

cutlery for everyday use; a dinner and a tea set, and cutlery to use when entertaining guests. Pots and pans, table mats, serving bowls, bread bin, knife set and wine glasses. I haven't used anything because I live with my in-laws. Most of the stuff is in the spare room.

Another bride of 1989 told me:

When I got married my parents gave me all sorts of household goods, but I didn't get to use most of them until 1993 when me and my husband bought our own house. By then most of the things were out of date, and if they didn't work they were not covered by the guarantee so we had to buy replacements. Mum and dad wasted a lot of money.

Many parents realise that there is no point in giving a daughter a large dowry of household goods, such as a television, washing machine and sofa, if she is going to be living with her in-laws, and that the smaller items, such as toaster, iron and food processor may be given by friends and relatives as wedding presents, so would be duplicated. One father told me:

I got my daughter a microwave, washing machine and a stereo. Her uncle, my brother, and her mum's best friend also got her a stereo each. They both returned theirs and bought her something else.

Nonetheless, only a small minority of parents are opting to give their daughters money instead of household items, but even then they do add a few household items. One father, who gave money, explained why he did this:

I thought there was no point giving my daughter a lot of things for the house when she was going to be living with her in-laws. She's been married for three years and is still living with her in-laws. If I had bought her things for a house they would have gone to waste, so I gave her money instead. I also gave her a television, video and stereo for her bedroom. The money that I gave her is in a building society account, which she and her husband can use to buy things when they get a house of their own. If they don't buy a house of their own then they can use it however they want to.

Another father, a factory owner, whose daughter was setting up home, told me:

I gave my daughter cash, and didn't buy her any furniture, or electrical equipment because I thought it would be better if she and her husband worked together to set up their home. Decorating and buying together for their new home brought them closer.

The practice of giving a daughter only cash, jewellery and clothes seems to have started in the early 1990s, and is mainly confined to the middle and upper class Sikh families. It is less common among the less wealthy parents, who want people to see what they have given their daughter. A cheque will not suffice – people from the lower castes and classes evidently want to see what has been given. To say that one has given ten thousand pounds to a daughter might be dismissed as of no account, whereas spending this sum on a room full of gifts will generate admiration for the family and praise that, 'so and so gave his daughter such a large dowry and she is so lucky to have such a generous father'. There is still some suspicion about parents who give only money as *daj*, and most believe that it is better to give gifts than cash because they are visible and tangible. As one man, a factory worker, said to me:

A father may give his daughter a cheque on her wedding day, in front of his relatives, but he can take it back afterwards. You never know if the daughter really gets to keep the money that she has been given. At least if you give things you can't take them back because people expect to see them when they go and visit the couple.

However, one father who wanted the practice of giving money to become acceptable suggested:

Somebody should open a 'rent a dowry' business for parents who want to give a daughter cash but who feel the need to show that they have given gifts to avoid losing face within their family and community.

So the practices surrounding the giving of daj among British Sikhs today are in a state of flux and are being resolved in various ways. But as we will see below, alongside these changing traditions the expenses surrounding marriage are soaring.

9.2 Affinal gifts and their escalation

Inflation is also evident concerning another set of gifts, not necessarily classified as 'dowry' but nonetheless adding to the overall expenses surrounding a marriage. The affinal gifts refer to two categories of presents assembled solely by the bride's parents: gifts for the groom, and gifts for the groom's immediate family. The affinal gifts may be given either with the dowry or separately and generally comprise:

- Gifts to the groom: Clothes, jewellery – a gold ring, necklace, bracelet, watch – cash, maybe a car, a house or a deposit on a house;

- Gifts to the father-in-law: Clothes, jewellery – normally a gold ring;

- Gifts to the mother-in-law: Clothes, i.e. *salwar kamiz* and shawls, jewellery – gold earrings, bracelet or ring, or a gold ornament set;

- Gifts to the groom's siblings: Clothes and jewellery, such as a ring, necklace, bracelet or earrings. Gifts, normally clothes, are also given to the partners and children of the groom's siblings.

Since migration, there has been an improvement, qualitatively and quantitatively, in the affinal gifts which accompany the dowry. What is given to the groom and his family has both increased and improved in quality. Today the majority of families try to give items of gold to the groom's kin, although this was not the practice in the past. For example, fathers-in-law are given a suit and a gold ring, mothers-in-law receive one or more *salwar kamiz*, a gold ring, gold earrings or a set of gold ornaments. If gold items are not given to the groom's kin, they are definitely given to the groom. While in the past gifts were given only to the groom and his parents, today they are also given to the groom's brothers and sisters. If the groom's siblings are married, then their partners and children also receive gifts. If people are wealthy and want to show off, these too may be items of gold. In other instances parents may give gold because they have been forced to do so by the groom's parents, who want people to see that they are respected by the new wife's family. Parents of girls would never contemplate withholding such gifts, or gifts to their daughter, even if they were told that they were not wanted by the groom's family, because they are aware that there are unspoken expectations about gift-giving with which they have to comply.

Thus the structure of the dowry, comprising gifts to the bride, groom and the groom's family, has not changed over time, but has increased qualitatively and quantitatively since migration. This is an outcome of the emergence since migration of a class system based on wealth, within the general caste system. The increasing prosperity of Sikh families and the entry of women into waged labour is reflected in dowries which proclaim the family's class status and the daughter's economic position. There are dowries which are, according to Bhachu (1993: 107-108):

> Sloane Rangerish in their interpretation – reflecting the exclusive 'London SW 1, 3, 5/ Knightsbridge/Sloane Square' locale consumption patterns of some of the high earning and professional brides, just as there are prestigious 'Designer ethnic/ European' *daajs*, the middle/ lower class 'Oxford Street Marks and Spencerish/mass produced-departmental store' types, working class 'London East Ender' types...

The escalation in dowry is clearly an outcome of increasing competition amongst Sikhs to out-do relatives and friends. This has been exacerbated by the growing prosperity of most Sikh families, the easy accessibility to loans and, importantly, women's entry into the waged labour market, which has allowed them to play a more central role in the accumulation of their dowry, and on which we now focus.

9.3 The role of brides in assembling the dowry

One solicitor bride is typical. She has worked for a year and purchased personal accessories such as make-up, handbags, shoes, coats and jewellery for her dowry. She brought with her several prestigious consumer items such as a Royal Doulton dinner and tea set and Edinburgh Crystal ware. She also bought less expensive things, such as an iron and ironing board, pressure cooker, ornaments and two lamps. As well as paying for some of the things she had selected, her parents bought her furniture and household items: a dishwasher, cooker and washing machine, six gold ornament sets and clothes. She received twenty sets of English clothes and twenty-one Indian outfits, including six silk *saris*, five shawls and eleven *salwar kamiz* suits. The bride's father is a doctor and her mother a housewife.

Another bride, a teacher, received a thirty-one item dowry: eleven English outfits, ten *salwar kamiz* suits, five *saris* and five shawls. She also received everything she would need to furnish the new home her husband had bought before the wedding, where they would live on their own: dining suite, sofa suite, coffee tables, two double beds, washing machine, cooker and refrigerator. She did not spend her money buying clothes or household items for her dowry but instead bought a new car for herself, even though her parents were prepared to buy it for her. Her family is very successful in business, running three factories.

Another bride, a nurse, used her wages to buy some of her clothes, Western and Asian, personal accessories such as make-up, artificial jewellery, and her bed linen. Everything else was bought by her parents, who both work in a factory. One bride, a factory worker, bought herself a basic twenty-one item dowry comprising nine *salwar kamiz* suits, five *saris*, two shawls and five English outfits.

One informant, who was unemployed before her marriage, told me that her dowry consisted of thirty-one items: nine silk *saris*, ten *salwar kamiz* suits, two shawls, two dressing gowns, two nighties, four English outfits, and two gold jewellery sets. She also received a few personal accessories like shoes and handbags, a sewing machine, refrigerator, television and music centre. Everything was bought for her by her parents, who own a newsagent. She used her unemployment benefit to buy her cosmetics.

From my research it appears likely that a woman who is unemployed will use her unemployment benefit to buy things for her dowry. The dowry of an unemployed or low-paid bride tends to be smaller, and sometimes of a poorer quality, particularly if the family is not wealthy. But if the family is fairly well-off, the dowry may still be large and of good quality.

Whether parents are contributing to the dowry, or paying for the bulk of it, they try to make it impressive, whether they are wealthy or not. Thus, a bride who does not earn much, or who has not earned in her own right before her marriage, can still expect a basic eleven or twenty-one item dowry, whereas dowries of earning brides will be far more elaborate. These are characterised by the inclusion not only of higher-quality garments and personal accessories but also of a wide range of consumer durables that the brides may have purchased from their own earnings, and which they themselves are likely to utilise and control. The size and quality of a dowry depends on the family's financial situation and also upon whether the bride is working and can buy things for her dowry.

Is the property accumulated by a bride through her own earning power really 'dowry'? The answer is 'yes', since most brides would claim that

'Mum and dad bought me this'. If a daughter said that she bought her own dowry, people would look down on the family for not buying her things. As one girl put it: 'People will gossip, so it is better to say mum and dad bought everything'. The family's status within the wider family is thus raised. Most fathers will at some time before the marriage pay for all or some of the items the bride bought herself, because parents do not want relatives, friends or the groom's family to think that the bride had to finance her own dowry. There is fear that people will ridicule and embarrass the family by calling them 'cheapskates'. One father told me how his sister talked about him to relatives when she learnt that her niece had bought many items for her dowry, and that her father had not paid her back:

> One day when we had visitors over I heard my sister talking to a colleague of mine from work. At first everything she said was good, but then all of a sudden she started criticising me for not buying my daughter her dowry. She finished her conversation by saying something like: 'He's been in England for thirty years and he couldn't even buy his daughter the things she wanted. She had to buy them herself. He should be ashamed of himself'. How could my own sister have said such a thing?

So parents do not use their daughter's money, nor do they like their daughter spending her money on her dowry, lest it lay them open to criticism. Instead, as Catherine Ballard (1978: 190) confirmed earlier, 'parents take pride in ensuring that there are no withdrawals recorded in the book for the months preceding the marriage, so that the daughter's husband's family can see that she has not been asked to play any part in financing it herself'. One father told me:

> My daughter works in a bank and earns a lot of money, but she doesn't save. If her future in-laws were to ask for her bank book they would be horrified. They would probably think that I have taken her money from her to buy things for myself, for they will see my recently bought new house and P registration car and her empty bank book, and their minds will begin calculating. My daughter says she's collecting things for her dowry, but I keep telling her to save. She doesn't listen and understand why I'm worried. She's bought some household goods and bed linen, but the rest of the money has been

spent on clothes and make-up which she is wearing now – so how can she say that she is collecting things for her dowry – she can't take used things with her when she gets married. That's not right. I don't want her in-laws to think that I have used her money to buy things for her dowry. I have now taken her cash card and credit cards off her in the hope that this will stop her spending money. What I have done may seem cruel, but it was the only way that I could think of getting some money into her account before she gets married next year. If I was rich I wouldn't have to worry because I could have put money in, but because I'm not, I can't.

Such examples indicate that when young women assemble their own dowries this creates new problems, which families have to learn to handle. While this can create tension in the natal family of the bride-to-be, much more serious are the changing forms of interaction between bride-giving and bride-receiving families.

9.4 The expectations of giving

Sikhs claim that the parents of the bride give what they wish to, and that they decide the amount given provisionally before they begin searching for a 'suitable' boy. Several things are taken into consideration: prominently the bride's father's occupation, the number of brothers and sisters in the family, and the daughter's expectations. However, to avoid the embarrassment of being told what to give and how much to give, many parents plan from the start to give their daughter a large dowry and substantial gifts to the groom and his family, irrespective of their socio-economic position. Any changes in the dowry, once negotiations have started, are normally caused by the bride's parents promising to give more to entice a particular boy to marry their daughter, or the boy's family asking for more gifts to be given to the bride, the groom and his family.

It is clear that in Britain, far from taking responsibility for reducing the dowry burden, most men and their families add to their wife's parents' burden by ruthlessly exploiting them for all they can. There are exceptions, of course, but a general picture is emerging of families of men getting what they want from the bride's family. Some drop hints, others demand that the bride brings a large dowry with her, or that the dowry should contain specific items for herself, the groom and his family. It is also noteworthy that in whereas the past prospective grooms, whatever their occupation, were not allowed (or if allowed, did not volunteer) an opinion of what they wanted from their wife's parents, today grooms actively participate in all areas of the marriage negotiations. Thus, if parents of the groom-to-be are demanding that certain items be included in the dowry, or gifts given to the groom, then the son might tell his parents what he wanted, and his parents would include that in their demands. Or if his parents are not making any demands, he might tell the girl, who will then inform her parents.

While the boy's parents can make outright demands, it is more usual for hints to be dropped by the parents and their son. Although in some instances the boy's family may have been joking, the girl's parents always feel obliged to take such jokes seriously, as an indirect message about what the groom's family wants. As one father said:

> We started negotiations with a family, who we thought may be suitable for our daughter. They were very modern, and after the girl viewing the boy would phone our daughter even though we had not said yes to the match. My daughter would tell me and her mother what they talked about. In his sixth phone call he told my daughter about his friend's wedding. He even described the dowry his friend's wife received and the gifts that his friend received. He joked to my daughter that his friend did very well out of the marriage, and how marriage was a good way of getting the things that you wanted without spending your own money. My daughter thought that he was dropping hints that he wanted gifts like the ones his friend got, and that he was trying to find out whether we would give such gifts. He may not have been serious and may have been joking but this scared us all, and since we hadn't agreed on the marriage we didn't pursue the family any more.

Many parents of girls believe that families should listen carefully to what the boy and his family say during negotiations and after the engagement, for what a family says may contain coded information about what kind of marriage they want, what they want in the dowry, or the gifts to the groom and his family.

Such demands or jokes usually surface after the engagement ceremony has taken place and the girl's family has no easy way out. Parents of girls in such situations often feel that they have no alternative but to give in to such pressures, because a decision to break off the engagement could endanger the future chances of their daughter finding a suitable husband. On the other hand, a decision to go through with the engagement can put a daughter's happiness at risk, for the family may open themselves up to further demands. Yet most parents will opt for a negative relationship rather than being dishonoured by breaking off the engagement. They will try to fulfill the demands because they do not want the boy's family to pull out of the negotiations lest it become gossip that the girl and her family were to blame for the break-up, even though this was not true. Such gossip will impair her future chances of finding someone suitable because it can sully her reputation. Such talk will also ruin the family's status (*izzat*). So, by putting up with such more or less hidden demands, people maintain a respectable front to the outside world – an important matter to many Asian families. The same applies when demands start after the marriage. Parents will tend to tell their daughter to put up with them while they try to fulfill them, for divorce is still viewed as a stigma which affects the whole family, and ruins the chances of younger brothers and sisters finding suitable partners. However, sometimes wives do leave. For example, as one told me:

I had trouble with my feelings for my husband because he and his family had started demanding things from my parents after our engagement. Mum and dad wouldn't call off the marriage because we had had our engagement. Although I was angry I married him because mum and dad said that was the right thing to do, and because they believed that the demands would stop once we were married. They were wrong. Although I married him I still had some bad feeling towards him. These feelings flared up when he told me to ask my parents for money. Even though I refused he kept pestering me about it. The anger kept building up and eating away at the good feelings that I had forced myself to bring into the marriage. He never got violent with me when I refused, but his constant nagging was probably just as bad as if he was hitting me. After a couple of months I had no nice feelings for him, well, I felt nothing for him because all he was interested in was my parents' money, not me. I left him after being married to him for a year.

Gifts may range from a few hundred pounds to thousands, from utensils and jewellery to refrigerators, cars and deposits on homes, but it is clear that the decision is influenced by the expectations of the groom's family, and behind each transaction is the desire for social status and security for the daughter. Moreover, a dowry does not always obtain security for the daughter because the groom and his parents may make demands at a later date, especially if they think that the bride's parents are rich. The demands are made to the bride, who is expected to tell her parents what her husband and his family have asked for. Giving a large dowry and generous gifts to the groom and his family can thus expose parents to further demands which they may be unable to meet, or which force them into debt.

From my research it appears that demanding a dowry is a way for the groom and his family to improve their wealth and social position. Most importantly, however, it is a way to demonstrate to the wife and her family who is boss, and to keep them in their place. Where a dowry is demanded or expected, the groom's family has power, while the bride's family are vulnerable because they never know whether what they have given is enough. One girl, whose husband and family demanded money from her parents before they were married and afterwards, commented:

> I think he felt big when he did this because he knew that we had to do what he wanted. By doing this he put me and my family in our place. He knew he could get away with his demands, for I couldn't leave him because I had to think about my younger sister.

A university graduate told me:

> My cousins told me that before she got married her husband's family, including her husband, told her family what they wanted in her dowry. Her parents met all the requirements. They shouldn't have done this, but because they thought he was a good catch – he is an engineer – they did. I can't understand why her husband needed to ask my cousin to bring certain gifts with her when they can buy whatever they want because they are pretty wealthy, and they probably had everything they asked for. My only explanation is that some Asian men in today's society of equality feel the need to privately undermine their wife and her family in order to prove that they are the head of the household.

One might assume that the men who are most likely to demand a dowry today will be from poor backgrounds, so as to improve their standard of living. I found that men from wealthy backgrounds and highly educated men with well-paid jobs are also guilty. But it is difficult to ascertain whether grooms and their family do demand a dowry, and to what extent, because no family is prepared to admit that they demanded a dowry, or that a dowry was demanded from them.

9.5 Escalation of demands: Who is to blame?

The growing escalation in the dowry and its problems is normally blamed on the boy's family, but it is not that simple. Although the practice has become a burden for many families, who can spend a lifetime's savings on a daughter's marriage, it is clear that they, especially the mothers and daughters, play a part in promoting and maintaining the practice of dowry giving, and have made few efforts to eliminate it.

Parents of daughters, particularly those who are well-to-do, tend to be liberal in assembling large dowries for their daughters. They ignore the fact that they are creating problems for parents of lesser means and that they encourage the families of boys to expect large dowries from all parents, whatever their financial position – and all because they feel under pressure from the wider community.

Although fathers may be spending large amounts of money on the dowry, mothers are the real culprits for the escalation of the dowry problem. Women who are aware of the problems caused by dowry payments at the time of their own or a daughter's marriage, sometimes argue that the practice should be abolished, yet it is clear that most women do nothing to stop the practice when their son gets married. Mrs. Sandhu, who complained about having to give her daughter a dowry, tried to explain why families have to do so. Her explanation was typical:

> Giving a dowry is an old tradition. Family *izzat* demands that we give our daughters a dowry. It's expected. Asking for a dowry is wrong, but if someone doesn't ask for a dowry that doesn't mean you don't give one.

Another mother told me:

> When our daughter got married we struggled to give her the wedding that she wanted. The dowry caused us the most trouble, especially in terms of expense. I think this would be true for most parents. Then again it shouldn't be a problem, because we have had a long time to save up for it – from when they are born. When my son got married

I told his wife's parents not go give us any gifts because I know that it can put a lot of pressure on a family. They didn't listen to me, and gave her a large dowry. They also gave us gifts, even though we had told them that we didn't want anything, but I have to say that it was right that they gave us gifts because if they hadn't, it would have reflected badly on them. Giving a dowry is important, and no parents would get their daughter married without a dowry.

Dowry-giving will clearly not be eradicated as long as parents are 're-formers' when they are getting their daughters married but 'conservatives' when their sons are married.

9.6 Dowry as a marker of status

The bride's parents are largely responsible for the escalation in dowry because most give over-large dowries because of increasing and conscious competition amongst Sikhs to out-do relatives and friends and raise their social status. The increasing prosperity of many Sikh families has exacerbated matters. Baljit, a banker, described how giving her a dowry allowed her family to make a public statement about their wealth and status. She told me:

My parents gave me a large dowry because their reputation was at stake. Within the last year (1993) we have had seven weddings. All of them were for girls. Every time there was a wedding, the dowry increased in size. Dad, not wanting to be outdone by other members of the family, gave me a dowry that was larger than the one that my uncle's daughter, Kiranjit, received. My dowry contained eight gold jewellery sets, four more than Kiranjit. I also received more furniture, clothes and cash than her. Out of all the dowries mine was the largest.

One young bride of 1992 said:

For my parents my dowry was a way of showing everybody how wealthy we are. It was meant to be noticed and discussed. Dad wanted this because he has always been called a 'cheapskate' by relatives, for he never gave me or my brother an eighteenth or twenty-first birthday party, or a party when we graduated. My dad doesn't believe in parties, he believes they are a waste of money because at the end of the day no one is ever satisfied – relatives always manage to find something to criticise, i.e. the hall was too small, the music was too loud, the meat was not cooked properly, or that the service was terrible. As a result, my parents channelled their money into our education. Everybody has ignored this expense, all they are concerned with is that my parents didn't host a single party. For my father my wedding, and the dowry, was a way to show the family that he is not a 'cheapskate'.

The Sikh community illustrates that, in the words of Hocart (1970: 129), '[t]he desire to emulate one's betters has been a most potent, perhaps the most potent, force in the diffusion of customs'. Relating such attitudes to snobbery, Hocart (1970: 129) writes that '[f]ew like to admit that they adopt new ways because they want to rise to a higher status or fear to drop to a lower one – in short, that they are snobs'. This fits my fieldwork on Sikhs. For example, a second-generation respondent told me:

When my dad was deciding what to give my sister for her dowry, he did not take into consideration what she wanted. Instead, he was more concerned with what my uncles had given their daughters. He wanted to outdo the dowries that they had given. He wanted people to think that he was more successful. He also gave her a large dowry because he didn't want people to think that he was a 'cheapskate'. Dad gave my sister a lot of gold jewellery, and he gave her husband a car. Nobody in the family has given a car before, and now everybody thinks that we are rich. What nobody knows is that dad took out a second mortgage on the house to pay for the extravagant dowry, and I am not married yet. Where will he get the money from when he has to get me married? I don't think the bank will give him another loan, and he's too proud to ask his brothers for money.

A dowry, then, does not have to be demanded by the groom's family; it may be assured and inflated by other mechanisms, such as the socio-economic status of the family concerned or the bride herself. A dowry also indicates the status of the groom, as well as of the bride's family. Many people believe that the more dowry you give, the better the groom must be, i.e. well-educated or from a good family.

Within the Sikh community, greed and status enhancement are also linked to the escalating consumerist culture, in which consumer items and designer labels are regarded as the prime symbols of status and wealth, which is why they feature prominently in most dowries. So a dowry bought from Indian shops may no longer be respectable, for people think that the family, especially the girl, has no taste or money. Even if a dowry bought from Soho Road in Birmingham is large, people may be unimpressed. What people will see is that the household items have been bought from Indian shops, so they assume that they were cheap, even though they may have cost the same as at a big department store. For example, Manjit, a banker, told her parents that she did not want household items from Indian shops on Soho Road, Birmingham, or Broadway in Southall in her dowry. Instead, she wanted her dowry to be one of 'class' which meant that things such as household items, cosmetics and personal accessories had to be brought from big department stores. Kiranjit, a twenty-six year old lawyer, told her parents that she wanted eight gold jewellery sets, at least twenty *salwar kamiz* suits, ten saris, plus twenty-one English outfits bought from department stores. She also wanted her make-up and perfume to be from Christian Dior, and her shoes from Bally and Roland Cartier. Her parents bought her everything apart from her make-up and shoes. They told me that they were not prepared to spend over two hundred pounds on just three pairs of shoes, and over five hundred pounds on cosmetics and perfumes, so she bought these herself.

Thus, what is important to girls and their families is that the dowry is seen to be expensive and of high quality so that relatives, but particularly the groom's family, will be impressed. If they are impressed this will raise the bride's status in her new family, and she will be viewed as having style and class. A dowry of quality and money is only achieved when items are bought from top quality department stores and parents make sure that relatives know where the goods were purchased.

Although many daughters view dowry-giving as an evil practice, they believe that they should receive one, and involve themselves in its accumulation. So much for the notion that the bride's family has no real control over what they give to their daughter because the groom's family dictates what they give. Sikh daughters in Britain are no longer passive, docile or powerless. Some demand a dowry, and stipulate what they want. And many get it. They promote the dowry system even though it may be causing their parents financial hardship. Girls demand a certain type of dowry because they want people to praise and respect them.

There are three ways that a daughter can get what she wants: She can sweet-talk her parents, she can demand the kind of dowry she wants, perhaps in front of certain relatives, or she can make her family feel guilty by giving them the 'silent treatment'. By whichever method, most parents are forced into doing what their daughter wants because they do not want relatives or friends to find out that she is unhappy because they will not give her the dowry she wants. This would ruin the family's *izzat*. One young woman told me:

> I asked my parents for certain designer items, like handbags, shoes and jewellery, but dad said I couldn't have them. I was very angry, and to get my own way, I refused to participate in the wedding preparations, in the normal day to day housework, and just to emphasise my points a little more, I gave them the silent treatment. People may think that I behaved like a spoilt brat, and I would agree, but what is important is that it got me what I wanted. If I had to have given them the silent treatment for longer, I would have. What was important to me was that my parents did what I wanted them to do, for once, since I had done everything that they had wanted me to do, especially have an arranged marriage. Winning was more important to me than reaching an understanding, but this may not be true for all girls; some may give way and reach a compromise with their parents.

Another explained:

> I told mum and dad what I wanted in my dowry in front of my uncles and aunts who had come over one evening to discuss the wedding preparations. I told my parents that I wanted a designer suit – Donna Karan, a Chanel handbag and earrings, and Christian Dior jewellery, particularly a pearl set (necklace, bracelet, earrings). Dad was about to say no because he knew that this would cost him a lot of money, but my uncle, my dad's eldest brother said that I could have whatever I wanted. Dad couldn't refuse then, for to do so would have opened him up to criticism from his family for not fulfilling his fatherly duties. Dad was angry with me, and he made that perfectly clear when everyone left, but he still got me what I wanted, although reluctantly. He knew that my uncles would expect to see the items that I had asked for in my dowry, and that if they were not given, they would view him badly.

So many girls have broken the tradition of being given a dowry without having a say in what they receive, and are actively engaged in its accumulation. When parents, who generally try to give their daughter a good dowry, find themselves under pressure from her to provide what she wants, they feel obliged to comply, lest the family's *izzat* be ruined. This is protected in the Sikh community by a rigid code of behaviour in relation to fulfilling a child's wishes, especially a daughter's on her marriage. My research shows that while many women say that dowry-giving is bad, most feel that it is acceptable for them to demand a dowry – but not for the men.

Some women demand certain gifts, because it allows them to feel in control and involved in the marriage preparations. Others want a better dowry than those given to relatives or friends, to enhance their status among their husband's and their own kinsfolk. As one young woman put it:

> Buying things from big department stores, and buying things with designer labels means you have 'class' and 'style'. When one of my aunts saw my dowry she was very impressed, and she now thinks that my dad is rich and that I am posh.

9.7 Ownership of the dowry

The increasing demands by women for a particular dowry, and their greater participation in accumulating their own dowry, possibly with their own wages, has resulted in greater 'individualism', so that property is now more clearly perceived to belong to the bride and not to the groom's family. This was expressed by Meena, a twenty-four year old credit controller, married in March 1994:

> My dowry included everything: jewellery, clothes, furniture, bed linen and kitchen ware. All of it is mine. It is me, and not my in-laws, who control it. Some in-laws take control of their daughter-in-law's dowry to find husbands for their daughters, or to meet their own interests, but that hasn't happened to me. I like my in-laws, but that doesn't mean that I will let them give my dowry away to their daughter. They can buy their daughter a dowry like my parents had to buy mine. To make sure that they didn't take control of my dowry, I, without the knowledge of my parents, husband and in-laws, gave a list of all the gifts that I received in my dowry to a solicitor before I

was married. I did this so that if me and my husband ever divorce, he can not claim that the dowry, especially the gold and the money, was given to him. People may think that I am selfish, and that this distrust and secrecy on my part was a bad start to a marriage, but all I can say is that I felt that I needed to protect what was mine. I have always believed that you have to look after number one, and that is what I have done.

One young solicitor said:

When I got married I was allowed to keep my jewellery and money. My jewellery is in a bank safe, which is in my name. My money is in a bank account, which is in my name. The other gifts that my parents had bought for me, and those that I had bought for myself, I control. I didn't have a problem with my mother-in-law taking everything because I live on my own with my husband.

A young doctor told me:

My husband and his family received gifts from my family, and I received a large dowry. I control most of the things, like the jewellery and the clothes that were given to me. Some of my gifts like the television, video, stereo and refrigerator have been used by my husband's family, but that doesn't matter because we live together. Nothing has been given away, and I know what is mine. If I ever moved out, I know that I can take my gifts with me.

A sales assistant faced the potential conflict between different expectations:

Before I got married, my parents told me that after my marriage I should give everything to my husband's parents. They said that this was a sign of respect, and that by doing this I would be treated nicely by my husband and his family. I did what I was told. I gave the keys to my trunk and suitcases, my jewellery and bank book to my mother-in-law. I was lucky for she didn't keep them. By letting me keep all my things my in-laws gained my respect. If my mother-in-law had kept my dowry I don't think that I would have respected her.

A young man, a pharmacist, who got married in 1995, told me:

My wife kept everything that her parents gave her. Mum and dad didn't use anything. Everything, apart from the bed, was put into storage. Since moving into our new home (October, 1996) we have taken everything out of storage.

Another young man, a factory worker, told me:

When I got married I moved into my own home straightaway. The dowry that my wife was given was used to furnish the house. She keeps all her jewellery and money. I don't think any in-laws confiscate their daughter-in-law's dowry. Why would anybody need to? Everybody has money.

A lot of my respondents, first, second and third generation in Britain, believed that if the groom's family is wealthy, the girl would surely keep her dowry under her control. Yet there is little to prevent a bride's in-laws from putting her dowry to whatever use they wish. Werbner (1990: 240) argued that in-laws do not confiscate their daughter-in-law's property in Britain due to the greater affluence of most immigrants, which means that the property rights of brides are respected, but this is not always the case. While most parents would not confiscate a daughter-in-law's dowry, there are some, no matter how wealthy they are, who would.

Although I have come across no incidence of dowries being confiscated by in-laws, I do believe that this does happen. Many respondents claimed that they had not heard of such instances, but we know from a number of court cases in Britain that there must be instances of Sikh in-laws confiscating their daughter-in-law's dowry. They have been kept well-hidden to protect the *izzat* of the family concerned, and the community as a whole. So although most respondents told me that the dowry belonged to the bride, and that she controlled it, how much control she has remains debatable.

The shift towards a notion of dowry as the bride's property is re-affirmed by the new practice, initiated by the women themselves, of registering their dowry with a solicitor. Women, mainly university graduates in high-flying jobs, believe that having purchase receipts or keeping dated photographs at home is not enough. They are aware that even if a camera prints the date on a photograph, the photographs can still be dismissed as proper evidence in a court of law, because it can be argued that the photographs were taken after the wedding and that the dating mechanism on the camera had been tampered with. Consequently, to register a dowry means entrusting photographs of the gifts that they and their parents had bought for their dowry with a solicitor before the marriage. If they did so after the marriage, the photographs could, in case of divorce, be dismissed as gifts from the husband and his family.

Daughters register their dowries in secret because most parents believe that doing so suggests that they do not have much faith in the marriage. While some parents may not know that their daughter has deposited a list and photographs of the things that they have given her, others do but play ignorant even though they may be glad about it.

Parents are peturbed about this new practice also because they fear that if the groom's family get to hear about it, they may call off the wedding. And if they hear about it after the marriage, they might treat the bride badly or even divorce her. The parents who acknowledge that they have registered their daughter's dowry with a solicitor seemed to suggest that they did so because they did not have much faith in their daughter making the marriage work.

Most parents do keep the receipts for everything they give to their daughters so that, if the couple ever divorce and there is a dispute over dowry, they could produce the receipts, especially credit card vouchers bearing their signature, as evidence that the dowry belongs to the woman for whom it was purchased. One father told me how he has a receipt for everything that he gave to his daughter, her husband's family and her husband in a bank safe. When asked to explain why, he gave me several reasons:

> It is important to keep all the receipts just in case something is faulty or there is a burglary. If you have the receipts then you can place an insurance claim for everything that was taken. I also kept everything just in case my daughter was ever divorced, but you don't tell people that is why you are keeping the receipts. Apart from the immediate family you shouldn't tell anyone that you have done this.

No matter what the reasoning behind the demands, whether by parents, girls or boys, it is clear that neither migration nor education has curbed the spread and escalation of dowry amongst the second and third generation of Sikhs in Britain.

Chapter 10

The legal context of dowry in Britain

Usha Sood

In English civil law, plaintiffs' claims in the context of dowry can arise from transfers of jewellery, monies and property under duress or through tradition, within the context of an arranged marriage in Britain. The action is normally for recovery of, or the value of dowry (*daj* or *burri*), jewellery, clothes, household effects, monetary gifts to the bride, the bride's wedding presents (*shagan* or *salaami*), cloth and clothing gifts to the bride, half of the wedding gifts, and monies paid by the plaintiff or her family under duress and/or undue influence, either at the time of the wedding or later on. Such actions may be within ancillary proceedings connected with a divorce or they may be free-standing civil actions for conversion.

10.1 Legal matrix
The practice of dowry and related concepts is well-recognised in English law by reference to the customary and/or legal rules in the country of origin. If the dowry contract is valid in the other country or jurisdiction, an English legal remedy can be sought which has to harmonise with the right according to its nature and extent as fixed by the foreign law, as held in the interesting case of *Phrantzes v. Argenti* [1960] 1 All ER 778, which involved a Greek woman. According to Poulter (1986: 42), who refers to this case, where the institution is perfectly lawful, as in Greece, 'such payments may be enforceable through the English courts in certain circumstances'.

In Indian law, however, dowry payments have been made illegal under the *Dowry Prohibition Act*, 1961 to ensure that dowry should in no possible manner pass into the hands of a husband and his family, making them unjust gainers, or to prevent unjust enrichment. Poulter (1986: 41) commented in this respect:

> Long-established anti-dowry legislation in India prohibits not only dowries payable to brides themselves but also any payment 'as consideration for the marriage', an expression wide enough to include those sums of money sometimes demanded by the husband's family which in reality constitute a form of 'bridegroom-price'.

Consequently, as Poulter (1986: 42) emphasised, '...no court would ever make an order for the payment of dowry where the foreign legal system in question actually prohibited such payments (as in the case of the Indian Dowry Prohibition Act)'. English courts have, however, recognised that ownership of such items is personal. In English law, the legal effect of a dowry is governed by *Samson v. Samson* [1960] 1 All ER 654, with ownership of items or monies bestowed passing individually to the bride or groom.

It is a recognised common law principle that monies had and received under economic compulsion are recoverable in a restitutionary action (*Maskell v. Horner* [1915] 3 KB 106 CA). Involuntary payments in themselves are recoverable according to *North Ocean Shipping Co v. Hyundai Construction Co, the Atlantic Baron* [1978] 3 All ER 1170, per Mocatta J (quoting from Isacs J in *Smith v. William Charlick Ltd* at p.1180):

> ...the only ground on which promise to repay could be implied is 'compulsion' [which] ...includes every species of duress or conduct analogous to duress, actual or threatened, exacted by or on behalf of the payee and applied to the person or the property or any right of the person who pays... Such compulsion is a legal wrong and the law provides a remedy by raising a fictional promise to repay.

If the plaintiff is arguing compulsion or duress, some factor(s) must exist 'which could in law constitute such coercion of the will as to vitiate consent' (*Pao On v. Lau Yiu Long* [1980] AC 614 PC). In determining whether there was coercion of will such that there was no true consent, it is material to inquire whether the person alleged to have been coerced did or did not protest; whether, at the time he was allegedly coerced into making the contract, he did or did not have an alternative course open to him as an adequate legal remedy, etc.

In terms of absence of choice, the interpretation is of a non-deliberate action by the plaintiff. There must be an 'intentional submission arising from the realisation that there is no other practical choice open to him' (*per* Lord Diplock in *Universe Tankships Inc. of Monrovia v. International Transport Works Federation* [1982] All ER 67 HL). The compulsion must deprive the promisor of *animus contrahendi*.

Any post-nuptial payments could also be set aside in equity for undue influence. The recent important case of *Barclays Bank plc v. O'Brien* [1993] 4 All ER 417 states that there are two classes:

> Class 1: Actual undue influence. For this the claimant must prove affirmatively that the wrongdoer exerted undue influence on the complainant to enter a particular transaction.
>
> Class 2: Presumed undue influence. Here the complainant only has to show relationship of trust and confidence giving rise to presumption of abuse of their relationship in procuring the complainant to enter into the impugned transaction. There is a need here to prove a confidential relationship; the burden then shifts to the wrongdoer to prove that the complainant entered the impugned transaction freely.

Class 2 includes a *de facto* relationship under which the complainant generally reposed trust and confidence in the wrongdoer. Categories currently include parents/children and husband/wife. This appears to cover any situation where a person who is in a position to dominate the will of another enters into a contact with him (probably including parents-in-law). Ballard (1978) focuses on the dominant role of the mother-in-law in Sikh marriages. After the decision of the House of Lords in *CIBC Mortgages plc v. Pitt* [1993] 4 All ER 433, there appears to be no need to show manifest disadvantage since it was held that '[a] claimant who proves actual undue influence is not under the further burden of proving that the transaction is manifestly disadvantageous: he is entitled as of right to get it set aside'. This may extend to cases of presumed undue influence.

In dowry cases, a presumption of undue influence would apply between parents-in-law and daughter-in-law, within the particular cultural context. It is also arguable that the situation would be covered by actual undue influence, particularly if the plaintiff could assert that she has shown on balance of probabilities the exertion of undue influence to provide any post-nuptial payments.

A gift from a wife to her husband must be given freely and voluntarily with full knowledge and understanding of the nature of the transaction, and without any pressure or the exercise of undue influence on the husband's part (Halsbury's *Laws of England,* Vol. 22, p. 1067, paras 664-665).

Even in cases pre-*Barclays Bank* and *CIBC Mortgages*, where the gift or commitment was of considerable value, the husband could without much difficulty be required to show that the transaction was fair and proper, although the burden of proving undue influence is on the asserter, here the wife. Earlier cases have also required that there be sufficient and independent explanation of the transaction and facts (details are found in Halsbury, as above).

It must be noted that the assent of a wife to the receipt by her husband of a capital sum belonging to her raises no presumption of gift. The contrary presumption is that the husband receives it as a trustee for his wife and the burden of proving a contrary intention lies upon him (Halsbury, Vol. 22, p. 1066, paras 662-663).

The relationship between husband and wife still has a recognised inequity: in *Barclays Bank plc v. O'Brien* it was held by Lord Browne-Wilkinson, at p. 422, paras g-h:

> Although the concept of the ignorant wife leaving all financial decisions to the husband is outmoded, the practice does not yet coincide with the ideal... in practice many wives are still subjected to and yield to undue influence by their husbands. Such wives can reasonably look to the law for some protection when their husbands have abused the trust and confidence reposed in them.

Other references in the same case are to treating married women more tenderly than others, a court of equity having more jealousy over dispositions by a wife to a husband, the 'invalidating tendency' of transactions between husband and wife, and the court recognising the opportunities which a wife's confidence in her husband gives him of unfairly or improperly procuring her to become surety (p. 424, paras b-f).

The court found an invalidating tendency because of (a) demonstration of trust regarding financial affairs in the husband and/or because (b) sexual and emotional ties between the parties can provide a ready weapon for undue influence: a wife's true wishes can easily be overborne because of her fear of destroying or damaging her relationship with her husband if she opposes his wishes (p. 424, paras g-h).

A wife who undertakes liability for her husband's debts (for example the father-in-law in the recent, unreported *Samra* case said the couple were liable for the loan) by undue influence has an equity to set that aside, enforceable against third parties (i.e., the father-in-law or perhaps the lender), as where the husband was acting as a third party's agent (*Barclays Bank plc*, at pp. 428-429) or the third party had actual or constructive notice of acts giving rise to her equity, as in *CIBC v. Pitt*, where despite undue influence, the husband had not acted as an agent. Lord Browne-Wilkinson in *Barclays Bank plc*, at p. 429, para f, also noted that 'the informality of business dealings between spouses raises a substantial risk that the husband has not accurately stated to the wife the nature of the liability she in undertaking...'. At p. 431, His Lordship extended that principle to other relationships where the payee reposes trust and confidence in the principal debtor in relation to his financial affairs. Where actual undue influence is shown, there is no need to show manifest disadvantage since *CIBC Mortgages*. However, there is no need to prove this in setting aside the transaction between the plaintiff and the agent or principal 'extorter', whether in cases of actual or presumed undue influence. The plaintiff here is simply requiring the return of her monies, upon proof of actual or presumed undue influence.

10.2 The social and cultural matrix

Writing about arranged marriages within British Asian families, Ballard (1978) emphasises the use of a matchmaker (*bachola* or *vachola*) and the dominant role of the parents in Sikh marriages. Preliminary information is sought and provided: photographs and criteria such as appearance, age, caste and, increasingly, status and education are considered. Should anything unacceptable be discovered, the marriage may be discreetly called off. According to Ballard, it is not thought proper that there should be too short an interval between the engagement and the marriage, for it might look as though the bride's family were anxious to be rid of her.

Also it is usual for a bride who has been working to save her wages and take her bank book as part of her dowry. A bride's parents feel proud that the in-laws can see that the bride has not been asked to make any contribution to financing the marriage. Having her own bank book strengthens the position of a new bride in her husband's household. The money could be used as a deposit on a house for herself and her husband if she should find living with her parents-in-law intolerable in the future. Ballard reported, in 1978, that the usual sum given at the engagement was £11 or £21, but that it can be much more.

Soon after arrival, the bride will be expected to take an active part in domestic work. Ballard stressed that it is at this time that the almost expected tension with her mother-in-law tends to emerge and her lowly position in the pecking order becomes clear. The new bride must usually wait until she has a son of her own before she gains some bargaining power and can really begin to hold her own within the household. This leading early British study showed that nearly all brides initially had a difficult and frustrating time with their mothers-in-law and that surveillance by the mother-in-law is well-recognised. Difficulties in trying to leave a failing or failed marriage and lack of support from the husband are also identified.

10.3 Implications for legal practice in Britain

To summarise the current legal position under English law, four points can be made:

- The settled principle of English law is that the wife's property is her absolute property, in reliance on *Samson v. Samson*. Her dowry, if retained, is recoverable (excluding household items removed).

- Further, any attempt to argue that there was prior or later agreement by the plaintiff or her father to finance a wedding loan is denied, and in any event would be void and illegal in the light of the widened definition of dowry prohibitions in Indian law.

- Financial pressure on the plaintiff to coerce her or any person related to her to meet any unlawful demand of money or goods constitutes a criminal offence or at least unenforceable and unconscionable attempts.

- Alternatively under English law, the plaintiff is also entitled to the return of monies had and received under duress and undue influence. *Barclays Bank plc v. O'Brien* recognises the reasonable need of wives to rely on the law's protection because of the presumption or reality of undue influence by the husband or by other persons in a dominant role where the husband might be an agent or acting in concert.

Regarding the scale of the dowry problem in the various South Asian communities, the first thing to note is that there are no published statistics on dowry abuse. Research in this area often finds a denial of the problem. However, those who work in the context of service support for Asian women or in specialist legal practices have no doubts about the escalation of the problem. My own practice has quadrupled this year with the publicity given to the 16 day hearing last year in the *Samra* case (judgement of 37 pages was given on 16th April, 1997) and the subsequent media attention to the claimant's success.

The problem relates to all South Asian community groups. Attempts to minimise the problem as one that can be resolved by the relevant community or according to the *shar'ia* law/religious courts in the Muslim community, for example, have not prevented the emergence of litigious battles.

In terms of addressing the cultural void in law through specialist pleadings, evidence and advocates, it must be noted that English courts do not rely on research literature or bland pronouncements from counsel, although judges (and lawyers) are now guided by the general information available on family customs in the Judicial Studies Board papers. These do not sufficiently inform the court, however, and it has been an effective method of information to provide a glossary of terms, including all the relevant rituals. Judges and opposing counsel who are not from an Asian background are significantly assisted by the explanation of terms such as *shagan* or *salaami* and by the identification of the hierarchical superiority of the groom's family vis-à-vis the bride's family and even the superior status of the mother-in-law in the extended traditional family.

The courts struggle with many of these concepts but recognise, in the words of Mr. Recorder Woodward in the unreported *Samra* case, that arranged marriages can '[result] in enmity, mistrust and fierce polarisation of family loyalty. The antipathy generated was almost palpable even within the courtroom and almost without exception, was to be discerned in the demeanour and reaction of the members of the two families throughout the hearing, both in and out of the witness box'. The judge in the Samra case was able to accept the familial hierarchical set-ups indicated above, understood that the bride's father could be made to replace

£1,100 of the bride's *shagan* (purse money) which had gone missing at the wedding and rejected the incredible assertion of dowry being for a loan (agreed at marriage negotiations). However, the same judge was unable to understand the adherence to tradition and to traditional marriage concepts by an educated South Asian woman living in Britain. While accepting that she did indeed hand over her jewellery to her parents-in-law, he assumed that this was for security, rather than custom. While each case turns on the judge's perception of the evidence, it is clear that there are difficulties in persuading Western judges of the difficult balance between independence and tradition, even with the assistance of a cultural expert giving evidence.

10.4 Choice of action

The *Samra* case shows that legal actions before English courts can be successful. Civil action against in-laws for conversion can be brought independently of matrimonial proceedings (but without the benefit of the £2,500 statutory charge exemption) and allow direct legal pressure to be exerted, although in-laws can also be made parties to ancillary relief proceedings or involved in the same.

Evidential issues will play a prominent role in such cases. Bare denials of a woman's claim are commonplace. The claimant's case is assisted by photographic, video and documentary evidence of the existence of the claimed property, and by certifiable valuation as evidence of its worth. Particularly useful in this context is the ostentatious custom of having the dowry items (*dahej* from the girl's side and *burri*, the jewellery and clothes given to the bride by the husband's family) videoed at their respective 'showing'. Useful evidence is also provided by filming the wedding rituals, including *chunni* (the first adornment of the bride in the clothes provided by her in-laws) and the showing of the bride's face (*muh dakhai*) after her arrival at the new home, which involve the bestowing of *shagans* and *salaami*. The knowledge required of community rituals is extensive. Brides are often given further *shagans* at the many first dinners at her own home and those of close friends and relatives, and obviously at relevant festivals, for example the Hindu *Karva Chauth* and the Diwali festival. The evidence of the mediator (*bachola* or, if a woman, *bacholi*) can assist in identifying exact arrangements, although strong links with either family can be a basis for an allegation of bias. Cultural reports should reveal clear rather than generic knowledge of the practices of settled and liberalised Asians, and stress those features in the case indicating strong reliance on tradition. The plaintiff's evidence needs to receive greater sensitivity. In the *Samra* case, attacks on the claimant's character were irrelevant to the claim, but were not excluded by the judge.

The South Asian communities in Britain need to be fully informed about extant legal sanctions, enforcement and the financial and emotional utility of contesting such claims. Some defendants have been left financially destitute by the award/settlement, or by the legal costs where the defence is privately funded, and are also humiliated by the public exhibition in open court of their defeat or settlement. The trail blazed by the *Samra* case offers confidence and knowledge to women with shared experiences – at least four of my cases have settled as a clear result of that important case.

Chapter 11

Practical steps towards eradicating dowry and bride-burning in India

Himendra Thakur

Since 1956, there have been a number of studies on dowry deaths, and many efforts, both at government level and by non-governmental organisations, to halt its spread. Yet the holocaust of dowry murders seems to be blazing harder every year. A quick review of my Preface to this book will recall the sense of horror at the practice of dowry-related violence and bride-burning. While we are convinced that India has the inherent strength to eradicate this evil, we fail to understand how a seat of ancient civilisations could fall into moral decadence of such magnitude.

The purpose of this chapter is to discuss practical steps towards complete eradication of dowry deaths, without compromise or reconciliation. Many people have helped me to formulate my ideas about a series of practical solutions to the key problem: how can we save the lives of tens of thousands of young women who are destined to die as victims of dowry-related murders in the next few years unless there is significant change? Who is the enemy? And what is the root of the problem? In the 20 years of my involvement in this issue, and after consulting many writers, political leaders, administrative officers, and social workers, I conclude that the problem is so deep-rooted and complex that it is impossible to extract an objective opinion from any of the involved parties.

11.1 The search for solutions

We organised international conferences and invited scholars, professionals and social workers to scrutinise the problem and suggest what might be done. A Six Point Programme to Eradicate Dowry and Bride-Burning in India was adopted at the First International Conference on Dowry and Bride-Burning in India, held at Harvard University in 1995. The Programme has since been revised and ratified at the Second and Third International Conferences, held at Harvard University and London University in 1996 and 1997 respectively. The Program is still under discussion and new ideas are being incorporated to make it effective, result-oriented and practical. The latest version of the Program is incorporated at the end of this article.

It seems certain that dowry-related violence and bride-burning will only stop if young women refuse to marry a man immediately he or his family asks for dowry. In India, most marriages are arranged after lengthy marriage negotiations. However, as soon as dowry is demanded, marriage negotiations should be terminated and the matter reported to a Dowry Prohibition Officer, because asking for dowry should be treated as a violation of the *Dowry Prohibition Act*. If, instead, dowry is not initially demanded, the marriage negotiations succeed, and a wedding takes place without dowry, and dowry is claimed later, the marriage must immediately be declared null and void and the bride should leave her marital home for her own safety. In the dowry-infested areas of India, and now also among Asians in Britain and elsewhere, it is common practice for a man to marry without making an explicit demand for dowry before the wedding, but his family may demand dowry after the wedding, at the time of the birth of a baby, for instance. In such cases, the marriage should stand dissolved at once. There must not be any reconciliation. The aura of reconciliation places the life of the bride in grave danger, as exemplified by the tragic case of Vimla Devi in 1995 (see Banerjee, 1995) and many others.

People who advise a young wife in that situation to remain in the house must take full responsibility if she is killed or maimed. It must not be forgotten that what we are handling here is murder, culpable homicide. There is a high risk that an innocent life is about to be terminated. Such a crisis must be handled with the urgency appropriate in a battlefield.

However, about ten million marriages take place in India every year, and to communicate with all the young brides would be impossible. Moreover, when a young woman is dreaming of married life, it is difficult to make her imagine a dangerous future, particularly when her parents are promoting the relationship. However, communication with the endangered future brides now assumes huge importance. We must have a plethora of stories, novels, dramas, movies, music, non-fictional statistics, newspaper advertisements and all other vehicles of mass communication to convince such brides that, instead of the option to marry with dowry and die, it is far better to remain unmarried and alive.

This solution may appear to be astute and candid, but it will create a scenario which will be considered by many as another problem: a large number of unmarried women in the society will scarcely be seen as desirable. In addition to the religious taboo against unmarried women, there is a popular but quite unwarranted belief in India that women must marry for financial security, and that an unmarried woman is financially insecure. To oppose such powerful notions, it will again be necessary to run an extensive mass communication drive to convince the parents of daughters that if they invest the dowry money in giving the young woman an education, so that she may qualify for a job that ensures her sustenance and maybe even helps the family, she need not marry for the illusion of so-called financial security. A marriage contracted by paying dowry, with an outstanding amount continually hanging over the bride's head like the sword of Damocles, does not give young women financial security. On the contrary, this is the most insecure future a father can give his daughter.

We are aware that in areas of India where the custom prevails, there will not be much social support for a bride (or her parents) who quits her husband's home because of new dowry demands. In many cases, the parents are afraid to take their daughters back, because they may not even get police protection if there are repercussions from the ex-husband's family. This was exemplified by the death of Sangeeta Goel in 1994 in Kanpur, discussed at both Dowry Conferences in Harvard.

Social apathy towards the bride's family is so strong that parents in the dowry-infested parts of India now try to abort the female foetus, as revealed in America by the CBS '60 Minutes' broadcast of 1993. In view of the social apathy, even if one builds shelters for such brides in these areas, it will be difficult to get police protection from attacks by hooligans, because police officers administrative officers, the custodians of law and justice, will not be opposed to dowry.

When parents cannot continue the education and training of unmarried daughters who refused to marry because of dowry, training centres should be opened to teach job-oriented skills. Such training centres for unmarried women can also house the mutual support groups which will work their way into the social acceptance of independent living, as discussed in section 11.2 below.

There is a widespread view that Hindu scriptural traditions underwrite dowry transactions. Our research so far shows that this is not correct. It will be necessary to publicise interpretations of Hindu scriptures which do not underwrite dowry. Certainly, the murder of innocent brides could not be justified by reference to Hindu tradition, least of all Vedic authorities. Further study, discussions and research into the roots of the problem and possible remedial measures should certainly be carried out. We cannot re-write the ancient scriptures, but we can search for their correct interpretation and think about their proper application in today's world.

Long-term solutions to the problems of dowry must basically be directed at changing attitudes towards women in India. Extensive educational reforms will be a starting point for a long-term plan. The people in areas of India where dowry and bride-burning are practised, having created a degenerate interpretation of Hindu scriptures and traditions to suit their appalling practice, require re-education.

On the legal front, the *Dowry Prohibition Act* of 1961, amended so frequently during the 1980s, must be further revised to include a clear stipulation that, as soon as dowry is demanded, the crime is committed. We are glad to note that efforts to move the Government of India towards further legal reform are now partially successful, as evidenced by a set of 'Recommendations to check dowry-related crimes', recently issued by the National Commission for Women (NCW), a Government body. It is encouraging that the NCW and its chairperson, Mrs. Mohini Giri, have emphasised the legal approach to control the crime and ask for more severe punishment for accepting dowry, and for exemption from punishment for the dowry giver. I support this measure and would add that the very act of demanding dowry should be made punishable still more stringently, even before the dowry is accepted.

A law can be punitive, reformative or preventive. The effect of a punitive law like the present Indian anti-dowry law, however, is no more than deterrent. If the society does not change, enforcement of any law becomes ineffectual: punitive laws merely induce offenders to sweep the crime under the rug, and the job of a Dowry Prohibition Officer becomes an uphill task. Significantly, NCW also recommends that these officers, already provided for in the amended 1961 Act, should become activated. Without minimising the need of strengthening the *Dowry Prohibition Act*, we have suggested a 'reformative' law in item 2(a) of our Programme below to safeguard a daughter's inheritance rights, which will ultimately replace any need for her to have a dowry. We have also suggested a 'preventive' law in 2(b) of our Programme below, to declare a marriage null and void as soon as dowry is demanded or claimed.

Every law has its loop-holes. The stronger the law, the greater the scope for its misuse. Although we agree with NCW that the *Dowry Prohibition Act* should be strengthened, we are concerned about the misuse of the law, which may bring suffering to innocent people. Right now, as we understand, an accused under the Act is presumed guilty, and the burden is on the accused to prove his or her innocence. Lack of witnesses and of evidence in bride-burning cases have forced the law makers to take this strict position, but this may also open the door for travesty of justice. In a democratic country, there may be a popular outcry against the law if a large number of innocent persons are punished, and the legal approach may backfire. If so, other anti-dowry measures may also suffer a reversal, which may be harmful to dowry victims. We appeal to the law-makers to take all necessary precautions while implementing stronger laws.

To reinforce the legal approach, we also need reforms to help change the social environment, so that the people will support the enforcement of the anti-dowry laws. Suggested steps are tabulated under 'Long-Term Plans' in the Program. The approach is to develop awareness against the evil of dowry and bride-burning by organising mutual support groups like 'Students Against Dowry' (which has existed at SOAS, University of London since 1995) and 'Parents Against Dowry', by holding group discussions, meetings, interviews, seminars and conferences, by promoting anti-dowry ideology through drama, music, movies, radio and television shows, books, periodicals, journals, handbills and other media, and by promoting research to identify and diagnose the dowry problem in India.

The purpose of the research will be to recommend legal, economic, psychological, spiritual and social remedies.

Funding for both long-term and immediate solutions is a real hurdle. The project is so huge that it may intimidate us. But we have to start somewhere. The world is full of good people, ready to carry the message of goodwill and protection of basic rights all over the world. There are immediate remedies and there are long-term solutions. I turn now to immediate measures in our attempts to save innocent women from a cruel death.

11.2 Immediate life-saving mechanisms

The plans for social and national reform, as tabulated under the category of 'Long Term Plan', are essential to build a strong foundation for future protection against dowry-related violence, but will not be helpful as an immediate step to save the lives of victims. Law can punish a criminal after the death of a victim but it cannot save the victim's life. Dowry Prohibition Officers cannot guard every kitchen in town. Every 21 minutes, a bride is killed or maimed somewhere in India. If we cannot find a direct way to save the victims, all efforts will be worthless.

The only way to save dowry victims will be to provide them with a sanctuary where they can flee before it is too late. It is the only way to ensure immediate safety. A father may advise his daughter to wait six months, or a shelter officer may send a victim of dowry-related violence back to her tormentor to uphold the popular Indian tradition of 'saving the family name'. We strongly feel, however, that a 'family' which demands dowry is not a family.

Unfortunately, we know well that in most crisis situations parents do not want to take their daughter back. The only alternative for her may be to move to a shelter, but she may be unable to overcome the mental barrier. Shelters are perceived as places for destitute women, and most brides cannot imagine themselves in that position, given their socio-economic circumstances and their expectations of a bright future. Moreover, most of the existing shelters are unpleasant places. Indeed, during the first International Conference on Dowry in Harvard, Attorneys Rani Jethmalani and Subhadra Chaturvedi remarked that many a bride would prefer to die at the hands of her in-laws rather than move to a shelter.

To provide a life-saving mechanism, we must build dignified, professional institutes for job-oriented training and respectable and safe accommodation where victims can qualify for a job and an independent career, if they need it. This is item 1(a) of the 'Programme'. To avoid the stigma attached to shelters in India, the institute should be called a 'Job Centre for Dowry Victims (abbreviated 'Job Centre' or 'Centre') and operated by a dedicated 'Head Mother' who, with the support of her trained associates, will create a family atmosphere for dowry victims.

The success of such Centres will largely depend upon its management and the 'Head Mother'. With appropriate opportunity and encouragement, educated, mature women can be found who are willing to dedicate their lives in this campaign of love and compassion. India is an ancient civilisation imbued with the positive wisdoms of trust, faith and love, so we need not despair. Under the leadership of a dedicated woman, we will see a group of inspired volunteers helping their less fortunate sisters with the re-discovery of love and compassion.

Although we are trying to outline some aspects of running such Centres in this article, they will finally be operated with the help of a written, well-documented Operation Manual, to be drafted by an Operations Committee of professionals – attorneys, medical doctors, psychologists, administrative officers, university scholars, spiritual leaders, social workers, Centre operators and volunteers. International organisations will be invited to monitor the operation of such Centres. The Operations Committee will revise and update the Operation Manual periodically to incorporate new experiences.

A crucial aspect of the Centre will be the physical safety of the victims. They will need protection from the ex-husbands or family members. Dependable security guards will be needed. The building should be designed as a high-rise block of up to twelve floors, with Gurkha security guards at the first floor and living quarters for the victims above, since Gurkha soldiers worship the Mother Goddess and have a reputation for respecting women. For the purpose of security, the building should have its own electricity generator, water treatment and water supply, cold storage for food supply, space for physical exercise, recreational facilities and shops, so that the need for going out is minimised. This will further reduce the possibility of physical attacks from ex-husbands' families.

It is common for many victims to arrive at the Centre in a confused state of mind and some may bear signs of physical abuse. It is important to receive them with love and care, give them food and mental support and to have them examined by a qualified woman doctor, who will provide any medical treatment required. The second floor of the building should have a centre for medical and psychological care. The Centre will also have a group of attorneys on call, who will record the legal aspects of each resident's case and start immediate legal action to assert her legal rights. Unlike many non-government organisations and police stations, the Centre would not try for reconciliation with the perpetrators.

The Centre will be planned to avoid over-crowding, allowing each victim – referred to as 'trainee' to inspire a positive outlook – access to all amenities needed for her to succeed in a job-oriented training programme for her financial independence. The third and fourth floor of the building would house the training centre, the fifth floor a library, the sixth shops and recreation, the seventh kitchen and dining, and the eighth physical exercise and indoor sports. The three upper floors would be the living quarters and there might be a prayer and meditation hall at the very top of the building.

In view of the victim's likely distrust and confusion, special care must be taken to help her achieve calm and a degree of optimism. Suicide attempts are not unlikely, and the building design should take this into account. The staff will share the living quarters with the victims and be trained to help the victims as if they were their family. The Centre will have a department of professional psychologists who work with the victims to help them regain their tranquillity. We are planning that buildings will be set up beside rivers, so affording a view of the sky and the river from upstairs living quarters, to help the victims to recover and rebuild their lives. So far, two plots of river-front land have been donated, one by Attorney Rani Jethmalani on the bank of the Yamuna river, and one by myself on the bank of the Brahmaputra river.

There is good reason for the emphasis on training. We know from experience that any shelter for young women is susceptible to bad reputation. Strong discipline will be necessary to ward off such vulnerability but the victims themselves might object. An intensive training programme with plenty of homework, job interviews, etc. will not only speed up the financial independence of the women but will also help to keep them busy, purposeful and disciplined.

Victims will live free of charge in the Centre, requiring funds to be raised from philantrophic organisations. The Centre will have an employment and placement department which will find jobs for the women, if necessary. Once a woman qualifies for a job and becomes financially independent, she may move to an 'Independent Working Women's Apartment' building which is item 1(b) of the Programme (see below). This building will be financed by its rental income. Discipline in the building will be the responsibility of the residents themselves, but they will be persuaded to follow security and safety arrangements similar to those of the 'Job Centre' sanctuary.

Once established as independent working women, the 'trainees' will be encouraged to make their own decisions about their future. The Centre will offer legal, social and moral support to facilitate marriage to a mate of a woman's choice, if that is what she wants to do.

The Job Centre for Dowry Victims will deal a powerful blow to the perpetrators of dowry crimes. They will find that the brides are not as helpless as they think. The Centre will cause money loss for dowry seekers and they may try to destroy it, so it must be planned to withstand such attacks. The success of the Centre will send the message throughout the country that women can no longer be burnt, that they are human beings and their lives must be respected.

11.3 Criticism: An attack on family values?

Like any radical new programme, the plan of the 'Job Centre for Dowry Victims' has been heavily criticised. The first criticism is that dowry is a deep-rooted social problem and cannot be solved simply by a large, air-conditioned building. We take the point. The roots of this problem must be eliminated from the heart of India's social structure, as we have emphasised in our long-term plans in our Six Point Programme (see below). The already maligned air-conditioned building is just a means to the instant life-saving operation.

There is a more serious criticism. Notwithstanding the fact that only dowry victims in fear of their lives will be encouraged by the Centre to leave their marital homes, many people have criticised this proposed sanctuary as an attempt to break up families and a threat to the foundations of Indian society. Such criticism is nothing new. In the early 19th century, Lord William Bentinck faced reproaches by both Hindus and Europeans about 'religious interference' when he tried to stop female infanticide, then widespread among the Rajputs, as well as *thagi* (*thuggee*), the ritual murder and robbery by gangs in Central India, misusing the name of the goddess Kali, and the practice of *sati*, the burning of Hindu widows on the funeral pyres of their husbands.

Contemporary with Lord Bentinck, a famous Hindu reformer, Raja Rammohun Roy, continued the crusade against *sati* and promoted widow remarriage. He had a bitter fight with the Hindu orthodoxy, who blamed him for disrupting family values and accused him of planning to destroy the foundations of Indian society. Misdirected reaction to social criticism is a common experience and we should not be afraid of it.

To accusations that the planned Job Centre is a threat to families and the foundations of Indian society, we reply that a society that overlooks daily bride-burning is based on questionable moral foundations. How can we deny the right of independent life to a woman who has just escaped from a marriage ruined by dowry-related violence, who has saved herself from almost certain death, and whose natal family does not, or for whatever reason cannot, protect her effectively?

Unlike Rammohun Roy's struggle in the last century, the strength to fight this battle against the destruction of women can, I believe, be drawn from Hindu orthodoxy itself. Professor Michael Witzel, a world authority on Vedic texts and their interpretation, has stated that in the Vedic texts:

> Bride burning or dowry deaths, of course, do not occur at all. Such behavior goes against the Sruti rule not to kill any woman – a fact that has to be stressed today (Witzel, 1995, chapter 18, p. 9).

Many scriptural sources reinforce this point. This kind of research needs to be conducted in more depth and detail. Arguing that traditional texts are irrelevant and dangerous will surely not assist South Asian women today in overcoming dangerous predicaments. It is as true as ever it was that a marriage without righteousness (*dharma*), or in violation of it, is not a proper marriage. It is certainly not righteous to burn a woman because her parents have failed to supply a fridge, scooter or a certain amount of money. No extended discussion is needed about such issues; what is required is purposeful, effective, practical action that saves the lives of young women who will otherwise die a gruesome death.

11.4 The Six Point Programme

The Six Point Programme to Eradicate Dowry and Bride-Burning in India was originally adopted on 2nd October 1995 at the First International Conference on Dowry and Bride-Burning in India, held at Harvard University. It has thereafter been revised and ratified at the subsequent two Conferences.

(A) Immediate life-saving action:

1. (a) Construct dignified, high-rise protected buildings in a number of cities and towns in India and operate 'Job Centres for Dowry Victims' equipped with telephone hot-lines, attended by specialists trained to handle distress calls, where a dowry victim will receive effective security, respectable accommodation, food and clothing, legal protection, medical, psychological and spiritual care, sports and recreational facilities, study material and job-oriented training till she is qualified to lead an economically independent life.

1. (b) Construct apartment buildings for independent, working women.

(B) Long-term plans:

2. (a) Reform the Indian legal system to safeguard a daughter's inheritance rights to the estate of her parents, forefathers and other ancestors.

2. (b) Enhance the Indian legal system to declare a marriage null and void as soon as dowry is demanded. The bride divorced under such circumstances shall be entitled to half the estate of her divorced husband.

2. (c) Strengthen the *Dowry Prohibition Act* of India to fortify it as an effective deterrent to the practice of dowry and bride-burning. The dowry giver must be exempt from punishment.

3. Organise 'Students Against Dowry': mutual support groups for both male and female students in colleges and universities to promote the resolve of refusal of marriage if there is dowry, and to support the struggle of young people against parental pressure.

4. Organise 'Parents Against Dowry': mutual support groups of parents who wish to resist payment of dowry, and/or whose daughters have been victims of dowry.

5. (a) Originate a 'Service Loan Fund' to provide loans to wage-earning males of marriageable age who wish to pay off their parents, thereby preventing the possibility of parents' claim of dowry as a compensation.

5. (b) Originate an 'Old Age Fund' in India to finance old people and eliminate their dependency upon their sons.

6. (a) Promote research to identify and diagnose the dowry problem in India, recommend legal, economic, psychological, spiritual and social remedies, hold interviews, group discussions, meetings, seminars, conferences.

6. (b) Promote mass communication and education programmes to publicise anti-dowry ideology through drama, music, movies, radio and television shows, books, periodicals, journals, handbills and other media.

Chapter 12

New research agenda on dowry problems among South Asians

Werner Menski

Where do we stand today in the dowry debate? Mr. Thakur has rightly pointed out in the previous chapter that everyone seems to come up with their own ideas about solutions to the dowry problem. This book illustrates the diverse views and approaches that exist and that cannot be harmonised easily. It shows also that there are no simple, straightforward solutions, however radical and interventionist some proposals may be. South Asian women will continue to suffer dowry-related violence in large numbers, and many more women will die before this book has even gone to print. But this is no reason to quit.

Social science research has social and moral obligations which cannot be brushed aside when we meet obstructions. The dowry problem posits moral dilemmas of an extreme nature. It was evident that many participants in the Dowry Conferences, including many students, felt a sense of urgency and an obligation to do something about a problem that is atrocious in its ambit and implications. This is an issue that directly affects people's lives, as several of my students stressed in recent months.

So there will be further Dowry Conferences and we must go on working towards solutions to the dowry problem among South Asians. This will not be easy. The biggest problem, happening before our very eyes, is that, as a group of researchers into the problems created by dowry, we are alienating the very people we want to help. It is no coincidence that Himendra Thakur, Jagbir Jhutti and Usha Sood report that some people will not speak to them when dowry problems are raised as an issue and will even deny that it exists. We found in the run-up to the Third Dowry Conference in London that intense media interest was partly motivated by the desire to show South Asians in a bad light. This is the other side of the dowry issue – it can so easily be used as a stick with which to beat South Asian people. Consequently, there is a good deal of distrust, as well as confusion and lack of direction in the debates, and in our own work (and that of others) so far. We have to overcome such hurdles, but there is no easy formula for achieving progress.

In light of these comments, I want to urge participants in the dowry debate to become more constructive and co-operative. This concluding chapter considers specific evidence of the problem in Britain and finally asks to what extent this topic needs to be made more relevant to the legal professions in Britain, given the growing evidence that South Asian women in Britain, as well as North America, are also at mortal risk from dowry-related violence.

12.1 The need for a real debate

I have observed with growing frustration that the dowry debates are marked by the unwillingness of many participants to listen to others. Some make a show of it, fly in for a conference, make their points – and leave. Some people appear not to listen to anything that overlaps with their own views, nor anything which pursues a different angle or perspective to theirs. There has so far been no real debate on the dowry problem, more a series of exchanges of opinions. We are nowhere near an informed multi-faceted debate about dowry.

So how can we go forward? In the hope of being constructive, I shall focus on several key issues about which further research is needed. We need to look forward, instead of constantly getting lost in old ideological battles which are admittedly related to dowry, but may not touch its cur-rent critical core. This is not a male, white middle-class scholar trying to impose his perspective on others – the point I want to make, albeit with some urgency, is simply this: we do now know a fair amount about the dowry problem among South Asians and its various manifestations and we ought to focus our energies on certain key aspects to make real pro-gress in understanding the problem and its potential solutions. I am parti-cularly concerned that in future conferences, which will also take us to India, where vigorous exchanges of views (rather than real debate) have long existed, we should not constantly have to spend valuable time on yet more ideological (and often very personalised) diatribes about women's rights and unbridled patriarchy. These aspects are already amply documented in the literature and I do not hear much that is new. Nor do they seem to offer any tangible remedies against the manifest violence unleashed on dowry victims. It does not help the dowry debate, for example, to be told that gender inequality or marriage should be abolished. The same goes for the rallying cry for total abolition of dowry. As individuals we are entitled to our dreams, but the gruesome realities of the dowry problem rudely – and constantly – remind us as researchers, that ideological axioms and real life diverge in many crucial ways. We seem to have reached a stage in the dowry debates where several practical issues should be researched, so that real action to save more women's lives can become a less distant goal. We need to talk more, but our discussions must become more focused and address the real problems faced by South Asian women, every day of their lives.

The London Dowry Conference in November 1997 began with a fairly brief summing up on 'the dowry problem' at the start, leaving the space for the newly researched topics presented, and also for some women victimised by the dowry system. This strategy was positively received, because it allowed for a fairly well-focused discussion in the regrettably short time available. But some participants who were not 'in' on the earlier debates but had themselves worked on dowry, felt that they had something to say on this topic and perceived the conference programming as almost academic gagging, even as another form of dowry-related violence. This was inevitable, but it is not feasible or productive to rehearse all the ideological positions every time we want to reopen the debate on dowry. Cannot some axioms be taken as read?

Those of us who participated in all three Dowry Conferences, including Mr. Thakur, feel that participants in the debates need to listen to each other more carefully and read the work of others, rather than regurgitating old arguments from their own specific angles. There has been rather too much idiosyncratic sloganeering in the dowry debates so far. We hope that the present book, and its detailed bibliography, to which many items could still be added, will be widely used to support further research.

12.2 An agenda for research

Which are the issues that need to be researched further? Which gaps have we identified in our coverage so far? The new agenda of research on dowry-related problems should be remedy-centred and action-focused, relating theory and practice more closely than has so far been done. If we want to understand why some South Asian families kill for dowry but others in similar situations do not, then it is not enough to research gender-based discrimination and bride-centred violence. There are manifestly other key factors, but which are they? It helps to divide the field of dowry-related violence into several, albeit interrelated, sections. Some researchers will clearly be better qualified than others to undertake work in particular segments of this vast field. The London Conference in November 1997 made it clear that the dowry problem appears to be a culture-specific form of domestic violence, with roots in South Asia, now spreading to wherever the transnational South Asian community has been settling, with the one exception – according to Dr. Rambilass – of South African Indians.

The dowry problem, as we know, involves the intersecting spheres of gender norms, concepts of property and interpersonal violence. Our research so far has been spread quite thinly over all aspects of the problem, both past and present. We cannot all start with research on the ancient roots of dowry, since this involves highly specialised skills, which regrettably few people now have. There will of necessity be a variety of approaches, which has already been a definite asset to this ongoing debate, and we need yet more and different approaches to achieve fuller discussions.

Yet we dare not neglect the roots of the dowry system in the traditions of South Asian cultures. Traditional indological scholarship and modern sociological research need to be brought together to identify in greater detail how transactions which could fall under 'dowry' were viewed and developed in earlier times. More specifically, we need to study not only what the old law was, which is very tricky given the nature of Hindu law (Menski, 1997c), but also to scrutinise the position of such old rules within their social environment.

From the start, ancient Indian cultures strongly emphasised the gender divide and come to a number of conclusions which seem mutually exclusive and yet co-exist – which is typical of South Asian cultures.

Women and men are seen as interlinked parts of one whole, symbiotically tied together, with the female element initially more important because of the monopoly of birth. However, over time, the male perspective and patriarchal concepts gained the upper hand in representations and constructions of Hindu culture, though this has never been as clear-cut as many studies assume. If we relate this to marriage, it is evident that families need brides to reproduce themselves, so *kanya*, the ideal virgin daughter, becomes the most precious social good. Giving a bride in marriage becomes an axiomatic social obligation of all families within a patriarchal, patrilocal framework of reference (which of course does not apply to all South Asian cultures). In other words, the most precious gift possible is the fertile, nubile woman, the idealised future 'mother of a hundred sons', as so many wedding *mantras* put it (see Bumiller, 1990). There is nothing intrinsically wrong with that, unless one opposes the idea that women should bear children. In other words, the gender divide as such, and the fact that South Asian cultures advocate near universal marriage cannot really be blamed for the dowry problem. This is not to foreclose any debate, merely to emphasise that the dowry problem has at least as much to do with finances as with gender ideology.

Some evidence of financial transactions around Hindu marriages already appears in the ancient textual sources, but none of dowry-related murder, which would clearly violate the basic norm that women are the most precious social property. To what extent, then, are the old forms of what a bride takes with her into the marriage, such as a treasure chest pertinent to our present debates? The term 'bridal procession' (*vahatum*) appears in the oldest Vedic text on the subject, but precisely what was it supposed to include? Further research needs to connect our knowledge of such ancient practices and assumptions with questions about how such transactions were socially valued and treated. Was such property freely given, or was it demanded? To what extent are the voluntary giving by a bride's parents and the expectations from the groom's side linked at that stage, and later? A fresh analysis of the 'eight forms of marriage', referred to in many ancient texts, should provide useful evidence about the textual basis of dowry and gift transactions. I worked on some of these questions in my doctoral thesis (Menski, 1984), but did not make explicit reference to the current dowry problems. However, such research work can only be done by people with solid knowledge of Sanskrit, and great patience. Academic pre-occupations seem to work against this kind of work today, but it remains an important component of dowry-related research.

We also need to know more about how South Asian people themselves, in the past and today, have viewed the links between the two main kinds of dowry: gifts and presents given to the bride on marriage, and the 'demanded' or 'expected' dowry that is supposed to accompany the bride when she comes to her new home. It is not enough to assert that there is a link – we know that. But when and how did this link originate? While some historical researchers, and probably also literary analysts, could throw light on perceptions of dowry transactions and their impact in the past, other researchers should interview South Asians today, as Jagbir Jhutti has done, to tease out how they perceive the various forms of 'dowry' and the problems this may give rise to. Thus, there are many distinctly different and subject-specific sub-tasks to be executed before the puzzle of dowry-related violence can be totally put together.

Several participants in the dowry debates have treated the question of female inheritance rights as a kind of panacea to the dowry problem. Even Himendra Thakur is raising this again (see chapter 11), inspired by recent policy statements from India. Although several of us disagree, we need to know more about how it would work in practice and whether it could save women from dowry-related deaths. In this regard, evidence from South Asian Muslim societies might be quite useful, since the *Qur'an* laid down that a family's women should have certain fixed shares of inheritance. We seem to know that, in practice, such shares are either denied women, or they 'renounce' them in exchange for goodwill, as also observed among expatriate South Asians today, who may renounce their due shares of ancestral property but retain moral claims over entitlements to family support. Thus, not surprisingly, South Asian Muslim societies not only practise 'dower' arrangements (*mahr, mehr* or *mahar*) but engage also in dowry transfers which go the other way, from the bride's family to the groom's. South Asian Muslim families, too, therefore face dowry problems, but there are many regional and local variations, and research is urgently needed into such practices. Future Dowry Conferences ought to be held in Pakistan and Bangladesh too, where there is also concern about dowry-related violence. Rohit Barot does make reference in chapter 8 to the fact that South Asian Muslims in Britain also engage in dowry transactions, but we need far more information.

Looking at present events, there is much for researchers to investigate concerning dowry problems. All goes far wider than India, or indeed South Asia, and we already have some interesting and relevant pieces of research from around the world. Bisakha Sen (chapter 5) and Vijayendra Rao, whose important work on dowry-related violence in South India we could not include, rightly emphasise the economic aspects of dowry transactions. Economic dissatisfaction, Rao's findings seem to suggest, may trigger domestic violence. Bisakha Sen presents us with frightening mathematical formulae to explain why one husband may kill his wife, whereas another may not. There is a growing realisation, reflected in the London Conference, that psychosocial and medical-related research needs to be brought to our discussion panels. Beginnings have been made even in Britain, where statistics of disproportionate mortality and suicide rates for young Asian women have been analysed (see Raleigh, Bulusu and Balarajan, 1990).

The London Conference identified clear links between dowry-related murder and domestic violence and recommended that future research should concentrate on those links. Indeed, some new work is already being produced along those lines (Devadason, 1998). To some extent, this appears to fit in well with Madhu Kishwar's argument that newly-married women are subjected to domestic violence because of dissatisfaction with them rather than their dowry, so that dowry becomes a flashpoint issue. While it is only women who die as a result of dowry-related violence, evidence of harassment of husbands (see Kusum, 1993b; Hood, 1993) should not be disregarded in our exploration of why so many South Asian marital relationships end up in flames. We must read the testimonies of men, too, if we want to understand why they might kill.

We must ask why so many South Asian women die on account of so-called dowry problems when clearly there are other, related problems that lead to marital breakdown. Quite what these are needs further investigation, since we are dealing with supposedly mature, middle-class people, often professionals of high standing, who should know better. Dowry-related violence is obviously not restricted to inarticulate uneducated spouses whose aggression is expressed in non-verbal violent actions. When, why and how do the mechanisms that trigger off dowry-related violence actually come into play? Why does this scenario develop in some families but not others? Why do some men and some mothers-in-law kill and others not? Vijayendra Rao's fieldwork in South India, showing the links between alcohol consumption and domestic violence, opens up fresh avenues for further research (Rao, 1995; 1997). We need to know more about how so-called dowry-related violence in such situations is emerging as a response to a life cycle crisis, which every person in the world probably goes through in some form, and which anthropologists refer to as a classic 'rite of passage'.

While this book was being edited, a whole bundle of new dowry murder cases from India became available. As a result, chapter 6 of this book has grown in size, illustrating in detail that the Indian Supreme Court is today much more aware of dowry-related violence than only a few years ago. Nevertheless, a large number of recent cases have ended in acquittal for persons who seemed implicated in dowry murders. While I do not doubt that in some cases corruption played a part, particularly in suppressing crucial evidence (significantly, the Supreme Court itself seems to suggest this in more than one case), the most recent case reports also show that not all members of a murderous husband's family can automatically be accused of the murder. It is no coincidence that Himendra Thakur, in chapter 11, refers to this problem as well, since police investigations of dowry murders can easily be abused for extortion. More detailed, careful analysis is needed before we can comment on the progress of the case law on dowry, affording much scope for new legal work.

In the meantime, renewed calls have been made in various quarters for the legalisation of giving dowry. This can be seen as a strategy to decriminalise the parents of a bride and thus to help promote prosecutions under Indian law of those who take and demand dowry. Significantly Bisakha Sen's research supports such decriminalisation, since the woman's family has, in her view, good reasons for wanting to offer a dowry. Add to this the argument that no woman would wish to enter her new home without a single possession, and this makes sense also to people who are not economists. Jagbir Jhutti seems to suggest that British Sikhs, similarly, give dowries because that will safeguard the daughter's future in her new home as well as increasing the family's status. Seen in such light, the law's attempts to prohibit dowry altogether look distinctly out of line with what South Asian people themselves want to do at the point of marriage.

We are still confused about what we are trying to combat regarding 'the dowry problem'. Are we really calling for the abolition of dowry? Several contributors to this book maintain that we must, while others, myself included, acknowledge that dowries are a fact of life and a cultural phenomenon among South Asians with which we have to live. I think the fact that members of South Asian societies anywhere in the world seem to look upon our research efforts with scepticism and reservations should make us think. What right do we have to dictate to any parent that their daughter should marry without dowry?

What we should not be prepared to tolerate, however, is a single dowry-related murder. I suggest that future research must tackle the issue of violence directly. The new approach of linking dowry murders with issues of domestic violence seems a promising way forward. It is fruitless to fantasise about the eradication of dowry when we know that this would disempower women still further. Instead, as much of the research indicates, we need to go along with the desire to provide dowries, but protect women from dowry-related violence.

Let us have no illusions; research alone will not decrease the number of murdered brides. On the contrary, there is evidence of increasing violence and murder, even among the South Asian communities in Europe and North America. The key to understanding dowry-related violence still lies in the human mind: the trigger that sets off violent actions is not a matter of economics, law or sociology, it is far more a matter of psychology. At the end, some of us have resorted to appeals to self-control, but how effective would that be in a world full of materialistic confusions, where people kill young women because a cycle was given rather than a motorcycle, or a fridge and a scooter were not forthcoming in time, or a set of gold ornaments was not considered good enough? The complexities of why South Asian people kill young women for such reasons remain mind-boggling. No amount of rationality, education or modernisation seems sufficient to eradicate this evil. I end on this pessimistic note only to turn to the recent growth of this menace in Britain itself.

12.3 Dowry problems in Britain today

In Britain, we have recently witnessed a well-publicised dowry dispute, the so-called *Samra* case, which was widely reported in the press but not officially printed in any law report. This means that future legal studies will still have no concrete evidence on which to base further research and we are still largely in the realm of 'anecdotal evidence' regarding British Asian dowry cases. So far the official legal system has shied away from taking formal notice of the dowry problems among South Asians and it has been left to the ethnic minority press or some local papers to carry reports on cases. Not that the *Samra* case was the first of its kind – there have been many similar cases since at least the early 1980s. It is apparent that the curtain is only just beginning to be lifted on such legal problems in Britain, as in the USA and Canada.

As confirmed by Jagbir Jhutti in chapter 9 and Usha Sood in chapter 10, there are many attempts to deny the existence of dowry-related problems among South Asians in Britain today and the picture would not be much different for North America. This highlights a major problem for researchers: detailed evidence on current dowry problems outside India is virtually unobtainable. As Jagbir Jhutti shows here, many members of the Asian communities do not wish to talk about it, even though they were happy to describe their ostentatious dowry arrangements. Some prominent members of the Asian community in Britain would even have us believe that the dowry system does not occur, lest it provoke bad publicity about Asians in Britain. We encountered attempts to sensationalise the issue in the run-up to the Third Dowry Conference in London, so excluded the press from the conference. At the same time, much media coverage, especially in the British Asian press, has highlighted dowry-related problems, including suicides and dowry murders.

As Usha Sood, in chapter 10, indicates from her professional perspective, several solicitors and advisers in the community now have experience of an ongoing case-load involving dowry problems. Yet the English legal system as a whole remains almost entirely unaware of the problem. This ignorance is partly due to the very nature of the custom of dowry. It is a family matter which the communities keep away from the official legal system, seeing no need to involving the state and its law. However, as Jagbir Jhutti reports, some young Asian women are now learning to use official legal processes to protect their claims to their dowry by registering documents with a solicitor. The official disinterest about the dowry problem among South Asians in Britain reflects the general lack of concern of the English legal system about matters of ethnic minority custom and, on their part, a marked reluctance among ethnic minorities to bring their disputes before the official legal system. Such mutual non-communication is no longer satisfactory, since women tend to be the victims if there are any legal problems. And while dowry disputes remain mostly within the 'extra-legal' realm of unofficial customary dispute settlement processes, the widespread failure to perceive and acknowledge dowry problems is being reinforced. I found it highly significant that a complex litigation in London a few years ago, over a super-rich young Asian wife's entitlement to matrimonial property, was ultimately settled through the subtle involvement of community leaders, not by the English courts.

The attitude of official legal organs towards Asian cultural patterns in Britain is no longer appropriate (for Muslim women, see Pearl and Menski, 1998, chapter 3). While Britain avoids the challenge of recognising the various personal laws of its new ethnic minority communities by insisting that everyone should be fitted under English law, women, as Usha Sood asserts in chapter 10, are at the mercy of customary, patriarch-dominated dispute settlement mechanisms. The only avenue for introducing South Asian cultural elements into a litigation is through expert evidence from a suitably qualified individual. I know from personal experience that this can be a powerful weapon, but many judges and other judicial and legal personnel in Britain seem reluctant to take such matters fully into account in the search for just and equitable solutions to legal problems involving South Asians.

Let me take the example of a husband's likely argument that, since dowry transactions are illegal under Indian law, his wife cannot claim possession of so-called dowry items. If an English judge were to accept this argument, he would clearly become party to a case of unjust enrichment. The definitional problems of dowry resurface here; precisely what has the Indian law outlawed as 'dowry', and what is exempt from official legal prohibition? Indian law has surely not been so modified that any property given to the bride by her parents falls under dowry and is therefore lost to the husband! Certainly, s. 6 of the *Dowry Prohibition Act* of 1961, with its rule that any dowry given shall belong to the wife, tells us otherwise. However, lack of specific South Asian legal knowledge, coupled with reluctance to recognise Asian customs, will be detrimental and, in cases of dowry, possibly even fatal to Asian women caught up in such disputes.

My reading of the British Asian press since the early 1980s confirms that with the arrival of South Asians in Britain have come dowry customs and the social evil of dowry extortion. Rohit Barot tells us in chapter 8 that the practice of hypergamous marriage arrangements continues to have a bearing on the dowry system – and not only among the various groups of Patels from Gujarat. One of the consequences of hypergamy has been a general inflation of dowries at the top end of the local hierarchy. The ethnic press have reported cases of Asian women taunted and ill-treated by their husband's families because of their inadequate dowries. In Leicester, one Hindu bridegroom refused to complete the seventh circle around the sacred fire unless his future father-in-law promised to give him more dowry. Some dowry-related cases come before the English courts as assault cases or prosecutions for grievous bodily harm, as seen in the case of a woman who had been knifed in the face by her husband, resulting in a public protest by Asian community members outside the Magistrates Court.

Other cases appear as disputes over gifts. In 1986, an Asian woman in Leicester won her claim in court that jewellery presented to her on her wedding day by her in-laws belonged to her. This was not really a dowry case, therefore; it was about a woman's right to individual ownership. The judge found in favour of the young woman but stressed that his ruling should not be regarded as a general guide for all Hindu weddings (*Leicester Mercury*, 28 April 1986). The judge in this case clearly had no knowledge or understanding of dowry customs and adjudicated the case by reference to English law alone. An Asian lawyers' conference and a campaign launched by the Indian Workers' Association to fight dowry practices, both in 1988, confirmed beyond doubt that dowry problems exist in Britain. It would be useful if someone were to write up all this 'anecdotal evidence' from various press reports over the decade.

One might argue that such factors as education should undermine the dowry system in Britain as compared to Asian countries but this is not so. And in India, what Himendra Thakur calls the 'dowry-infested areas' are actually those parts of the country with good educational provision. Now that more Asian girls in Britain are highly educated and are in paid employment, where they can contribute to the family budget, before marriage and after, how are dowry transaction mechanisms affected? Do we still call this dowry if the bride herself assembles the dowry but for status reasons, as Jagbir Jhutti confirms, claims that 'mum and dad bought this for me'? Jhutti shows that young Sikh women increasingly purchase what they want for themselves, and may in addition receive traditional dowries from their parents. The problem of dowry may reduce itself in the sense that brides now appear to be claiming greater control over the dowry transactions, in terms not only of what they are given by their parents but also of ownership.

This is probably a key element in the solution of the dowry problem. For the argument that the husband's family owns the newly married woman, and thus everything she brought with her, does surface in cases I have seen in Britain. Where the dowry is not made over to the bride but goes straight to the husband's family, including possessions that should constitute the woman's own and separate property, the roots for dowry problems can be seen. What if someone then claims that what she brought with her was no good, or not good enough? It is a small step from there to saying that the woman herself is no good. Some research rightly suggests that there is a ritual element of disparagement here, which our studies must not overlook in the context of hypergamous family relations.

A major reason for scenarios of dowry-related violence is the traditional – but not universally shared – attitude that on marriage a woman becomes the property of her husband and/or his family. This leaves no scope for maintaining that women are independent full owners of their own property and few Asian women, however assertive, will succeed in being respected as an individual with separate rights. A number of legal practitioners in Britain have encountered situations where the ownership of wedding presents, often including substantial amounts of money and jewellery, has been disputed. Such cases tend to show that the concept of the man possessing the woman and all her property, is by no means unknown among South Asians in Britain. Where this is not the case, however, the young bride may be free to enjoy her dowry and other property, and there is no 'dowry problem'.

At the same time, Jhutti's research and Barot's preliminary investigations show that getting married in Britain is now so costly that this is beginning to be perceived as another marriage-related problem. This may not be directly a 'dowry problem' but it undoubtedly relates to it. When we hear of BMW cars, flats, deposits on houses and other expensive goods as marriage 'presents', the thought that this is somehow problematic does occur. But who are we to criticise people for arranging splendid weddings which they perceive to be for their own and their children's benefit? The only valid test is whether any 'presents' made are actually presents, or whether they were made under pressure and duress, in which case there is clearly a 'dowry problem'.

12.4 Dowry-related violence and English law

The occurrence of dowry violence, undoubtedly a grave social problem in South Asian countries, has become a matter of increasing concern in England. Until his untimely death, Sebastian Poulter was one of the few English lawyers who attempted in-depth research into ethnic minority customs. He wrote briefly about dowry but seemed to conflate the presents given to the bride by her parents with the 'real' dowry extracted from them under compulsion (Poulter, 1986: 40). While this definition of dowry did not quite touch the core of the problem, when Poulter (1986: 41) discussed the dowry problem in India today, he linked the two kinds of dowry:

> On the face of it there seems little reason to oppose the obligation of a bride's family to provide her with a dowry on marriage. However, the custom may become so distorted in practice that it creates a grave social evil, as now appears to be the case in India. The greed of some husbands' families has led them to demand that very large dowries should be provided for their future daughter-in-law (often running to several thousand pounds) and when that is not forthcoming they burn her to death.

Poulter gave no indication that such crimes were perpetrated among South Asians in England. However, published research by medical researchers (e.g. Raleigh, Bulusu and Balarajan, 1990) strongly suggests that we cannot be sure (see also *The Independent*, 11 February 1990). The press have argued that dowry violence is a major problem in cities like London, Leicester and Birmingham. One commentator indicated that dowry violence is on the increase because people had become greedy during a recession in which everybody is suffering, and asserted that the level of violence used to extract a larger marriage present or to keep hold of such property if the marriage fails is quite terrifying. A number of press clips that I have collected over many years confirm the existence of dowry-related deaths in Britain itself, but seldom clarify whether by murder or suicide.

While the existence of dowry-related violence in Britain is partly accepted, it is often presumed that it is not as harsh as in the subcontinent. Some observers have argued that the difference in the degree of violence is primarily due to the context of British society. It is assumed that Asian women in Britain have the option, unlike many of their counterparts in the subcontinent, of walking out of the marriage, seeking refuge in women's institutions and, ultimately, in divorce. If dowry disputes seem to be resulting in death more rarely in Britain, is this because divorce is relatively easier? If so, this bears important messages for South Asian legal and social systems.

Although some press reports assert that matrimonial violence appears to be of a milder form in Britain, one can also find evidence of brutality. For example, *The Observer* (13 December 1987) reported how a Gujarati woman from Southall, West London was subjected to regular beatings and confinement soon after she married, because her dowry did not meet the expectations of her husband's family. When the assaults failed to produce a larger dowry, her in-laws tried to murder her. They dragged her outside the house, stacked up a pile of wood, held her down and poured paraffin over her. They were stopped only by another relative who intervened because of the shame it might bring on the family.

The harsher forms of violence appear to be directed particularly at women who have come directly from India and are less able to rely on the help of friends and relatives (for a case study see Barton, 1987). Some are totally isolated from their natal family and at the mercy of in-laws and/or the husband. This is undoubtedly potentially dangerous.

Some researchers have suggested that dowry deaths in Britain may have taken on a new guise of suicide (Raleigh, Bulusu and Balarajan, 1990). Their findings, which need more detailed analysis and should be followed up, indicate that women from the Indian sub-continent living in Britain are four times more likely than other women to commit suicide. The method chosen by one third of such women was to set fire to themselves. There is corresponding evidence from community groups, for example an Anti-Dowry Campaign based in Belvedere, Kent has argued that some of the burnings may have been murder (*The Independent*, 11 February 1990). This group expressed scepticism as to whether so many women would commit suicide by burning. A more plausible explanation would be that some are dowry deaths committed by greedy in-laws who want their sons to be free to marry again and get another dowry.

Indeed, the most worrying dowry-related cases are those disguised as suicide. There have been cases where women have been mysteriously burned to death and the ultimate cause is not established. In most cases the coroner records an open verdict. It remains a worrying fact that British coroners are not trained to detect dowry murder, since the concept is alien to English law and relevant cultural knowledge is almost entirely absent.

Thus English law remains unaware of South Asian dowry problems. This is clearly illustrated by the way the various types of dowry disputes have come before the courts and not been given the attention and detailed analysis they warrant. Since the English legal system as a whole is currently becoming more sensitised about issues relating to domestic violence, it may be possible that more attention will be paid to South Asian dowry problems in Britain – but there is no guarantee. Dowry remains an area of ethnic minority custom and cultural practice of which English law must urgently take official notice, so as to give due legal protection to Asian women caught up in dowry disputes. To adopt the stance that eventually Asians will assimilate to an assumed British mainstream culture and discard their 'ethnic' cultural baggage is both unrealistic and dangerous, especially in the case of dowry. If English law refuses to recognise the dowry evil, many Asian women will continue to suffer harassment and violence without protection from the law, when South Asian women in England are already dying as a result of dowry-related violence.

Some commentators have suggested that Britain should follow the example set by India, where every case of a woman who has been burnt to death should be investigated by the police, in recognition that it may be murder. This would amount to raising a rebuttable presumption of dowry death, as in Indian law. Does English law need to enact specific legislation to protect such women, as the major South Asian countries have done? Only by taking such targeted action will English lawyers be adequately prepared to give due legal protection to Asian women caught in dowry disputes. At present legal personnel in England are clearly ill-equipped, with little or no understanding of the dowry issue and no specific legal machinery to protect Asian women. While one can debate whether it is desirable to institute special protective mechanisms – another form of protective discrimination – for Asian women, there should be no disagreement over the need to protect Asian women in Britain from dowry-related murders.

While it was too early for the Third Dowry Conference in London to involve British legal professionals because the evidence we have so far is still largely 'anecdotal' and therefore liable to be unfairly challenged, a future Dowry Conference in London will pursue this issue in more depth. Participants of the Third Dowry Conference in London were left in no doubt that the agenda for further research on dowry-related problems is extensive and that much work remains to be done. The contributors to this book share a sense of urgency in this endeavour. These and other issues will no doubt be taken up at the Fourth Dowry Conference in Harvard, in November 1998 and, one hopes, in future conferences.

Table of cases

Abbreviations used:

AC	*Appeal Cases*
AIR	*All India Reporter*
All ER	*All England Reporter*
CA	Court of Appeal
CriLJ	*Criminal Law Journal* (India)
Del	Delhi
FB	Full Bench decision
HL	House of Lords
KB	King's Bench
KLT	*Kerala Law Times*
PC	Privy Council
P&H	Panjab and Haryana High Court
PLD	*Pakistan Legal Decisions*
SC	Supreme Court
SCC	*Supreme Court Cases* (India)

England and Wales

Barclays Bank plc v. O'Brien [1993] 4 All ER 417	201, 202, 203, 204-205
CIBC Mortgages plc v. Pitt [1993] 4 All ER 433	201, 202, 203
Maskell v. Horner [1915] 3 KB 106 CA	200
North Ocean Shipping Co v. Hyundai Construction Co, the Atlantic Baron [1978] 3 All ER 1170	200
Pao On v. Lau Yiu Long [1980] AC 614 PC	200
Phrantzes v. Argenti [1960] 1 All ER 778	199
Samra case (unreported)	203, 205, 206, 207, 230

List of statutes

Bibliography

Achar, M. R. and T. Venkanna [1993]: *Dowry Prohibition Act and Rules (central and states): with state amendments*. 3rd ed. Revised by B. K. Sharma. Allahabad: Law Book Co

Advani, Poornima [1994]: *Crime in marriages: A broad spectrum*. Bombay: Gopushi

Agarwal, Bina (ed.) [1989]: *Structures of patriarchy: The state, the community and the household*. London: Zed Books

Agarwal, Bina [1994]: *A field of one's own: Gender and land rights in South Asia*. Cambridge: Cambridge University Press

Ahmed, Rafiuddin [1993]: 'Migrations from Bangladesh to the Middle East: Social and economic costs to the rural people'. In: Israel, Milton and Narendra K. Wagle (eds.): *Ethnicity, identity, migration: The South Asian context*. Toronto: University of Toronto, Centre for South Asian Studies, pp. 105-122

Ahuja, Ram [1987]: *Crime against women*. Jaipur: Rawat

Akerlof, George [1984]: 'The economics of caste and of the rat race'. In: *An economic theorist's book of tales: Essays that entertain the consequences of new assumptions in economic theory*. New York: Cambridge University Press, pp. 30-44

Ali, M. Immam [1987]: 'Dower/dowries in Bangladesh and primary purpose'. In: Vol. 1 No. 4 [January] *Immigration & Nationality Law & Practice*, p. 125

Altekar, A. S. [1978]: *The position of women in Hindu civilization*. New Delhi: Motilal Banarsidass. [1st ed. 1938, various editions and reprints]

Antony, M. J. [1995]: *Landmark judgements on dowry related deaths*. New Delhi: Indian Social Institute

Anwar, M. [1979]: *The myth of return: Pakistanis in Britain*. London: Heinemann

'Appeal to Supreme Court – Enquiry into Vimla's death in Hyderabad'. In: No. 20 [January-February 1984] *Manushi*, pp. 41-42

Awasthi, S. K. and U. S. Lal [1986]: *Dowry prohibition*. Allahabad: National Law Agency

Bakar, Khondaker Md. Abu [1989]: *A handbook on the Dowry Prohibition Act, 1980 and the Cruelty to Women (Deterrent Punishment) Ordinance, 1983*. Rangpur, Bangladesh: Author

Balarajan, R. and L. Bulusu [1990]: 'Mortality among immigrants in England and Wales, 1979-83'. In: [1990] *Mortality and Geography*, pp. 103-127

Balchin, Cassandra (ed.) [1994]: *A handbook on family law in Pakistan*. 2nd ed. Lahore: Shirkat Gah

Ballard, Catherine [1978]: 'Arranged marriages in the British context'. In: Vol. 6 No. 3 *New Community*, pp. 181-197

Ballard, Roger (ed.) [1994]: *Desh pardesh: The South Asian presence in Britain*. London: Hurst and Co

Balse, Mayah [1976]: *The Indian female: Attitude towards sex*. New Delhi: Chetana

Banerjee, A. R. and Lipi Chowdhuri [1988]: 'Caste exogamy and clan/gotra endogamy in contemporary Bengalee society'. In: Vol. 68 No. 2 [June 1988] *Man in India*, pp. 200-210

Banerjee, Gooroodas [1879]: *The Hindu law of marriage and stridhan*. Calcutta: Thacker, Spink & Co

Banerjee, Partha [1996]: 'Bride burning and dowry deaths in India'. In: [1997] Vol. 1 No. 1 *Injustice Studies*. Found at: http://wolf.its.ilstu.edu/injustice/newcontents.htm

Banerjee, Ritu [1995]: 'Bride-burning and the law: Vimala Devi's tragedy'. In: Witzel and Thakur (eds.), chapter 4, pp. 1-6

Barot, Rohit [1975]: 'The Hindus of Bakuli'. In: Twaddle, Michael (ed.): *Expulsion of a minority: Essays on Ugandan Asians*. London: Athlone Press, pp. 70-80

Barot, Rohit [1987]: 'Caste and sect in the Swaminarayan movement'. In: Burghart, Richard (ed.): *Hinduism in Great Britain: The perpetuation of religion in an alien cultural milieu*. London: Tavistock, pp. 67-80

Barton, Rachel [1987]: *The scarlet thread*. London: Virago

Basu, Srimati [1996]: *Wo ayee hak lene. There she comes to take her rights: Indian women, property and propriety*. Columbus, OH: Ohio State University. [Ph.D. Dissertation, Dept. of Women's Studies]

Baxi, Upendra [1986]: *Towards a sociology of Indian law*. New Delhi: Satvahan

Beall, Jo [1990]: 'Women under indenture in colonial Natal, 1860-1911'. In: Clarke, Colin, Ceri Peach and Steven Vertovec (eds.): *South Asians overseas. Migration and ethnicity*. Cambridge et al.: Cambridge University Press, pp. 57-74

Becker, Gary Stanley [1974]: 'A theory of social interactions'. In: Vol. 82 No. 6 *Journal of Political Economy*, pp. 1063-1093

Becker, Gary Stanley [1981]: *A treatise on the family*. Cambridge, MA: Harvard University Press. [Enlarged ed. 1991]

Bennett, Lynn [1983]: *Dangerous wives and sacred sisters: Social and symbolic roles of high-caste women in Nepal*. New York: Columbia University Press

Beri, B. P. [1988]: *Commentaries on Dowry Prohibition Act 1961. Together with Guroodas Banerjee's Tagore Law Lectures on Law of Stridhan*. Lucknow: Eastern Book Co

Bhachu, Parminder Kaur [1985]: *Twice migrants: East African Sikh settlers in Britain*. London and New York: Tavistock

Bhachu, Parminder Kaur [1993]: 'Identities constructed and reconstructed: Representations of Asian Women in Britain'. In: Buijs, Gina (ed.): *Migrant women crossing boundaries and changing identities*. Oxford: Berg, pp.99-117

Bhana, Surendra (ed.) [1990]: *Essays on indentured Indians in Natal*. Leeds: Peepal Tree Press

Bhana, Surendra and Arvinkumar Bhana [1990]: 'An exploration of the psycho-historical circumstances surrounding suicide among indentured Indians, 1875-1911'. In: Bhana (ed.), pp. 137-199

Bhasin, Kamla [1993]: *What is patriarchy?* Delhi: Kali for Women

Bhatnagar, Jagdishwar P. [1987]: *Offences against women: Marriage and married women.* Allahabad: Ashoka Law House

Bhatnagar, Jagdishwar P. [1988]: *Dowry Prohibition Act alongwith dowry death and bride-burning cases, with state amendments.* Allahabad: Ashoka Law House

Bhatnagar, Jagdishwar P. [1993]: *Cases and materials on Dowry Prohibition Act, 1961 with state amendments along with dowry death and bride burning cases.* Allahabad: Ashoka Law House

Bhatnagar, J. P. [1996]: *Dowry Prohibition Act alongwith dowry death and bride burning cases.* 3rd ed. By S. K. Awasthi. Allahabad: Ashoka Law House

Bhopal, Kalwant [1997]: South Asian women within households: Dowries, degradation and despair'. In: Vol. 20 No. 4 *Women Studies International Forum*, pp. 483-492

Billig, Michael S. [1991]: 'The marriage squeeze on high-caste Rajasthani women'. In: Vol. 50 No. 2 [May 1991] *Journal of Asian Studies*, pp. 341-360

Biswas, S. K. and T. P. Tripati [1990]: 'A comparative study of employment situation of the aged'. In: Vol. 70 No. 1 [March 1990], *Man in India*, pp. 26-46

Bumiller, Elisabeth [1990]: *May you be the mother of a hundred sons: A journey among the women of India.* New Delhi: Penguin

Bunwaree-Phukan, Ranjita [1995]: 'Domestic violence: A daily terror in most Mauritian families'. In: Witzel and Thakur (eds.), chapter 5, pp. 1-6

Caplan, Lionel [1984]: 'Bridegroom price in urban India'. In: Vol. 19 *Man* (N. S.), pp. 216-233

Caplan, Patricia [1985]: *Class and gender in India.* London: Tavistock

Carroll, Lucy [1987]: 'Dowry Prohibition legislation: Some suggestions for change'. In: Vol. 29 No. 1 [January-March 1987] *Journal of the Indian Law Institute*, pp. 48-59

Chatterjee, Heramba [1974]: *Forms of marriage in ancient India.* Vol. 2, Calcutta: Sanskrit Pustak Bhandar

Chatterjee, Meera [1990]: *Indian women: Their health and economic productivity.* Washington, DC: World Bank [World Bank Discussion Papers, 109]

Chatterji, Jyotsna (ed.) [1985]: *The women's decade 1975-1985. An assessment.* Delhi: ISPCK

Chattopadhyaya, H. [1970]: *Indians in Africa. A socio-economic study.* Calcutta: Bookland

Chattopadhyaya, Kamaladevi [1983]: *Indian women's battle for freedom.* New Delhi: Abhinav.

Chaturvedi, Subhadra [1995]: 'Whether inheritance to women is a viable solution of dowry problem in India'. In: Witzel and Thakur (eds.), chapter 6, pp. 1-5

Chekki, Danesh A. [1974]: *Modernization and kin network.* Leiden: E. J. Brill

Chowdhary, Manjaree [1996]: *Dousing the flames. An assessment of recent legal attempts to control the dowry problem in India.* London: SOAS [Unpublished LLM essay]

Clark, Alice W. [1993]: *Gender and political economy – exploration of South Asian systems.* Delhi et al.: Oxford University Press

Comaroff, J. [1980]: *The meaning of marriage payments.* London: Academic Press

Connors, Jane F. [1989]: *Violence against women in the family.* New York: United Nations

Connors, Jane F. [1994]: 'Government measures to confront violence against women'. In: Davies, Miranda (ed.): *Women and violence.* London and New Jersey: Zed Books, pp. 182-199

Das, Veena [1976]: 'Indian women: Work, power and status'. In: Nanda (ed.), pp. 129-145

Dayal, R. [1995]: *Law relating to dowry: Murder of wife, dowry deaths, bride burning, suicide and abetment of suicide, cruelty to women, bail and matters incidental thereto.* Allahabad: Premier Publishing Co

Derrett, J. Duncan M. [1963]: *Introduction to modern Hindu law.* London: Oxford University Press

Derrett, J. Duncan M. [1970]: *A critique of modern Hindu law.* Bombay: N. M. Tripathi

Derrett, J. D. M. [1984]: 'What the dharmasastra has to say about dowry'. In: Larivière, Richard (ed.): *Studies of Dharmasastra.* Calcutta: KLM, pp. 179-193

Desai, Amala [1996]: *Women's property rights, women as property and the problem of dowry.* London: SOAS [Unpublished MA Dissertation]

Desai, Neera and Maithreyi Krishnaraj [1987]: *Women and society in India.* New Delhi: Ajanta Publications

Desai, Rashmi [1963]: *Indian immigrants in Britain.* London: Oxford University Press for Institute of Race Relations

Desai, Sonalde and Devaki Jain [1994]: 'Maternal employment and changes in family dynamics: The social context of women's work in rural South India'. In: Vol. 20 No. 1 [March 1994] *Population and Development Review*, pp. 115-136

De Souza, Alfred (ed.) [1975]: *Women in contemporary India.* New Delhi: Manohar

'Despite much fanfare' [1984]. In: No. 24 [September-October 1984] *Manushi*, pp. 33-35

Devadason, Ranji [1998]: *Dowry abuse in Britain – A culture-specific form of domestic violence.* London: SOAS. [Unpublished MA Dissertation]

Dhar, Lalita [1988]: 'Dowry legislation in India: Retrospects and prospects'. In: Vol. 14 Nos. 1-2 *Indian Socio-Legal Journal*, pp. 129-141

Diwan, Paras [1985]: 'The dowry prohibition law'. In: Vol. 27 No. 4 *Journal of the Indian Law Institute*, pp. 564-571

Diwan, Paras [1987]: *Dowry and protection to married women (with up to date amendments).* New Delhi: Deep and Deep

Diwan, Paras [1990]: *Dowry and protection to married women.* 2nd ed. New Delhi: Deep and Deep

Diwan, Paras and Peeyushi Diwan [1995]: *Dowry and protection to married women.* 3rd ed. New Delhi: Deep and Deep

Dolphyne, F. A. [1991]: *The emancipation of women. An African perspective.* Accra: Ghana University Press

'The dowry problem persists in India'. [Women's International Network News]. In: Vol. 14 No. 1 [1988] *Women in Asia*, p. 58

Dreze, Jean and Amartya Sen [1995]: *India: Economic development and social opportunity.* Delhi et al.: Oxford University Press

Dumont, Louis [1959]: 'Dowry in Hindu marriage – as a social scientist sees it'. In: 11 April 1959 *Economic Weekly*, pp. 219-220

Dumont, Louis [1970]: *Homo hierarchicus: The caste system and its implications.* London: Weidenfeld and Nicolson

Duraisamy, Malathi and P. Duraisamy [1996]: 'Sex discrimination in Indian labor markets'. In: Vol. 2 No. 2 *Feminist Economics*, pp. 41-62

Fruzetti, L. M. [1990]: *The gift of a virgin. Women, marriage and ritual in Bengali society.* Delhi et al.: Oxford University Press

Gandhi, M. K. [1947]: *Women and social injustice.* Ahmedabad: Navajivan Publishing House

Garzilli, E. [1996]: 'Stridhana: To have and to have not'. In: Vol. 2 No. 1 *Journal of South Asian Women Studies* [on Internet] http://northshore.shore.net:8000/~india/jsaws/issue2/art_a.htm

Gautam, D. N. and B. V. Trivedi [1986]: *Unnatural deaths of married women with special reference to dowry deaths: A sample study of New Delhi.* New Delhi: Government of India. Ministry of Home Affairs

Ghadially, Rehana (ed.) [1988]: *Women in Indian society: A reader.* New Delhi: Sage.

Ghadially, Rehana and Pramod Kumar [1988]: 'Bride-burning: The psycho-social dynamics of dowry deaths'. In: Ghadially (ed.), pp. 167-177

Ghosh, S. K. [1989]: *Indian women through the ages.* New Delhi: Ashish

Ghouri, Umer Hayat Khan [1992]: *Dowry and Islamic social system.* 2nd ed. Delhi: Markazi Maktaba Islami

Goody, Jack R. and Stanley J. Tambiah (eds.) [1973]: *Bridewealth and dowry.* Cambridge: Cambridge University Press

Gopal, Ram [1983]: *India of Vedic Kalpasutras.* Delhi: Motilal Banarsidass

Gough, K. [1956]: 'Brahman kinship in a Tamil village'. In: Vol. 58 *American Anthropologist*, pp. 826-853

Grover, Kanta [1990]: *Burning flesh.* New Delhi: Vikas

Gulati, L. [1981]: *Profiles in female poverty. A study of five poor working women in Kerala.* New Delhi: Hindustan

Gupta, Giri Raj (ed.) [1986]: *Family and social change in modern India.* Delhi: Vikas

Hawthorn, Geoffrey (ed.) [1988]: *The standard of living.* [The Tanner Lectures, Clare Hall, Cambridge, 1985]. Cambridge et al.: Cambridge University Press

Healy, P. [1984]: 'The death of three sisters highlights disturbing trend: Pressure grows on Asian marriages'. In: *The Times*, 2 May 1984, p. 3

Helweg, A. W. [1979]: *Sikhs in England: The development of a migrant community.* Delhi: Oxford University Press

Henning, C. G. [1993]: *The indentured Indian in Natal, 1860-1917.* New Delhi: Promilla

Hershman, P. [1981]: *Punjabi kinship and marriage.* Delhi: Hindustan

Hiese, Lori, Jacqueline Pitanguy and Adrienne Germain [1993]: 'Violence against women: The hidden health burden'. [Background Paper for the World Bank, Population, Health and Nutrition Division, October 1993]

Hill, M. Anne and Elizabeth King [1995]: 'Women's education and economic well-being'. In: Vol. 1 No. 2 [Summer 1995] *Feminist Economics*, pp. 21-46

Hingorani, Kapila [1981]: 'Dowry'. In: No. 1 [1981] *Banhi*. [An occasional journal published by the Joint Women's Programme. Focus: Women and the law], pp. 29-40

Hocart, A. M. [1970]: *The life-giving myth and other essays*. 2nd impression, reprint. London: Methuen and Co

Hood, Nilkanth Vinayakrao [1993]: *Cases and materials on cruelty against husband*. Wardha: Sagar

Hooja, S. L. [1969]: *Dowry system in India: A case study*. New Delhi: Asia Press

'India studying 'accidental deaths' of Hindu wives'. [1989]: In: 15 January 1989 *New York Times (International)*

Israel, Milton and Narendra K. Wagle (eds.) [1993]: *Ethnicity, identity, migration: The South Asian context*. Toronto: University of Toronto, Centre for South Asian Studies

Jackson, Robert and Eleanor Nesbitt [1993]: *Hindu children in Britain*. Stoke-on-Trent: Trentham Books

Jacobson, D. and Susan Wadley [1977]: *Women in India*. New Delhi: Manohar

Jain, Devaki (ed.) [1980a]: *Indian women*. Delhi: Ministry of Information and Broadcasting

Jain, Devaki (ed.) [1980b]: *Women's quest for power: Five case studies*. New Delhi: Vikas

Jain, Ranjana S. [1992]: *Family violence in India*. New Delhi: Radiant

Jaswal, P. S. and Nishtha Jaswal [1988]: 'Anti-dowry legislation in India: An appraisal'. In: Vol. 30 No. 1 [January-March 1988] *Journal of the Indian Law Institute*, pp. 78-87

Jeffery, Patricia and Roger Jeffery [1994]: 'Killing my heart's desire: Education and female autonomy in rural North India'. In: Kumar, Nita (ed.): *Women as subjects: South Asian histories*. Calcutta: Stree, pp. 148-157

Jeffery, Patricia and Roger Jeffery [1996]: *Don't marry me to a plowman! Women's everyday lives in rural North India*. Boulder, Colorado and Oxford: Westview Press

Jeffery, Patricia, Roger Jeffery and Andrew Lyon [1988]: *Labour pains and labour power*. London: Zed Books

Jethmalani, Rani (ed.) [1995]: *Kali's yug. Empowerment, law and dowry deaths*. New Delhi: Har-Anand

Jethmalani, Rani and P. K. Dey [1995]: 'Dowry deaths and access to justice'. In: Jethmalani (ed.), pp. 36-78

Jha, Uma Shankar and Premlata Pujari [1996]: *Indian women today: Tradition, modernity and change*. New Delhi: Kanishka

Johal, Sukhjinder [1992]: 'The dowry in law'. In: Vol. 89 No. 38 [22 October 1992] *The Law Society's Gazette*, pp. 34-36

John, D. W. [1969]: *Indian Workers' Associations in Britain*. London: Oxford University Press

John, T. G. [1989]: 'Ramblings and gleanings'. In: 1989(2) *Kerala Law Times*, Journal section, p. 13

Joseph, Ammu and Kalpana Sharma (eds.) [1994]: *Whose news? The media and women's issues*. Delhi: Sage

Joshi, Charu Lata [1994]: 'Give dowry, will marry'. In: *India Today*, 15 October 1994, pp. 112-115

Judicial Studies Board [1994]: *Handbook on ethnic minority issues*. London: Judicial Studies Board

Jung, Anees [1994]: 'Betrayed: Through violence, visible and invisible'. In: *Seven sisters: Among the women of South Asia*. New Delhi: Penguin, pp. 45-55

Kamlakar, S. [1984a]: 'Evil of dowry – solutions for its eradication'. In: Vol. LXXXVI [1984] *The Bombay Law Reporter*, Journal section, p. 8

Kamlakar, S. [1984b]: 'Offence of cruelty by husband or relative of husband'. In: Vol. LXXXVI [1984] *The Bombay Law Reporter*, Journal section, pp. 22, 27-30 and 40-42

Kapadia, K. M. [1955]: *Marriage and family in India*. Bombay et al.: Oxford University Press

Kapur, Promilla [1993]: *Girl child and family violence*. Delhi: Har-Anand

Karet, D. J. Jerome [1994]: 'Ancillary to belief'. In: [March 1994] *Family Law*, pp. 133-134

Karve, I. [1953]: *Kinship organisation in India*. Poona: Deccan College

Kelkar, Govind [1992]: *Violence against women. Perspectives and strategies in India*. New Delhi and Shimla: Manohar and Indian Institute of Advanced Study [Occasional Papers, 30]

Kelkar, R. V. [1984]: *Outlines of criminal procedure*. 2nd ed. Lucknow: Eastern Book Co

Kelly, J. M. [1992]: *A short history of Western legal theory*. Oxford: Clarendon

Khan, Mumtaz Ali and Noor Ayesha [1982]: *Status of rural women in India: A study of Karnataka*. New Delhi: Uppal

Khan, M. Z. And R. Ray [1984]: 'Dowry death'. In: Vol. XLV No. 3 [1984] *Indian Journal of Social Work*, pp. 303-315

Khanna, Girija and Mariamma A.Varghese [1978]: *Indian women today*. New Delhi et al.: Vikas

Khare, R.S. [1970]: *The changing Brahmans. Associations and elites among the Kanya-Kubjas of North India*. Chicago and London: University of Chicago Press

Kishwar, Madhu [1986]: 'Dowry – to ensure her happiness or to disinherit her?'. In: No. 34 [May-June 1986] *Manushi*, pp. 2-13

Kishwar, Madhu [1988]: 'Rethinking dowry boycott'. In: No. 48 [September-October 1988] *Manushi*, pp. 10-13

Kishwar, Madhu [1989a]: 'Towards more just norms for marriage'. In: No. 53 [July-August 1989] *Manushi*, pp. 2-9

Kishwar, Madhu [1989b]: 'Dowry and inheritance rights'. In: Vol. XXIV No. 11 [18 March 1989] *Economic and Political Weekly*, pp. 587-588

Kishwar, Madhu [1990]: 'Women's organisations. The pressure of unrealistic expectations'. In: No. 59 [July-August 1990] *Manushi*, pp. 11-14

Kishwar, Madhu [1993]: 'Dowry calculations: Daughter's rights in her parental family'. In: No. 78 [September-October 1993] *Manushi*, pp. 8-17

Kishwar, Madhu [1994a]: 'A code for self-monitoring: some thoughts on activism'. In: No. 85 [November-December 1994] *Manushi*, pp. 9-12

Kishwar, Madhu [1994b]: 'Love and marriage'. In: No. 80 [January-February 1994] *Manushi*, pp. 11-19

Kishwar, Madhu [1994c]: 'Co-ownership rights for wives: A solution worse than the problem'. In: No. 84 [September-October 1994] *Manushi*, pp. 8-12

Kishwar, Madhu et al. [1980]: 'Beginning with our own lives: An open letter to women activists, women's groups and organizations'. Editorial. In: No. 5 [May-June 1980] *Manushi*, p. 3

Kishwar, Madhu and Ruth Vanita [1984]: *In search of answers*. London: Zed Books

Kolenda, P. [1976]: 'Seven kinds of hierarchy in homo hierarchicus. In: Vol. XXXV No. 4 [August 1976] *Journal of Asian Studies*, pp. 581-596

Kolenda, P. [1984]: 'Women as tribute, women as flowers: Images of women in weddings in North and South India'. In: Vol. 11 [1984] *American Ethnologist*, pp. 98-117

Kothari, Sima [1989]: *The social, economic and legal context of dowry in modern India*. London: SOAS. [Unpublished LL.B. Essay]

Krishnakumari, N. S. [1987]: *Status of single women in India. A study of spinsters, widows and divorcees*. New Delhi: Uppal

Krishnakumari, N. S. and A. S. Geetha [1983]: *A report on the problem of dowry in Bangalore city*. Calcutta: William Carey

Kumar, Radha [1993a]: 'The campaign against dowry'. In: Kumar, R. (ed.) [1993b], pp. 115-126

Kumar, Radha (ed.) [1993b]: *The history of doing: An illustrated account of movements for women's rights and feminism in India, 1800-1990*. Delhi: Kali for Women

Kumar, Vinay [1994]: 'Ruminations of a young man: On marriage and dowry'. In: No. 80 [January-February 1994] *Manushi*, pp. 29-35

Kumar, Virendra [1983-84]: 'Dowry dilemma'. In: Vol. 35 No. 1 (Special Issue) [1983-84] *Punjab University Law Review*, pp. 265-275

Kumar, Virendra [1986]: 'An evaluation of dowry prohibition law'. In: Saraf, D. N. (ed.), pp. 325-342

Kumari, Ranjana [1989]: *Brides are not for burning: Dowry victims in India*. New Delhi: Radiant

Kumari, Ved [1994]: 'State's response to the problem of rape and dowry'. In: Sarkar and Sivaramayya (eds.), pp. 104-128

Kuper, Hilda [1960]: *Indian people in Natal*. Durban: Natal University Press

Kusum (ed.) [1993a]: *Women – March towards dignity: Social and legal perspectives*. New Delhi: Regency

Kusum [1993b]: *Harassed husbands*. New Delhi: Regency

Lateef, Shireen [1992]: 'Wife abuse among Indo-Fijians'. In: Counts, Dorothy Ayers, Judith K. Brown and Jacquelyn C. Campbell (eds.): *Sanctions and sanctuary: Cultural perspectives on the beating of wives*. Boulder et al.: Westview Press, pp. 185-201

Lawyers' Collective [1992]: *Legal Aid Handbook 1: Domestic violence*. New Delhi: Kali for Women

Laxmi, C. S. [1989a]: 'On kidneys and dowry'. In: Vol. 24 No. 4 [28 January 1989] *Economic and Political Weekly*, pp. 189-190

Laxmi, C. S. [1989b]: 'Family as an area of power struggle'. In: Vol. 22 No. 19 [13 May 1989] *Economic and Political Weekly*, p. 1065

Leslie, Julia [1989]: *The perfect wife: The orthodox Hindu woman according to the Stridharmapaddhati of Tryambakayajvan*. Delhi: OUP (and Harmondsworth: Penguin 1995)

Leslie, Julia [1991a]: 'A problem of choice: The heroic sati or the widow-ascetic'. In: Leslie (ed.) [1991c], pp. 46-61

Leslie, Julia (ed.) [1991b]: *Roles and rituals for Hindu women*. London: Pinter

Leslie, Julia (ed.) [1991c]: *Rules and remedies in classical Indian law*. Leiden et al.: Brill. Panels of the VIIth World Sanskrit Conference, Kern Institute, Leiden, August 23-29, 1987, Vol. IX]

Leslie, Julia [1991d]: 'Shri and Jyestha: Ambivalent role models for women'. In: Leslie (ed.) [1991b], pp. 107-127

Leslie, Julia [1991e]: 'Suttee or sati: Victim or victor?'. In: Leslie (ed.) [1991b], pp. 175-191

Leslie, Julia [1992]: 'The significance of dress for the orthodox Hindu woman'. In: Barnes, Ruth and Joanne B. Eicher (eds.): *Dress and gender: Making and meaning in cultural contexts*. New York and Oxford: Berg, pp. 198-213

Leslie, Julia [1996a]: 'Menstruation myths'. In: Leslie (ed.) [1995b], pp. 87-105

Leslie, Julia (ed.) [1996b]: *Myth and mythmaking: Continuous evolution in Indian tradition*. Richmond: Curzon Press. [SOAS Collected Papers on South Asia, 12]

Liddle J. and R. Joshi [1986]: *Daughters of independence: Gender, caste and class in India*. London: Zed Press

Lundberg, Shelly and Robert A. Pollak [1993]: 'Separate spheres bargaining and the marriage market'. In: Vol. 101 No. 6 [December 1993] *Journal of Political Economy*, pp. 988-1010

Luthra, A. [1983]: 'Dowry among the urban poor: Perception and practice'. In: Vol. 33 No. 2 *Social Action*, pp. 207-220

Madan, T. N. [1975]: 'Structural implications of marriage in North India: Wife-givers and wife-takers among the pandits of Kashmir'. In: Vol. 14 *Contributions to Indian Sociology*, (N. S.), pp. 217-243

Malik, Shahdeen [1990]: 'Dowry Prohibition Act, 1980. Conflict of decisions need[s] resolution'. In: 42 *Dhaka Law Reports 1990*, Journal section, pp. 55-58

Mangum, Stephen L. [1988]: 'The male-female comparative worth debate: Alternative economic perspectives on an issue that cuts across the social sciences'. In: Vol. 47 No. 2 [April 1988] *American Journal of Economics & Sociology*, pp. 149-165

Manser, Marilyn and Murray Brown [1980]: 'Marriage and household decision making: A bargaining analysis'. In: Vol. 21 No. 1 [February 1980] *International Economic Review*, pp. 31-44

Mathew, Anna [1987]: 'Attitudes towards dowry'. In: Vol. XLVIII No. 1 [April 1987] *The Indian Journal of Social Work*, pp. 95-102

Mathew, Anna [1990]: 'Dowry and its various dimensions'. In: Devasia, L. and V. V. Devasia (eds.): *Women in India*. New Delhi: Indian Social Institute, pp. 79-88

Mathew, P. D. [1993]: *The Dowry Prohibition Act*, 1961. Reprint. New Delhi: Indian Social Institute

Matin, Abdul [1992]: *The law on dowry prohibition and child marriage restraint*. Dhaka: Rose

Maydeo, Anjali [1990]: 'Domestic violence: The perspective and experiences of an activist group'. In: Sood, Sushma (ed.): *Violence against women*. Jaipur: Arihant, pp.269-278

Meer, Fatima [1969]: *Portrait of Indian South Africans*. Durban: Avon House

Mehta, H. [1981]: *Indian women*. New Delhi: Butala

Menski, Werner [1984]: *Role and ritual in the Hindu marriage*. London: SOAS. [Unpublished PhD thesis]

Menski, Werner [1993a]: 'Asians in Britain and the question of adaptation to a new legal order: Asian laws in Britain?'. In: Israel and Wagle (eds.), pp. 238-268

Menski, Werner [1993b]: 'Egoism versus family solidarity: Women's property rights in Kerala'. In: 1993[2] *Kerala Law Times*, Journal section, pp. 45-49

Menski, Werner [1996]: 'Introduction: The democratisation of justice in India'. In: Singh, Gurjeet: *The law of consumer protection in India. Justice within reach*. New Delhi: Deep and Deep, pp. xxv-liv

Menski, Werner [1997a]: 'The dowry problem: Can legal remedies work?'. In: Issue 10 [Autumn/Winter 1997] *Wig & Gavel* London Law Review, pp. 129-132

Menski, Werner [1997b]: 'The dowry problem: Progress in legal remedies'. In: 1997(2) *Kerala Law Times*, Journal section, pp. 67-75

Menski, Werner [1997c]: *Indian legal systems past and present*. London: SOAS. [Occasional Papers No. 3]

Miller, Barbara D. [1980]: 'Female neglect and the cost of marriage in rural India'. In: Nos. 14-15 [January-June 1980] *Contributions to Indian Sociology*, pp. 95-129

Miller, Barbara D. [1992]: 'Wife-beating in India: Variations on a theme'. In: Counts, Dorothy Ayers, Judith K. Brown and Jacquelyn C. Campbell (eds.): *Sanctions and sanctuary: Cultural perspectives on the beating of wives*. Boulder et al.: Westview Press, pp. 173-184

Miller, Jeanine [1985]: *The vision of cosmic order in the Vedas*. London et al.: Routledge & Kegan Paul

Minakshi, Charu [1985]: 'From the bridal to the pyre'. In: No. 28 [May-June 1985] *Manushi*, pp. 30-31

Mitter, Sara S. [1991]: 'Only a female'. In: *Dharma's daughters: Contemporary Hindu women and Hindu culture*. New Delhi: Penguin, pp. 109-120

Mohite, Vijayrao [1993]: *Law of cruelty, abetment of suicide, and dowry deaths*. Bombay: Bar Council of Maharashtra and Goa

Monsoor, Taslima [1994]: *From patriarchy to gender equity. Family law and its impact on women in Bangladesh*. London: SOAS [Ph.D thesis]

Monsoor, Taslima [1998]: *From patriarchy to gender equity. Family law and its impact on women in Bangladesh*. Dhaka: UBL

Moore, M. [1997]: 'Consumerism fuels dowry-death wave: Bride burning on the increase in India'. In: Washington Post, pp. 1-4

Morris, H. S. [1968]: *The Indians in Uganda*. London: Weidenfeld and Nicholson

Mustill, Emma [1989]: *Dowry and the part it plays in the suppression of Indian women today*. London: SOAS [Unpublished B.A. Essay]

Mustill, Emma [1991]: *The dowry system. An overview*. London: SOAS. [Unpublished MA Dissertation]

Naidoo, Thillayvel [1992]: *The Arya Samaj movement in South Africa*. Delhi: Motilal Banarsidass

Nair, P. T. [1978]: *Marriage and dowry in India*. Calcutta: Minerva

Nanda, B. R. (ed.) [1976]: *Indian women: From purdah to modernity*. New Delhi: Vikas

Narayan, Uma [1993]: 'Women, modernization and arranged marriages in India'. In: Turshen, Meredith and B. Holcombe (eds.): *Women's lives and public policy – the international experience*. Westport, Connecticut: Greenwood Press, pp. 159-170

Narayan, Uma [1995]: 'Paying the price of change: women, modernization and arranged marriages in India'. In: Witzel and Thakur (eds.), chapter 12, pp. 1-7

Nath, Tarkeshwar [1976]: 'Legal aspects of dowry'. In: *All India Reporter* 1976, Journal section, pp. 18-22

National Crime Records Bureau [1995]: *Crime in India*. New Delhi: NCRB

Nye, M. [1995]: *A place for our gods: The construction of a Hindu temple community in Edinburgh*. London: Curzon Press

Oldenberg, Veena T. [1993]: 'Dowry murders in India'. In: Turshen, Meredith and B. Holcombe (eds.): *Women's lives and public policy – the international experience*. Westport, Connecticut: Greenwood Press, pp. 145-158

Omvedt, Gail [1990]: *Violence against women: New movements and new theories in India*. Delhi: Kali for Women

Padayachee, A. and S. R. Singh [1997]: 'Violence against women. A long history for South African Indian women with specific reference to Hinduism and Hindu law'. In: Vol. 14 *Social Science International Interdisciplinary Readings*, pp. 1-10

Palriwala, R. [1989]: 'Reaffirming the anti-dowry struggle'. In: Vol. 24 No. 17 [29 April 1989] *Economic and Political Weekly*, pp. 942-944

Papanek, Hanna [1985]: 'Class and gender in education-employment linkages'. In: [August 1985] *Comparative Education Review*, pp. 317-346

Parashar, Archana [1992]: *Women and family law reform in India*. New Delhi et al.: Sage

Parry, J. P. [1979]: *Caste and kinship in Kangra*. London: Routledge & Kegan Paul

Paul, Madan C. [1980]: *Dowry and position of women in India. A study of Delhi metropolis*. New Delhi: Inter India

Pearl, David and Werner Menski [1998]: *Muslim family law*. London et al.: Sweet and Maxwell

Phukan, Bandita [1995]: 'The daughters and Hindu rites'. In: Witzel and Thakur (eds.), chapter 13, pp. 1-4

Pocock, D. [1957]: ''Difference' in East Africa: A case study of caste and religion in modern Indian society'. In: Vol. 13 No. 4 *South Western Journal of Anthropology*, pp. 289-300

Pocock, D. [1972]: *Kanbi and Patidar: a study of the Patidar community of Gujarat*. Oxford: Clarendon Press

Pollack, Robert [1985]: 'A transactions cost approach to families and households'. In: Vol. 23 No. 2 [June 1985] *Journal of Economic Literature*, pp. 581-608

Poulter, Sebastian [1986]: *English law and ethnic minority customs*. London: Butterworths

Prasad, Devi B. and B. Vijayalakshmi [1988]: 'Dowry-related violence towards women – some issues'. In: Vol. XLIX No. 3 [July 1988] *Indian Journal of Social Work*, pp. 271-280

Raizada, K. K. [1989]: 'Dowry deaths, suicide and bride burning'. In: Vol. 15 Nos. 1-2 [1989] *Indian Socio-Legal Journal*, pp. 87-98

Rajagopaul, G. R. [1982]: 'Dowry and the law'. In: *All India Reporter* 1982, Journal section, pp. 49-51

Rajan, R. S. [1993a]: 'The name of the husband'. In: Rajan (ed.) [1993b], pp. 83-102

Rajan, R. S. (ed.) [1993b]: *Real and imagined women: Gender, culture and post-colonialism*. London: Routledge

Rajaraman, Indira [1983]: 'Economics of bride-price and dowry'. In: *The Economic and Political Weekly*. 19 February 1983, pp. 275-278

Raleigh, V. Soni, L. Bulusu and R. Balarajan [1990]: 'Suicides among immigrants from the Indian subcontinent'. In: Vol. 156 *British Journal of Psychiatry*, pp. 46-50

Rani, Prabha [1984]: 'The tyranny of marriage'. In: No. 21 [March-April 1984] *Manushi*, pp. 15-16

Rao, M. S. A. [1970]: *Urbanization and social change: A study of a rural community on a metropolitan fringe*. New Delhi: Orient Longmans

Rao, R. Jaganmohan [1973]: 'Dowry system in India – A socio-legal approach to the problem'. In: Vol. 15 No. 4 [October-December 1973] *Journal of the Indian Law Institute*, pp. 617-625

Rao, Vijayendra [1993a]: 'Dowry 'inflation' in rural India: A statistical investigation'. In: Vol. 47 No. 2 [July 1993] *Population Studies*, pp. 283-293

Rao, Vijayendra [1993b]: 'The rising price of husbands: A hedonic analysis of dowry increases in rural India'. In: Vol. 101 No. 4 [August 1993] *Journal of Political Economy*, pp. 666-677

Rao, Vijayendra [1995]: 'Wife-beating in a rural South Indian community'. In: Witzel and Thakur (eds.), chapter 14, pp. 1-30

Rao, Vijayendra [1997]: 'Wife beating in rural South India: A qualitative and econometric analysis'. In: Vol. 44 No. 8 [April 1997] *Social Science and Medicine*, pp. 1169-1180

Rao, Vijayendra [1998]: 'Wife abuse, its causes and its impact on intra-household resource allocation in rural Karnataka: A 'participatory' econometric analysis'. In: Krishnaraj, Maithreyi, Ratna M. Sudershan and Abusaleh Shariff (eds.): *Gender,population and development*. Delhi and Oxford: Oxford University Press, pp. 94-121

Rao, Vijayendra and Anil Deolalikar [1998]: 'The demand for dowries and bride characteristics in marriage: Empirical estimates for rural South-Central India'. In: Krishnaraj, Maithreyi, Ratna M. Sudershan and Abusaleh Shariff (eds.): *Gender, population and development*. Delhi and Oxford: Oxford University Press, pp. 122-140

Rao, Vijayendra and Anne Waters [1995]: *The link between female sterilisation and wife-abuse: A statistical and ethnographic investigation*. Williamstown, MA: Williams College [Mimeo, March 1995]

Rehat maryada: A guide to the Sikh way of life [1971]: Translated by Kanwaljit Kaur and Inderjeet Singh. London: The Sikh Cultural Society

Report, Joint Committee of the Houses of Parliament to examine the questions of the working of Dowry Prohibition Act, 1961. New Delhi, (Mimeograph), 6 August 1982

Ross, A. D. [1961]: *The Hindu family in its urban setting*. Toronto: University Press

Sadagopan, Shobha and Radha Kumar [1979]: 'Matches are made in heaven, but marriages are made on earth'. In: No. 1 [January 1979] *Manushi*, pp. 11-12

Saini, Debi S. [1983]: 'Dowry prohibition: Law, social change and challenges in India'. In: Vol. XLIV No. 2 [July 1983] *The Indian Journal of Social Work*, pp. 143-152

Sambrani, Rita and Shreekant Sambrani [1983]: 'Economics of bride price and dowry'. In: [9 April 1983] *Economic and Political Weekly*, pp. 601-603

Sandanshiv, D. N. [1995]: 'Bride-burning: Perspective of interveners'. In: Jethmalani, R. (ed.), pp. 94-104

Sandanshiv, D. N. and Jolly Mathew [1995]: 'Legal reform in dowry laws'. In: Jethmalani, R. (ed.), pp. 79-93

Saraf, D. N. (ed.) [1986]: *Social policy, law and protection of weaker sections of society*. Lucknow: Eastern Book Co

Sarkar, Lotika [1985]: 'Women and the law'. In: *Annual Survey of Indian Law* 1985. New Delhi: Indian Law Institute, pp. 493-500

Sarkar, Lotika [1986]: 'Women and the law'. In: *Annual Survey of Indian Law* 1986. New Delhi: Indian Law Institute, pp. 637-651

Sarkar, Lotika and B. Sivaramayya (eds.) [1994]: *Women and law. Contemporary problems*. New Delhi: Vikas

Sen, Amartya [1988a]: 'The standard of living: Lecture I, concepts and critiques'. In: Hawthorn, Geoffrey (ed.), pp. 1-19

Sen, Amartya [1988b]: 'The standard of living: Lecture II, lives and capabilities'. In: Hawthorn, Geoffrey (ed.), pp. 20-38

Sen, Amartya [1990]: 'Gender and co-operative conflicts'. In: Tinker, I. (ed.): *Persistent inequalities – women and world development*. New York: Oxford University Press, pp. 123-149

Shah, Kalpana [1984]: *Women's liberation and voluntary action*. New Delhi: Ajanta

Sharma, Sudesh Kumar [1986]: 'Dowry system in India: A socio-legal analysis'. In: Saraf, D. N. (ed.), pp. 343-367

Sharma, Ursula [1980]: *Women, work and property in North West India*. London and New York: Tavistock

Sharma, Ursula [1984]: 'Dowry in North India: Its consequences for women'. In: Hirschon, Renée (ed.): *Women and property – women as property*. London: Croom Helm, pp. 62-74

Sharma, Ursula [1986]: *Women's work, class and the urban household*. London and New York: Tavistock

Shaw, A. [1988]: *A Pakistani community in Britain*. Oxford: Basil Blackwell

Shurei, Sha [1997]: *Don't burn the brides*. Delhi: Ajanta

Siddiqui, Musab U. and Earl Y. Reeves [1987]: 'Mate selection practices of Indians in India and Indian nationals in the United States'. In: Vol. 67 No. 4 [December 1987] *Man in India*, pp. 302-316

Singh, Indu Prakash [1990]: *Indian women: The captured beings*. New Delhi: Intellectual Publishing House

Singh, N. [1989]: *An exposition of the vivaha (marriage) sanskara and related rituals as a paradigm of religio-cultural continuity among the Hindi speaking community of South African Hindus*. Durban: University of Durban Westville [Unpublished PhD thesis]

Sood, Sushma (ed.) [1990]: *Violence against women*. Jaipur: Arihant

Srinivas, M. N. [1942]: *Marriage and family in Mysore*. Bombay: New Book Co

Srinivas, M. N. [1968]: *Social change in modern India*. Los Angeles: California University Press

Srinivas, M. N. [1978]: *The changing position of women*. Delhi: Oxford University Press. [The T. H. Huxley Memorial Lecture. Delivered at the London School of Economics in 1976]

Srinivas, M. N. [1984]: *Some reflections on dowry*. Delhi et al.: Oxford University Press

Srinivas, M. N. (ed.) [1989a]: *The cohesive role of sanskritization and other essays*. Delhi: Oxford University Press

Srinivas, M. N. [1989b]: 'Some reflections on dowry'. In: Srinivas (ed.) [1989a], pp. 97-121

Srinivasan K. and S. Mukerji (eds.): *Dynamics of population and family welfare*. Bombay: Himalaya

Status of Women in India [1975]: *A synopsis of the Report of the National Committee on the Status of Women (1971-74)*. New Delhi: Allied

Stein, Dorothy [1988]: 'Burning widows, burning brides: The perils of daughterhood in India'. In: Vol. 61 No. 3 [Fall 1988], *Pacific Affairs*, pp. 465-485

Tambiah, Stanley. J. [1973a]: *Dowry, bridewealth and property*. Cambridge: Cambridge University Press. [Cambridge Papers in Social Anthropology]

Tambiah, Stanley J. [1973b]: 'Dowry, bridewealth and women's property rights'. In: Goody and Tambiah (eds.), pp. 59-91

Tambiah, S. J. [1989]: 'Bridewealth and dowry revisited'. In: Vol. 30 No. 4 [August-October 1989] *Current Anthropology*, pp. 413-435

Tambs-Lyche, Harald [1980]: *London Patidars: A case study in urban ethnicity*. London: Routledge & Kegan Paul

Teja, Mohinderjit Kaur [1993]: *Dowry: A study in attitudes and practices*. Delhi: Inter-India Publications

Thakur, Himendra B. [1991]: *Don't burn my mother!*. New York: International Publishing House

Thakur, Himendra B. [1995]: 'Practical steps towards saving the lives of 25,000 potential victims of dowry and bride-burning in India in the next four years'. In: Witzel and Thakur (eds.), chapter 16, pp. 1-8

Thomas, P. [1964]: *Indian women through the ages*. London: Asia Publishing House

Towards Equality [1974]: *Report of the Committee on the Status of Women in India.* New Delhi: Government of India, Ministry of Education and Social Welfare

Tripathi, Ram Narayan [1995]: 'Hindu marriage system, Hindu scriptures and dowry and bride-burning in India'. In: Witzel and Thakur (eds.), chapter 17, pp. 1-8

Tudor, Gillian [1986]: *Dowry deaths in India.* London: SOAS. [Unpublished M.A. thesis]

Vanita, Ruth [1984a]: 'Nominal changes'. In: No. 24 [September-October 1984] *Manushi*, pp. 29-31

Vanita, Ruth [1984b] : 'Preserving the family at the cost of women – the new Family Courts Bill'. In: No. 25 [November-December 1984] *Manushi*, pp. 41-47

Vanita, Ruth [1987]: 'Can police reform husbands?'. In: No. 40 [May-June 1987] *Manushi*, pp. 12-24

Vatuk, Sylvia [1972]: *Kinship and urbanization: White collar migrants in North India.* Berkeley: University of California Press

Vatuk, Sylvia [1975]: 'Gifts and affines in North India'. In: Vol. 9 *Contributions to Indian Sociology,* (N. S.), pp. 155-196

Vedalankar, Nardev and Manohar Somera [1975]: *Arya Samaj and Indians abroad.* New Delhi: Arya Pratinidhi Sabha

Veen, Klass W. van der [1972]: *I give thee my daughter: A study of marriage and hierarchy among the Anavil Brahmins of South Gujarat.* Assen: Van Gorcum

Veeraraghavan, Vimala [1985]: *Suicides and attempted suicides in the Union Territory of Delhi.* New Delhi: Concept

Verghese, Jamila [1980]: *Her gold and her body.* New Delhi: Vikas

Wani, M. Afzal [1996]: *The Islamic institution of Mahr: A study of its philosophy, working & related legislations in the contemporary world.* Noonamy: Upright Study Home

Werbner, Pnina [1990]: *The migration process: Capital gifts and offerings among British Pakistanis.* London: Berg

Willigen, John van and V. C. Channa [1991]: 'Law, custom and crimes against women: The problem of dowry death in India'. In: Vol. 50 No. 4 [Winter 1991] *Human Organization*, pp. 369-377

Witzel, Michael [1995]: 'Little dowry, no sati: The lot of women in the Vedic period'. In: Witzel and Thakur (eds.), chapter 18, pp. 1-10

Witzel, Michael and Himendra Thakur (eds.) [1995]: *Souvenir of the First International Conference on Dowry and Bride-Burning in India.* Cambridge, MA: Harvard University

Yalman, Nur [1963]: 'The purity of women in Ceylon and Southern India'. In: Vol. 93 No.1 [1963] *Journal of the Royal Anthropological Institute*, pp. 25-58

Index